Religious Pluralism

Giuseppe Giordan • Enzo Pace
Editors

Religious Pluralism

Framing Religious Diversity in the Contemporary World

 Springer

Editors
Giuseppe Giordan
Enzo Pace
Department of FISPPA
University of Padova
Padova, Italy

ISBN 978-3-319-06622-6   ISBN 978-3-319-06623-3 (eBook)
DOI 10.1007/978-3-319-06623-3
Springer Cham Heidelberg New York Dordrecht London

Library of Congress Control Number: 2014943515

Printed on acid-free paper

Springer is part of Springer Science+Business Media (www.springer.com)

Contents

Introduction: Pluralism as Legitimization of Diversity   1
Giuseppe Giordan

Part I   Ideas and Concepts on Religious Pluralism

Re-Thinking Religious Pluralism   15
James A. Beckford

Religious Diversity, Social Control, and Legal Pluralism:
A Socio-Legal Analysis   31
James T. Richardson

Oligopoly Is Not Pluralism   49
Fenggang Yang

Part II   Case Studies in Religious Pluralism

Religious and Philosophical Diversity as a Challenge
for the Secularism: A Belgian-French Comparison   63
Jean-Paul Willaime

The Diversity of Religious Diversity. Using Census and NCS
Methodology in Order to Map and Assess the Religious Diversity
of a Whole Country   73
Christophe Monnot and Jörg Stolz

Increasing Religious Diversity in a Society Monopolized
by Catholicism   93
Enzo Pace

**Re-Thinking Religious Diversity: Diversities and Governance
of Diversities in "Post-Societies"** 115
Siniša Zrinščak

Diversity Versus Pluralism? Notes from the American Experience 133
James V. Spickard

**Between No Establishment and Free Exercise: The Dialectic
of American Religious Pluralism** 145
William H. Swatos Jr.

**Missionary Trans-Border Religions and Defensive Civil Society
in Contemporary Japan: Toward a Comparative Institutional
Approach to Religious Pluralism** 157
Yoshihide Sakurai

**Religious Tendencies in Brazil: Disenchantment, Secularization,
and Sociologists** 171
Roberto Motta

Index 185

Author's Bio

James A. Beckford Fellow of the British Academy, is Professor Emeritus of Sociology at the University of Warwick and a former President of four professional associations for sociologists of religion. In addition to publishing several books which examine theoretical questions about the sociology of religion, he has conducted empirical research projects on the accommodation of religious diversity in Britain, Canada, France and the USA. His books on this subject include *Religion in Prison: Equal Rites in a Multi-Faith Society*, with S. Gilliat, 1998; and *Muslims in Prison: Challenge and Change in Britain and France*, with D. Joly & F. Khosrokhavar, 2005.

Giuseppe Giordan is Senior Lecturer in Sociology at the University of Padua. From 2009 to 2013 he served as General Secretary of the International Society for the Sociology of Religion. With Enzo Pace and Luigi Berzano he edits the *Annual Review of the Sociology of Religion*. His books in English include *Identity and Pluralism: The Values of the Post-Modern Time*. Center for Migration Studies, 2004; *Vocation and Social Context* (ed.), Brill, 2007; *Conversion in the Age of Pluralism* (ed.), Brill, 2009; *Youth and Religion* (ed.), Brill, 2010; and *Religion, Spirituality and Everyday Practices* (ed. with William H. Swatos, Jr.) Springer, 2011.

Christophe Monnot is Assistant Professor of the Sociology of Religion at the University of Lausanne. His field of study is mainly on religious organizations and institutionalization of religious diversity with quantitative as well as qualitative approaches. He has recently published a book on religious congregations in Switzerland: *"Croire ensemble. Analyse institutionnelle du paysage religieux en Suisse"* and has edited another specifically on institutionalization of the Muslim *"La Suisse des mosquées. Derrière le voile de l'unité musulmane"*. He has also co-edited with Gladys Ganiel and Heidemarie Winkel the forthcoming volume *"Religion in Times of Crisis, Critiques and Change"*.

Roberto Motta has degrees in Philosophy (Recife), Sociology (The Hague) and a Ph.D. in Anthropology by Columbia University (New York). He has done extensive field work on the Afro-Brazilian religions and has also a keen interest in the relationship between religion and social change. He has published in several languages and has worked in teaching and research in Brazil and abroad. A member of ISSR since 1993, he has presented papers and organized sessions in most conferences held in the last 15 years. Having retired from Recife University, he is at present an associate researcher of *Conselho Nacional de Pesquisas* (Brasília) and of *Groupe de Sociologie des Religions et de la Laïcité* (Paris).

Enzo Pace is Full Professor of Sociology of Religion at Padua University, Directeur d'Études invité at the École des Hautes Études en Sciences Sociales and Past-President of the International Society for the Sociology of Religion (ISSR). He is a co-editor of the *Annual Review of the Sociology of Religion* (Brill). His recent publications include: *Religion as Communication*. Farnham: Ashgate, 2011; *Il carisma, la fede, la chiesa: introduzione alla sociologia del cristianesimo*. Roma: Carocci, 2012; and *La comunicazione invisibile. Religioni e internet*. Cinisello Balsamo, San Paolo Editore, 2013.

James T. Richardson is Professor of Sociology and Judicial Studies at the University of Nevada in Reno, Nevada. He directs the Judicial Studies graduate degree program for trial judges offered by the University. He has authored, edited and co-edited a dozen books and nearly 300 articles and chapters, most of which deal with various aspects of NRMs and minority religions. His recent work has focused on social control of minority faiths. His most recent books include: *Regulating Religion: Case Studies from around the Globe* (Kluwer, 2004), *Saints under Siege: The Texas Raid on the Fundamentalist Latter Day Saints* (with Stuart Wright; New York University Press, 2011), *The Sociology of Shari'a* (with Adam Possamai and Bryan Turner; Springer, forthcoming 2014), and *Legal Cases New Religious Movements and Minority Religions* (with Francois Belanger; Ashgate, forthcoming 2014).

Yoshihide Sakurai is a Professor of Sociology at the Graduate School of Letters, Hokkaido University, Japan. He obtained Ph.D. in Development Studies of Thailand at Hokkaido University and published many papers and books on the research of Thai Buddhism, East Asian transnational religions, and Japanese religions from sociological and anthropological perspective. He was a former president of The Japanese Association for the Study of Religion and Society, and he is executive committee member of Japanese Association for Religious Studies. His English paper is included in the Hokkaido University Collection of Academic Papers: http://eprints.lib.hokudai.ac.jp/dspace/index.jsp?locale=en.

James V. Spickard is Professor of Sociology and Anthropology at the University of Redlands, where he teaches social theory, the sociology of religion, research design, and a series of courses on the ethical implications of contemporary social issues. He has published widely on religion in contemporary society, human rights, social research methods, and non-Western social theory, among other topics. His most recent book is *Religion Crossing Boundaries* (Brill 2010), co-edited with Afe Adogame, on the transnational dynamics of African Christian movements. His current project is a book on non-Western sociologies of religion.

Jörg Stolz is Professor of the Sociology of Religion at the University of Lausanne. Working with a framework of "analytical sociology", he uses quantitative, qualitative and mixed methods approaches. He has written *Die Zukunft der Reformierten. Gesellschaftliche Megatrends – kirchliche Reaktionen* (together with Edmée Ballif), has edited an issue of *Social Compass* on "Salvation goods and religious markets" and has co-edited the book *La nouvelle Suisse religieuse. Risques et chances de sa diversité* (with Martin Baumann). He is the author of many articles in leading sociology journals, among them "Explaining religiosity. Towards a unified theoretical framework" in the *British Journal of Sociology*.

William H. Swatos Jr. is Editor of the *Interdisciplinary Journal of Research on Religion*, published through Baylor University, and Executive Officer of the Religious Research Association. From 1996 to 2012, he also served as Executive Officer of the Association for the Sociology of Religion. He is author, co-author, editor or co-editor of at least 23 volumes in the sociology of religion, including the text Sociology of Religion, with Kevin Christiano and Peter Kivisto, entering its third edition. From 1989 to 1994, he edited the journal *Sociological Analysis/ Sociology of Religion*, immediately prior to which he served as its book review editor.

Jean-Paul Willaime was born in 1947, is a Doctor of Religious Studies (1975) and Doctor of Sociology (1984) from the University of Strasbourg. He was a Lecturer in Sociology of Religion at the University of Strasbourg (1975–1992). Since 1992, he is the Research Director at l'*Ecole Pratique des Hautes Etudes*, Department of Religious Studies, Sorbonne, Paris. He is member of the Research Centre *Group of Sociology of Religions and Laïcity* (EPHE/CNRS) and past-president of the *International Society for the Sociology of Religion*. His main publications include: *Europe et religions. Les enjeux du XXIe siècle*, Fayard, 2004; *Sociologie du protestantisme*, PUF, 2005; *Le retour du religieux dans la sphère publique. Vers une laïcité de reconnaissance et de dialogue*, Editions Olivétan, 2008; *Religionskontroversen in Frankreich und Deutschland*, Matthias Koenig/Jean-Paul Willaime Hamburger Edition, 2008; *Les jeunes, l'école et la religion* (ed. with C. Béraud, Bayard, 2009); and *La nouvelle France protestante. Essor et recomposition au XXIe siècle* (ed. with S. Fath, 2011).

Fenggang Yang is Professor of Sociology and Director of the Center on Religion and Chinese Society at Purdue University. His research focuses on religious change in China and immigrant religions in the United States. He has received two distinguished article awards in these two areas. He is the author of *Religion in China: Survival and Revival under Communist Rule* (Oxford, 2012) and *Chinese Christians in America: Conversion, Assimilation, and Adhesive Identities* (PennState, 1999), the co-editor of nine books or journal special issues, and the Editor-in-Chief of the *Review of Religion and Chinese Society.*

Siniša Zrinščak is a Professor of Sociology and Social Policy at the University of Zagreb. His main scientific interests include religious and social policy changes in post-communism, Church-State relations, European and comparative social policy, gender, and civil society. He has been President of the ISORECEA (International Study of Religion in Central and Eastern Europe Association) and Vice-President of the International Sociological Association RC 22 since 2006, as well as General Secretary of the International Society for the Sociology of Religion since 2013. He has been involved in several mainly international scientific projects, and has numerous publications in peer-reviewed journals and books.

Introduction: Pluralism as Legitimization of Diversity

Giuseppe Giordan

The theme of religious pluralism is taking an increasingly important place within the sociology of religion. Its greatest merit is to have finally shifted the sociological debate from the juxtaposition between the supporters of the theory of secularization and those who opposed the issue of religious revival against it, toward a more articulate perspective that seems able to explain and better interpret what is happening in the world of religions and contemporary spiritualities.

Pluralism is a key concept toward understanding what is happening in our world, even if the risk, as with all the words that suddenly become popular and fashionable, is that it becomes an umbrella under which we put together quite different and heterogeneous phenomena, sometimes hardly consistent with each other. This error, which still often occurs in much sociological literature, is to superimpose the meaning of pluralism onto that of diversity, as if they were synonyms. Actually, as some authors contributing to this volume argued several years ago (Beckford 1999; Beckford and Richardson 2007), we must not confuse the normative-regulatory level, namely that of pluralism, with the descriptive level of empirical diversity. Besides, even taking for granted now the distinction between the normative and the empirical aspects, the concept of religious pluralism needs to be further refined to make it useful to the study of the different socioreligious situations. The contribution that this volume offers is to define the concept of religious pluralism as clearly as possible and then to make its explanatory potential evident by applying it to some specific case studies.

The prospect of religious pluralism places the study of religions and spiritualities outside the enclosure within which sociology of religion had voluntarily locked itself for several decades. While there were certainly valuable exceptions and dissident voices, there is no doubt that the theory of secularization has largely dictated the agenda of the sociological study of religion, especially in Europe, for

G. Giordan (✉)
Dipartimento FISPPA, University of Padua, Via Melchiorre Cesarotti 10/12, 35123 Padua, Italy
e-mail: giuseppe.giordan@unipd.it

G. Giordan and E. Pace (eds.), *Religious Pluralism*,
DOI 10.1007/978-3-319-06623-3_1, © Springer International Publishing Switzerland 2014

more than 40 years since the 1960s. Given that the ambition of this book is to address not only scholars, but also students and those who are interested in such an important subject as that of religious pluralism, in this introduction we can retrace briefly the path that sociology of religion has taken in recent decades by highlighting what were the main hubs that led to the change of perspective in the study of contemporary religious phenomena.

What has happened in this span of time as a result of which the category of secularization, which at the moment of its greatest fortune had become almost a sociological dogma, has slowly but inevitably lost its explanatory power? To understand the scope of the category of pluralism, which is placed outside the debate on secularization, it is useful to review briefly the changes in the religious landscape between the second and third millennium, passing the theories of "God's death" to the recognition of his "return" and his "revenge" (Kepel 1991).

From the Disappearance of Religion to Its Transformation

It is worth mentioning that, from the point of view of the sociology of culture, the emergence of a new analytical category is certainly an index of the inadequacy of the existing conceptual tools, and such inadequacy is directly related to the speed of the social and cultural change that characterizes a certain period of history. In the lapse of few decades, with a speed and acceleration that in many ways had never been recorded before in human history, we have passed from the traditional to the modern and then to the contemporary context, consistently redesigning all the spheres of social life, from politics to the economy, from education to leisure, not to mention that complex system of meanings and behaviors that we usually label with the word "religion."

One of the outcomes of the speed and depth of such changes is the difficulty to describe them within the categories we inherited from the past. Conceptual instruments that until not very long ago managed to bridle the reality of today in an unequivocal manner, nowadays are blunt weapons that, instead of helping us to understand, run the risk of creating confusion. The theory of secularization is an example of how fast changes rust categories seemingly stainless, making them usable only on the condition that they are accompanied by many details.

The theory of secularization, as it was presented in the 1960s (Acquaviva 1961; Berger 1967), solved the problem of the relationship between religion and modernity according to an almost mechanistic model: in an inversely proportional manner, as the modernization process advances, religion should progressively and inevitably disappear, at least with regard to its public manifestations. In fact, however, as Casanova (1994) has consistently pointed out, the theory of secularization brings together three different perspectives and interpretations of the relationship between religion and modernity: their confusion and overlapping has led to often ideological and misleading interpretations of reality. As we know, a first interpretation means secularization as the differentiation of social spheres, thus distinguishing and emancipating such putatively secular spheres as those of the state, economy, science from the religious sphere. A second version, the one that has established itself in the public debate as well as in the scientific one, secularization means the disappearance, or at least the progressive irrelevance, of religion. The third version of the concept describes it as privatization.

The great mistake, as has been highlighted by many, is to have overlapped the first and the second version of the concept of secularization, inseparably linking the functional differentiation of the social spheres with the progressive irrelevance of religion. If in Europe this model could appear plausible in some respects, in other contexts, as for example in the United States, the emergence of modernity has not triggered any process of the loss of relevance of the different religious traditions and not even the confinement of religion to the private ambit. Indeed, it is under everybody's eyes, how precisely in the United States the modernization and democratization processes have led not only to the persistence of the traditional religious presence, but also to new forms of "religious awakening."

Even in Europe, where there is a marked decline of religious practices, the fall of the priestly ordinations and the emancipation of the faithful from the official teachings of the churches on ethical issues, we also can record from at least the 1980s forward, a great proliferation of new religious movements, and more recently, under the influence of increasing migration, we can also record an unprecedented proliferation of multi-religious presence even in countries such as Italy, where the management of the religious market was monopolized by a single majority religion.

Far from being marginal and residual, religious phenomena in the contemporary world attract the attention of scholars for their peculiar vivacity, for their ability to get into the game of modernity and democracy by offering new experiences, often hardly comparable with the role played by religions in the traditional era.

The transition from the traditional to the contemporary world has not registered the disappearance of religion, but rather its more or less radical transformation according to the different social and cultural contexts. It has been a process of de-composition and re-composition, at both individual and collective levels, which has redesigned the role of religion itself, often putting together the juxtaposition of quite heterogeneous issues. The significance of religion within contemporary society therefore lends itself to multifarious interpretations that try to explain both the individualization of belief, the challenge of the fundamentalist movements, and the use of religion in an identity and ethnic interpretation. Religion, therefore, does not disappear, but adapts and transforms itself within modernity, often through heterogeneous issues, not to be explained with simple and linear theories: it suffices to think of the diversity of experiences of the Pentecostal or neo-Pentecostal, Charismatic and Evangelical religious communities in Latin America, or in Asia or in sub-Saharan Africa. It is a process of negotiation between the need of absoluteness typical of any system of religious belief and the different social and cultural contexts unceasingly changing – a negotiation that has led to the progressive deconfessionalization of belief, together with its individualization under the push of the freedom of choice of the subject.

Deconfessionalization and the Freedom of Choice of the Subject

The traditional world, governed by the principle of *cuius regio eius religio*, confirmed by the Treaty of Westphalia, structured belief in Europe in a territorial manner, and for many centuries the parish regulated such structure in a confessional way. With the urbanization processes typical of modernity, this orderly and stable world falls into a crisis. We can remember the reflections of the French sociologist Gabriel Le Bras (1956) who argued in the 1950s that as soon as the French peasant arrived at the Gare de Montparnasse in Paris, he would stop going to church because the model of the French rural parish could not be reproduced in the wider ambit of a modern metropolis – and, indeed, the options in the immediate second post-war France were either Catholicism or non-religion.

It should not be forgotten, however, that the same urbanization phenomenon in the United States of America had a different value, providing the immigrants with the most diverse religious beliefs not only the possibility of joining other people sharing the same religion but also the opportunity to change their own religious identities: the multicultural and multireligious context of the American metropolis offers the chance to choose which religion to join, without having to opt for nonreligion if persons don't feel at ease in their religion of birth. Similarly, in Latin America, the deconfessionalization processes have not resulted into the disappearance of religion, but rather into its explosion, with the birth of innumerable Pentecostal and neo-Pentecostal Churches, as well as with the rediscovery of the Afro-American Churches and the syncretistic experiences of spiritism, as well as Umbanda and Candomblé in the Afro-Brazilian context.

The deconfessionalization process goes hand in hand with the affirmation of the freedom of choice of the subject, who has wider and wider operating margins even in the religious ambit, while obedience to the traditional religious authorities fade into the background. The practice of such freedom of choice is obviously not without consequences for the relationship of the believer with the tradition and with the religious institutions: the relationship with the sacred is no longer governed solely by the moral laws or the beliefs of the different churches, but also by the expressiveness and the creativity of the individuals. Scholars since at least the 1990s – even if 30 years before there were already scholars, such as Peter Berger, who recorded the shift "from the institution to the subject." Daniélè Hervieu-Léger (1993), for example, speaking of "religion without memory," says that the autonomy of the subject, the rationalization of social life, and the differentiation of the institutions have marked the end of the "societies of memory." The collective memory of modern societies is a memory made of fragments and lacks coherence, and also establishes the principle according to which each one must find one's own way. Just this principle triggers a process of "exit from religion" and, at the same time, a dynamism of religious resocialization based on the elective dimension – that is to say, on the free choice of the believers.

Hervieu-Léger calls the tension between the freedom of the subject, with his feelings and needs, and the institution of believing, with its dogmatic and normative references, "elective fraternity." The spread of elective fraternity shows how modernity resolves the tension between the affirmation of the modern culture of the individual and the traditional regulations of faith and of the religious practices. The group of freely chosen brothers and sisters is the place where a specific and authentic personal research can express itself, outside any reference and orthodoxy institutionally regulated.

Charles Taylor (1989, 1991, 2002) likewise reflects on the new perception that the subject has of himself as modern era advances. Speaking of the "culture of self," he describes the "subjective turn" of contemporary culture, which consists in the individuals' refusal to live their lives in such exclusive allegiance to objective roles that are imposed on them from outside. Such refusal allows the subjects to be in tune with their "inner selves," which suggests from each one's inside which tasks to take, the ways to implement them, the judgments to give. This approach is both cause and effect of a reflexive way of dealing with life, no longer accepting external rules and practices uncritically but, as we have just seen, in tune with the needs of the "inner self," which pays more attention to subjective authenticity than to objective truth. Such change from exteriority to interiority brings with it specific attention to emotions, feelings, dreams, memories, the body, compassion, and individual life experiences.

It is clear that the shift of attention from the order established by any system of objective meaning, as for example the order crystallized in the religious institutions, and the needs of the subject as he or she perceives them, brings as a consequence the redefinition of the relationship between the believing subject and the institutions that have always governed the relationship with the sacred. We might say that in the contemporary age the "sacred self" becomes the source of meaning and the primary authority to which we owe obedience.

Spirituality as Democratization of the Sacred

These processes of deconfessionalization and individualization reformulate belief in terms of relativity (Michel 1994). In the words of Poulat (1994), whereas once everything was according to God's Grace, for us all now everything is linked to man's freedom, and within the limits of his possibilities, the only controls and prohibitions are the rules deemed appropriate by one's society. Crucial in this regard is the transformation that happened in respect to ways of conceiving the relationship with power and authority. As noted by Gauchet (1998), after the three modern revolutions (the English, the American and the French), power does not impose itself on the will of men "from above," be it religious or political, but rather it is drawn back to earth "at eye level." The democratic exercise of power seems to inaugurate a new situation in which the human is no longer defined in relation to the sacred, but it is the latter that is understood differently starting from the protection of the needs of the individuals. Hence, the religious diversity of contemporary societies and the consequent processes of normative pluralism should be studied not only from the religious institutional aspects, but we must also consider the transformation of the self and of the way of believing. The individualization of the way of believing consists precisely in this: the subject engaged in the research of meaning no longer accepts the normative answers that come from outside. As Michel (1994) points out, the contemporary way of believing, far from being functional to religious identities conceived according to the criterion of stability, places the primacy of experience over dogmatic contents, of authenticity over truth, according to a perspective that legitimizes change as the rule. The debate on the concept of spirituality, as it has been carried out in the sociology of religion for more than a decade, can be placed in this situation of the gradual weakening of traditional legitimacy, as it is recognized in institutions, while instead affirming the affirmation of the democratic device protecting the freedom of choice of the individual.

Clark Roof (1993, 1999) and Robert Wuthnow (1998, 2001) were the first to put the terms "religion" and "spirituality" in a dialectical position, starting from the analysis of empirical data.

To Roof (1993), the former term highlights the importance of the personal paths of research for the meaning of life, research that is often carried out at the margins or even outside the boundaries of the traditional religions. And even if the polarization between religion and spirituality is certainly not a new issue (in the theological and philosophical ambits the polarity between the subjective and the objective dimensions of believing has always been acknowledged), the novelty consists in the new hierarchical order of the two dimensions: the objective dimension no longer governs the subjective dimension, but vice versa. As we have already seen above, it is the actual needs of the believing subject that reshape the offer of meaning of the traditional churches. This seems to be the keystone to understanding the relationship of contemporary man with the sacred and the transcendent: everyone builds for himself or herself a "tailor-made meaning system" both within the historical religious traditions and outside them. As noted by Wuthnow (1998), considering the relationship with the sacred no longer starting from the institution but rather starting from the subject means to understand better the issues concerning authority, the recognition of truth, the credibility of beliefs, the durability and stability of belongings. Wuthnow makes a distinction between "dwelling spirituality" and "seeking spirituality." The former characterized religion in the context of the traditional society: it referred to a relationship with the sacred that was granted by the rites and the certainties offered by the religious institutions, which guaranteed the objective meaning of believing. On the contrary, "seeking spirituality" marks the dynamics of the contemporary believing, where the risk of exploration and openness to multiple possibilities of meaning is preferred to the security ensured by dogmatic certainties.

If in the traditional perspective the sacred referred to the stability of clear boundaries that made the identities and the differences recognizable, today the relationship with the sacred does not know any safe boundaries. Indeed, it prefers openness and movement through the different beliefs, both traditional and non-traditional, and the many possible life experiences, often eclectically combining teachings and practices from different cultural traditions. To Wuthnow the two approaches to the sacred are not to be considered as alternatives: The traditional way of believing may become meaningless. Then it can give way to a need for freedom and openness toward diverse experiences. Incessant research for new experiences, by contrast, might generate a need of belonging and of strong identity. The "spiritual revolution" to which by now various scholars of religion refer (Heelas 2002; Tacey 2003; Heelas and Woodhead 2005) fits into this line of thinking, sometimes assuming mistakenly, that religion and spirituality would be two opposing dimensions, in a "zero sum" relation. Although the usefulness of the category of spirituality is still discussed within the sociological debate, it seems undeniable that that it has the merit of highlighting a new legitimizing process of the relation with the sacred, a legitimization that is no longer based on obedience to the religious institution but one that is founded on the freedom of choice of the subject who can even freely accept to adhere to an extremely conservative religion, not very attentive to the individuals' needs of expressiveness and creativity.

Rather than being in competition with religion, then, spirituality shifts the axis of legitimacy from the institution to the subject, acknowledging in the religious field the effects of the recognition of the freedom of choice of the individuals, spirituality in this sense can again be considered as the democratization of the sacred. As widely recognized in other spheres of social life, from politics to family, from the orientations of value to the choices of ethical character, even in the religious field we ultimately record a slip of legitimacy from externally directed moral codes to normative systems based on the subject and his freedom. From a functional point of view, we could say that spirituality enables the believer to be more flexible in a world in which religious diversity affects even those national contexts in which there is a monopoly or semi-monopoly control of the religious market. As illustrated by Pace (2010), even countries that until not long ago were homogeneous from the point of view of religion, now must deal with the religions and beliefs of the millions of immigrants who populate them. For example, of the seven nations forming the United Arab Emirates, only 20 % of the population are indigenous.

From Religious Diversity to Religious Pluralism

The transition from the twentieth to the twenty-first century has been characterized by a transnational migration process that has radically transformed the social and cultural landscape of wide areas of the planet. Such process of global mobility has caused a transformation from the cultural and religious homogeneity, either real or socially constructed in many nations, and especially in Europe, to the acknowledgement of diversity. Religious differentiation, then, is played on more levels: an individual level, with what we have called the democratization of the sacred, and a social one, with the differentiation of the religious offer: if on one side the demand for goods and religious services is becoming more complex, on the other side the supply of such goods and services is also becoming complex, and this is the result of the new proximity of different cultures and religions.

According to the estimates of the United Nations Population Division the number of migrants in the world has grown in the last 50 years from 80 million to 214 million, shifting from 2.6 to 3 % of the world population. A report published in 2012 by Pew Forum on Religion & Public Life shows that nearly half of these migrants are Christian (49 %), 27 % are Muslim, 5 % Hindu, 3 % Buddhist, 2 % Jewish, while 4 % belong to other religions and 9 % are unaffiliated.

The millions of migrants who have moved from one part of the globe to the other have brought with them, besides the hope to better their own and their families' life conditions, the culture, the values, the traditions and the religions of their countries of origin. No doubt the place where such changes are more noticeable are the cities: it is here that the highest concentration of immigrant people are recorded, and there is no western town that has not experienced a profound re-configuration due precisely to the migratory flows in the last two decades, and the same goes for the immense towns of the Asian continent.

Just to give some examples of how these global towns must confront the social and cultural diversity never experienced before, the city of Birmingham, Britain's largest minority-majority city, has launched a program of study and of social action which is entitled "Superdiversity": the local university and the City Council will work side by side to understand the challenges and the opportunities offered by the presence in the same urban space of an unusual variety of languages, ethnic groups, faiths, and traditions that make the daily interaction of the citizens more and more variegated and complex. A superdiversity experience like that of Birmingham is to be found in many cities of the western world, as well as in the Latin American universe or in some African metropolises. Across the next 15 years this will be more and more the situation of many cities in Asia in which, according to a forecast of the World Development Bank, within 2030 there will be more than a billion people, and more than 50 % of the population of those countries will settle around the urban areas. Given this situation, on one hand it is not difficult to imagine, considering the size of the urbanization processes, that in the coming decades the issue of religion will be among the most relevant ones in the agenda of the governors of the major global cities; on the other hand it is virtually impossible to make predictions about what will be the outcomes of this interlacement of cultures, traditions and religious beliefs.

What we can say for certain is that such religious diversity will have to be "governed" in some way by the civil authorities, and the increasingly diverse demands for the free practice of one's religion will find a regulative principle in the State, that will try to combine the general interests of the community with the legitimate requests of acknowledgment of the "minorities" and of the individual believers. The transition from "religious diversity" to "religious pluralism," as we shall see well illustrated in the chapters of this book, consists precisely in the "institutional arrangements," especially of legal nature, that regulate diversity, and in the ideas of political and philosophical nature that tend to consider cultural and religious diversity as a high value.

The legal, regulatory and cultural answers to religious diversity vary consistently from country to country: there are contexts in which all religions, from the traditional ones, historically established, to the new religious movements and the religious beliefs that group a few hundred followers, can live and proliferate without any interference on the part of political power, and contexts in which religious diversity is governed very strictly, if not even prohibited.

The reasons for such difference are justified depending on the issues that such diversity puts under discussion: they often touch the nations' very identities, built in many cases through a more or less recognized identification with a single religious tradition, but they also have to do with national security, public order, and the protection of individuals' health and dignity. The particularly close eye of the public authority especially supervises groups who might potentially cause problems for national security (e.g. Islam in many European countries, but not only in Europe), or that might be dangerous for the people who join it (e.g. cases of collective suicide of the Order of the Solar Temple in Switzerland, France and Canada).

The religions, from their part, obviously do not suffer the external regulation exercised by the State against them passively: they react by implementing adaptation strategies that can involve both the legal and the regulative levels, as well as cultural awareness and social mobilization. In this regard, Beckford and Richardson (2007), explained in detail how religion is both subject and object of regulation at the same time: in the former case religion and the religious organization exercise their power of control within their own area of influence and in the external area where they operate; in the latter case, it is the political and military agencies who exercise the power of control over religion. The modalities of controlling and being controlled vary not only from country to country but even more depending on the different historical periods. The economic and financial crisis which erupted in 2008, for example, has re-defined migration flows and has changed the attitudes of the citizens and the politicians of many states toward immigration. Suffice it to recall what two political leaders stated in Germany and Great Britain only a few months apart: in October 2010 Angela Merkel announced that the German attempt to build a multicultural society had "utterly failed"; 4 months later, in February 2011, British Prime Minister David Cameron stated that the experiment of multiculturalism had failed in Great Britain. Statements of this kind cannot fail to have important consequences on how to read and interpret cultural and religious diversity, and then, later, on the different types of religious pluralism that are being tested. When we speak of pluralism, it is important to remember that we do not mean a single mode to adjust to and to deal with diversity of culture in general and religion in particular, but we refer to a number of strategies involving religions, the State and the civil society. It is a continuous process of negotiation and re-negotiation, in an ongoing effort to maintain and preserve the boundaries between the different social spheres in a world that makes these boundaries ever more porous and fragile.

In the end, the issue of religious pluralism helps sociologists to open their eyes to a reality that is plural in itself, and that only in an ideological and artificial way has been understood as homogeneous and singular. As pointed out by Ammerman (2010), religious pluralism is the "normal state of affairs," and this is so not only because religion is a multidimensional reality, but also because the institutions that govern it are manifold, both from within the religious field itself and outside it. Even more, the focus on religious pluralism has made visible the religious traditions that have been present for centuries in countries where the religious market was monopolized by a single religion which, with its shadow, made all the others invisible (Dìez de Velasco 2010).

From the point of view of political and sometimes even religious rhetoric, it is difficult to find someone who openly opposes cultural and religious pluralism (except for xenophobic parties that are present in all nations). Reality, however, often contradicts the statements of principle.

It is also the sociologist's concern to distinguish between the two levels, that is to say between the statements of principle and the practices of daily life, and this book attempts to make a contribution in this direction. The volume is divided into two parts: the first four chapters of a theoretical nature mean to offer a definition, as exhaustive as possible, of the concept of religious pluralism, focusing different perspectives; the second part includes another eight chapters that report case studies, illustrating how diversity and religious pluralism are combined together in different ways according to the different social and cultural contexts.

In chapter "Re-thinking Religious Pluralism" James Beckford proposes a conceptual clarification distinguishing the definition of religious pluralism from that of religious diversity, and then places this distinction within political, legal and cultural contexts. In chapter "Religious Diversity, Social Control, and Legal Plural ism: A Socio-legal Analysis", James Richardson focuses on the systems of social control that are implemented on the various religious groups, highlighting the different degrees of intensity by which this control is exercised. In chapter "Oligop oly Is Not Pluralism", Fenggang Yang distinguishes the difference between oligopoly and pluralism, then addressing an ever-present issue in the sociology of religion: the definition of the concept of religion itself.

In chapter "Religious and Philosophical Diversity as a Challenge for the Secu larism: A Belgian-French Comparison", Jean-Paul Willaime, starting from a comparison between France and Belgium describes two different ways of understanding the concept of "secularism" in Europe: the former way considers secularism as a general principle of relationship between the State and the religions in the context of pluralist democracies that respect the individuals' exercise of freedom; the latter way interprets secularism as an agnostic philosophical concept that refers to a non-religious view of the world; in this latter meaning, then, secularism behaves like a true belief, and is organized in the same way as the traditional religions.

In chapters "The Diversity of Religious Diversity. Using Census and NCS Methodology in Order to Map and Assess the Religious Diversity of a whole Country", "Increasing Religious Diversity in a Society Monopolized by Catholi cism", and "Rethinking Religious Diversity: Diversities and Governance of

Diversities in "Post-Societies" religious diversity in three European countries is presented: Switzerland, Italy and Croatia. Christophe Monnot and Jorg Stölz, illustrating the "diversity of religious diversity" in Switzerland, show how census and quantitative "national congregations study" methodology can be combined to describe and interpret the religious diversity of an entire nation. Enzo Pace, in chapter "Increasing Religious Diversity in a Society Monopolized by Catholicism" illustrates the mapping of religious diversity in Italy, a country traditionally characterized by the monopoly of Catholicism. Siniša Zrinščak analyzes the similarities and differences in the regulation of religious diversity in other post-communist countries, starting from the socio-religious situation in Croatia.

James Spickard and William Swatos, focus the situation of religious diversity in the United States respectively in chapters "Diversity Versus Pluralism? Notes from the American Experience" and "Between No Establishment and Free Exercise: The Dialectic of American Religious Pluralism": Spickard emphasizes how the concept of religious pluralism should be considered carefully when it is applied to the United States, a country that is still predominantly Christian; Swatos, starting from the First Amendment to the Constitution of the United States, shows the problematic consequences when it is applied in an increasingly multi-religious situation.

Chapters "Missionary Trans-Border Religions and Defensive Civil Society in Contemporary Japan: Toward a Comparative Institutional Approach to Religious Pluralism" and "Religious Tendencies in Brazil: Disenchantment, Secularization, and Sociologists" lead us to Japan and Brazil: Yoshihide Sakurai explains in a historical perspective how the transnational religions arrived in Japan with immigrants and missionaries have contributed to make that country more and more differentiated as to religion. Roberto Motta, describing the revival of Candomblé, the emergence of liberation theology and the rapid spread of the Pentecostal Churches, interprets the religious change in Brazil as a process of "dis-enchantment" and "re-enchantment," stressing how in this process the sociologists have played a major role.

References

Acquaviva, Sabino Samele. 1961. *L'eclissi del sacro nella società industriale: dissacrazione e secolarizzazione nella società industriale e post-industriale*. Milano: Edizioni di Comunità.

Ammerman, Nancy T. 2010. The challenges of pluralism: Locating religion in a world of diversity. *Social Compass* 57(2): 154–167.

Beckford, James A. 1999. The management of religious diversity in England and Wales with special reference to Prison Chaplaincy. *MOST Journal on Multicultural Societies* 1(2): 10. Available from: http://unesdoc.unesco.org/images/0014/001437/143733E.pdf#page=19.

Beckford, James A., and James T. Richardson. 2007. Religion and regulation. In *The SAGE handbook of the sociology of religion*, ed. James A. Beckford and N. Jay Demerath III, 396–418. London: Sage.

Berger, Peter L. 1967. *The sacred conopy*. Garden City: Doubleday Anchor.

Casanova, José. 1994. *Public religions in the modern world*. Chicago: The University of Chicago Press.

Dìez De Velasco, Francisco. 2010. The visibilization of religious minorities in Spain. *Social Compass* 57(2): 235–252.

Gauchet, Michel. 1998. *La religion dans la démocratie. Parcours de la laïcité*. Paris: Gallimard.

Heelas, Paul. 2002. The spiritual revolution: From 'Religion' to 'Spirituality'. In *Religions in the modern world*, ed. Linda Woodhead, Paul Fletcher, Hiroko Kawanami, and David Smith, 357–377. New York: Routledge.

Heelas, Paul, and Linda Woodhead. 2005. *The spiritual revolution. Why religion is giving way to spirituality*. Oxford: Blackwell.

Hervieu-Léger, Danièle. 1993. *La religion pour mémoire*. Paris: Cerf.

Kepel, Gilles. 1991. *La revanche de Dieu*. Paris: Seuil.

Le Bras, Gabriel. 1956. *Etudes de sociologie religieuse*. Paris: PUF.

Michel, Patrick. 1994. *Politique et religion. La grande mutation*. Paris: Albin Michel.

Pace, Enzo. 2010. Introduction. *Social Compass* 57(2): 147–153.

Poulat, Emile. 1994. *L'Ere postchrétienne: un monde sorti de Dieu*. Paris: Flammarion.

Roof, Wade Clark. 1993. *A generation of seekers. The spiritual journeys of the baby boom generation*. San Francisco: Harper Collins.

Roof, Wade Clark. 1999. *Spiritual marketplace. Baby boomers and the remaking of American religion*. Princeton: Princeton University Press.

Tacey, David. 2003. *The spirituality revolution. The emergence of contemporary spirituality*. Sydney: Harper Collins.

Taylor, Charles. 1989. *Sources of the self. The making of the modern identity*. Cambridge: Cambridge University Press.

Taylor, Charles. 1991. *The ethics of authenticity*. Cambridge: Harvard University Press.

Taylor, Charles. 2002. *Varieties of religion today*. Cambridge: Harvard University Press.

Wuthnow, Robert. 1998. *After heaven. Spirituality in America since the 1950s*. Berkeley: University of California Press.

Wuthnow, Robert. 2001. *Creative spirituality. The way of the artist*. Berkeley: University of California Press.

Part I
Ideas and Concepts on Religious Pluralism

Re-Thinking Religious Pluralism

James A. Beckford

Introduction

I want to begin by going back to one of the foundational works of the philosophy of the social sciences, namely, Lewis Carroll's *Through the Looking Glass, and What Alice Found There*. This 1871 sequel to *Alice's Adventures in Wonderland* raises many profound questions about the nature of human reality and our capacity to understand it. For my purposes, one of the most interesting episodes in the book occurs when Alice meets the egg-shaped, argumentative character called Humpty Dumpty. When she disputes his meaning of the term 'glory', his ill-tempered reply tells us a lot about our use of words:

> When *I* use a word,' Humpty Dumpty said, in rather a scornful tone, 'it means just what I choose it to mean — neither more nor less.
>
> The question is,' said Alice, 'whether you *can* make words mean so many different things.
>
> The question is,' said Humpty Dumpty, 'which is to be master — that's all. (Carroll 1871: 73).

Some commentators regard Humpty Dumpty as a postmodernist *avant la lettre* for implying that words can mean more or less anything he chooses. But my interpretation is different. I think Humpty Dumpty's argument is more sinister. I think his argument is that the meaning of words is dependent on the power to enforce it. This linguistic *Realpolitik* is crude but it contains the kernel of a truth that underlies my chapter.

I shall argue that the term 'pluralism' needs to be used with special care and that a particularly important dimension of 'religious pluralism' has not yet received the sociological attention that it deserves. My strategy will be to place pluralism in a variety of different contexts in order to show that religious pluralism is not alone in

J.A. Beckford (✉)
Department of Sociology, University of Warwick, Coventry, CV4 7AL, UK
e-mail: J.A.Beckford@warwick.ac.uk

G. Giordan and E. Pace (eds.), *Religious Pluralism*,
DOI 10.1007/978-3-319-06623-3_2, © Springer International Publishing Switzerland 2014

giving rise to interesting questions and problems. There is no special metaphysical pathos attaching to the notion of religious pluralism; and we need to place it squarely in the context of other types of pluralism and struggles for recognition because they are all features of liberal democracies in a globalizing era (Tully 1995; Connolly 1995). I shall begin with a summary of the range of meanings often attributed to pluralism in political and legal contexts. Then I shall argue that the term 'religious pluralism' can refer to four different things:

(a) empirical forms of diversity in relation to religion
(b) normative or ideological views about the positive value of religious diversity
(c) the frameworks of public policy, law and social practices which accommodate, regulate and facilitate religious diversity.
(d) relational contexts of everyday interactions between individuals and groups identified as religious.

There are clearly overlaps and mutual interactions between empirical religious diversity, normative views of pluralism, frameworks to sustain and regulate religious diversity, and everyday interactions around religious diversity. Indeed, the political philosopher William Connolly (1995) insists that his inclusive notion of 'deep pluralism' must embrace the descriptive and the normative. And Martin Marty (2007: 16) argues that '"pluralism" implies and involves a polity, a civic context which provides some "rules of the game", refers to an ethos, and evokes a response'. But the distinctions that I want to make are not only essential for conceptual hygiene but are also pre-conditions for the clarification of empirical realities and public policies and regulations.

Varieties of Pluralism

Variation in the meanings attributed to pluralism is extensive. In fact, it would be better to think in terms of 'pluralisms' in the plural. This would draw attention not only to the differences between usages of the term in different intellectual disciplines but also to the tensions that exist between meanings of pluralism within the same disciplinary frameworks. These differences and tensions should alert us to the fact that discourses about pluralism are contentious for many different reasons. Nevertheless, there is a wide measure of agreement that the term – in its most general normative formulation – refers to 'a powerful ideal meant to resolve the question of how to get along in a conflict-ridden world' (Bender and Klassen 2010: 1). And this is how the Global Centre for Pluralism, jointly funded by the Canadian government and the Ismailis, describes it:

> Pluralism rejects division as a necessary outcome of diversity, seeking instead to identify the qualities and experiences that unite rather than divide us as people and to forge a shared stake in the public good. (Global Centre for Pluralism 2012: 1)

The ideal is admirable, but pluralisms invariably place limits on the choice of others with whom getting along is permitted or encouraged. For example, in a powerful indictment of colonialism and its continuing effects on the native peoples of North America, Tracy Leavelle (2010: 175) concludes that 'Pluralism . . . enacts definitions of acceptable difference'. And Geneviève Zubrzycki (2010) shows how the religious diversity of Poland before the 1930s was masked by discourses of Polish Catholic unity and uniformity in the face of threats from Nazi Germany and the Soviet Union. Indeed, she adds that 'Religious discourse in present-day Poland generally is not being used to advocate the building of an open society, as it had under communism, but rather to exclude those considered unworthy of full membership' (Zubrzycki 2010: 279).

In the space available I can only sketch the broad outlines of a small selection of the many variations in the use of the notion of pluralism. For the sake of convenience, I shall group them under the three headings of political, legal and religious. I shall have to omit medical pluralism (Cant and Sharma 1998), cultural pluralism (Deveaux 2000) and welfare pluralism (Johnson 1987; Gilbert 2000) as well as many others. But it would be a mistake to neglect the fact that all the variations on the theme of pluralism derive from ancient philosophical discussions of whether the nature of reality – and/or knowledge of reality – was monist, dualist or pluralist.

(i) *Political pluralism*

Discussions of pluralism have been at the centre of political philosophy and political theory for many centuries.[1] Discussions focus mainly on questions about the most appropriate distribution of valued goods, power and authority in political regimes that are not entirely centralized or totalitarian. In particular, the slow emergence of liberal democratic regimes in Western Europe and North America provided ideal conditions for theorizing about relations between the one and the many, the individual citizen and the sovereign state, the public and the private, and the clash between irreconcilable values – 'value pluralism' (Lassman 2011). Early modern contributors include Spinoza, Hobbes, Rousseau and Kant. In their different ways, each of these thinkers grappled with questions about the appropriate – or putatively natural – relations between unity and multiplicity or between sameness and difference. Contributors in the modern era include William James, Charles Pierce, Richard Rorty and Jean-François Lyotard. The question of whether philosophical pluralism necessarily entails relativism haunts many of the discussions. More to the point of this chapter, echoes of these discussions can be heard in

---

[1] My discussion takes no account of the radically different notion of 'plural societies' which characterized colonial regimes in which power was unevenly distributed between different categories of people identified by their so-called race. Western European and American colonial territories in South and South East Asia met the criteria of a plural society originally laid down by J.S. Furnivall (1948: 446): 'A plural society, with different sections of the community living side by side, but separately, within the same political unit. Even in the economic sphere there is a division of labour along racial lines'.

disputes about relations between religious diversity, multiculturalism and cultural relativism (Trigg 2007, 2010).[2]

There are major differences between American and English traditions of theorizing about political pluralism. American approaches to political pluralism tend to start from the assumption that power and other resources in the USA have invariably been unevenly distributed between a wide variety of competing interest groups (Dahl 1967, 1982). The aim of pluralist thinking is therefore to determine how best to ensure that none of the competing groups becomes tyrannical and that none of the minority interests is excluded from democratic processes. The function attributed to the state and to legislatures is largely to mediate between competing groups.

There is more continuity than discontinuity between American pluralism, which flourished in the 1960s and 1970s, and more recent currents of neoliberalism. They share an equally strong commitment to minimizing the role of the state, but neoliberalism lacks faith in the capacity of overlapping intermediary associations to keep the state in check. Neoliberals prefer to leave this role to individuals, enterprising corporations and voluntary associations rather than to competing interest groups.

By contrast, English political pluralism – which flourished in the early twentieth century – starts from criticism of the state for centralizing all power in its own hands (Hirst 1997). The pluralist aim is to challenge the idea that the state must be, by definition, sovereign and to loosen its grip on society by dispersing certain powers to properly constituted associations and corporate organizations such as workers' guilds, voluntary associations and community groups.[3] In this scenario, representative democracy would no longer be based on political parties alone but, instead, would be stronger for being able to draw on citizens' other interest groupings – and on the overlaps between them. In other words, 'In the pluralist mode, government is the arena of competition among private interests, in which it brokers, bargains and manages conflicts' (Kazepov and Genova 2006: 249).

The *locus classicus* for this style of theorizing about political pluralism is John Neville Figgis's *Churches in the Modern State*, which was first published in 1913 (Hirst 2000). Figgis, an Anglican priest who greatly admired the co-operative theory of the German legal philosopher Otto von Gierke, located sovereignty in a 'community of communities' comprising voluntary associations, churches, guilds and community groups – all regarded as having a legal personality of their own. Loud echoes of this type of pluralist thought could be heard in the policies advanced by the New Labour Party before and after their election victory of 1997 in the UK. But David Runciman's downbeat assessment is cogent:

---

[2] 'Pluralism can quickly degenerate into relativism, the view that "truths" are only true for those who believe them. Once a society stands back from the standards of a particular religion, and tries to treat all religions fairly, there are problems about whether it can accept the beliefs of all religions as of equal value.' Trigg (2007: 1, 3).

[3] According to Hirst (1997: 64), 'the principle underlying a pluralist state – as conceived by J.N. Figgis, G.D.H. Cole and H.J. Laski' would be 'that the state exists to protect and serve the self-governing associations'.

[T]he greater the emphasis placed on voluntary associations (such as the family, for communitarians; or voluntary pension schemes, for new Labour), the greater the constraints that come to be placed on the ways in which these associations can operate... The attempt to enhance the role of voluntary associations does not result in a diminution of the authority of the state; it merely relocates it. (Runciman 1997: 264).

Similar arguments have been made about New Labour programmes for partnerships between the state and the 'faith sector' (Carmel and Harlock 2008; Beckford 2010a, b).

In short, political pluralisms can take a variety of forms. American pluralism tends to emphasize the search for balance between competing interest groups, while the focus of English pluralism is on the need to devolve power from the State to voluntary and communal groups.

(ii) *Legal pluralism*

Individualism and universalism are important hallmarks of Western liberal philosophies and ideologies. They leave little space for the particularities and relativities of pluralist thinking. This is most clearly evident in the pressure from the advocates of legal pluralism to acknowledge that distinctive ways of life and cultures deserve to be recognized to some degree in national and international systems of law without necessarily jeopardising rationality. The belief that existing systems of self-regulation and adjudication – operating alongside national systems of state law – are appropriate for certain professional, religious, ethnic or cultural collectivities is at the heart of legal pluralism. And in the case of England, legal pluralists could point to 'living' practices of social and cultural regulation by norms other than those of the state's legal system. Religious tribunals, for example, are free to deal with the religious aspects of marriage and divorce for members of religious communities who voluntarily submit themselves to their jurisdiction.

Nevertheless, these tribunals have no standing in English law; and their decisions are not taken into account in civil law (Douglas et al. 2011).[4] For example, systems of ecclesiastical law and diocesan consistory courts regulate the Church of England. The Roman Catholic Church has its own canon law, courts and lawyers. Orthodox Jews can have recourse to '*beth din*' or rabbinical courts for the resolution of various civil matters. And although the term 'sharia court' is questionable,[5] Muslims can certainly use Islamic law, procedures and institutions to seek redress or resolution of civil problems. Even Jehovah's Witnesses have judicial committees in their congregations for investigating and adjudicating claims of misconduct among members. On the other hand, the contributions that religious tribunals may make towards the arbitration of civil disputes between parties who willingly choose

---

[4] 'None of the tribunals has any legal status afforded to them by the state or the civil law, and their rulings and determinations in relation to marital status have no civil recognition either. They derive their authority from their religious affiliation, not from the state, and that authority extends only to those who choose to submit to them.' Douglas et al. (2011: 48).

[5] Sharia Councils and Muslim Arbitration Tribunals make judgments on the basis not only of sharia but also of other Islamic sources of guidance.

to seek this form of arbitration may be recognized under the Arbitration Act 1996 (Sandberg 2011: 184–90). Sports, professions and universities are other areas in which self-regulation is conducted largely in 'supplemental jurisdictions', although the power to enforce or overturn determinations remains ultimately with State law.[6] Australia, Canada, New Zealand and the USA have also established supplemental jurisdictions for aboriginal, indigenous, native, Indian or First Nations peoples.

Given the existence of these well established instances of legal pluralism in England and elsewhere, it is surprising in some ways that such intense controversy flared up in 2008 when the Archbishop of Canterbury spoke openly about legal pluralism in practice (Tucker 2008). He recommended to a meeting of eminent jurists that a scheme should be instituted 'in which individuals will retain the liberty to choose the jurisdiction under which they will seek to resolve certain carefully specified matters' (Williams 2008: 274). He was also far from being the first to make such a proposal (Morris 1990) or to note the religious dimension of legal pluralism (Allott 1990). But the public response to the Archbishop's proposal was overwhelmingly critical, with outspoken condemnation of the possibility that so-called sharia courts would be free to discriminate against women and to inflict inhumane punishments for minor offences (One Law for All 2010). Some experts in law, for example Adam Tucker (2008), were also highly critical of the Archbishop's proposal.

Nevertheless, it remains the case that forms of legal pluralism have existed in England for centuries and that the institutions of religious law have provided supplemental jurisdictions with varying degrees of success. More than 20 years ago, Antony Allott (1990: 225) characterized the 'English way' of coping with competing pressures for legal recognition as 'to allow the maximum freedom to subsidiary home-made legal systems, constituted by contract, by membership of a group with its own customs'. This pragmatic approach was also characteristic of British colonial policies and practices for accommodating some of the distinctive and widely differing systems of traditional conflict resolution among religious, tribal and ethnic peoples subjected to British rule.

What is still unclear is how far the enactment of laws promoting equality and prohibiting discrimination will strengthen the case for legal pluralism or undermine it on the grounds that the rights to equality and non-discrimination are universal and dependent on the power of unitary legal systems to enforce them. In other words, recognition of sub-national categories of peoples and cultures as deserving of separate protections in law seems to be simultaneously an objective of both liberalism and pluralism. A reminder of David Runciman's point is in order here: 'The attempt to enhance the role of voluntary associations does not result in a diminution of the authority of the state; it merely relocates it.' (Runciman 1997: 264). Jane Lewis (2005) made a similar point about the failure of partnerships with New Labour governments to foster 'civil renewal' or 'democratization'. Instead,

---

[6] 'The doctrine of "consensual compact" means that the rules and structures of voluntary associations are binding on assenting members.' Sandberg (2011: 188).

she argued, partnerships had the effect of controlling as well as harnessing the energies of community and voluntary associations. Something similar could be said about religious pluralism as well.

I have tried to make two main points so far. First, questions of pluralism are common in the realms of politics and law in liberal democracies. Second, there are competing doctrines within political and legal pluralisms. I now want to move on to consider religious pluralism, which also gives rise to a variety of approaches and normative doctrines. In addition, I shall emphasise the fact that studies of religious pluralism often confuse its normative and its empirical aspects.

(iii) *Religious pluralism*
Earlier in this chapter I listed four distinct – but overlapping – meanings of religious pluralism:

(a) empirical religious diversity
(b) normative ideas about the positive value of religious diversity
(c) the frameworks of public policy, law and social practices which recognize, accommodate, regulate and facilitate religious diversity
(d) the social relational contexts of everyday interactions between individuals and groups in settings where religious differences are considered relevant.

Ideally, researchers would keep these four categories distinct for analytical purposes, but the tendency is to conflate them within a generic notion of pluralism. Moreover, the fourth category attracts far less scholarly attention than the other three, although I shall argue below that it is no less important than they are.

(a) *Empirical diversity*
Religious diversity sounds simple but is potentially complicated (Beckford 2003: 74–77; Bouma and Ling 2009; Bramadat and Koenig 2009; Ahlin et al. 2012). It displays many dimensions, but I shall limit myself to just three.

(i) First, religious diversity refers to the variety of distinct faith traditions to be found in any region, country or continent. The list of such traditions could be both long and contentious because of potential disputes about the identity of traditions, the extent to which they are unified, and the boundaries that separate them. Paul Hirst (1997: 43) caricatures the extreme case of empirical religious diversity as 'a virtual process of "Ottamanization", in which plural communities co-exist side by side with different rules and standards'.

(ii) Second, diversity within distinct faith traditions has long been a feature of all religions. Again, boundary disputes are common between schools, currents and factions within each tradition – as well as between formal organizations representing particular expressions of the traditions.

(iii) Third, individual religious believers and practitioners differ in terms of (a) the extent to which their beliefs, practices and emotions reflect different faith traditions and (b) the extent to which they accord salience to religion at different stages of their life and in different situations. This adds to the diversity of 'lived' religions and is closely related to variations in the emotional registers of religious practice.

Devising empirical indicators and measures of these three dimensions of religious diversity is not easy, but I believe that this should be a priority for sociological research on religion.

(b) *Normative religious pluralism*
Studies of the positive value attributed to religious diversity – perhaps most famously associated with John Hick's (1977) edited volume on *The Myth of God Incarnate* – are too numerous to be easily summarized here. They include debates about ecumenism, multi-faith philosophies, inter-faith activities, religious 'othering', the theology of religions, religious aspects of multiculturalism, religious literacy, religious dialogue, intercultural religious education, and so on. They all analyze and/or advocate respect for the positive value of religious diversity in itself or as a means to the attainment of social and cultural cohesion and harmony. In this respect, some versions of normative religious pluralism resemble the 'value pluralism' strand of political theory. And it is worth bearing in mind Peter Lassman's observation that 'The problem ... for political theory is not so much that values might be plural, but, rather, that plural values can and do conflict with each other' (Lassman 2011: 13).

Indeed, the positive evaluation of religious diversity has paradoxically acquired the force of a unitary standard of rectitude in some places. This raises the question of whether liberal democracies have reached a point where expressions of doubt about the desirability of religious diversity are automatically categorised as 'radical' or 'extremist'. As ever, the liberal dilemma is how far to tolerate illiberal ideas and practices without jeopardising liberalism (Mahmood 2007; Butler 2008; Beckford 2008; Woodhead 2008).

In comparison with the doctrines of political and legal pluralism, however, there is a distinctive feature of normative religious pluralism. In theory it places few or no limits on the extent of the religious diversity to be promoted. By contrast, discussions of political and legal pluralisms tend to confine themselves to interactions between a relatively small number of 'interest groups' or legal systems. 'Plural' in these contexts usually means 'a few', whereas religious pluralisms are more likely to imply a much greater range of diversity. Indeed, James Davidson Hunter (2009: 1309, 1311) describes modern pluralism as 'a near-infinite yet random number of spiritual and religious positions' in the absence of a 'dominant culture'. This is the ideal or the theory, but sociological analysis shows that the reality tends to be different. That is, the social settings to which labels such as 'pluralistic' or 'interfaith' are usually applied invariably exclude large numbers of religious or spiritual groups. Religious pluralism in practice is confined to 'acceptable' groups – especially in 'closed' institutions such as prisons where religion can be contentious (Beckford 2011). Inter-faith dialogue is never open to all would-be participants (Stand for Peace 2013); and the full extent of religious diversity is rarely reflected in doctrines or displays of religious pluralism.[7] This is another good reason for keeping empirical diversity analytically separate from notions of normative pluralism.

(c) *Frameworks of regulation and recognition*
Scholarly attention to the frameworks of law and custom that regulate relations between individuals and groups, in so far as they are identified in terms of their religion, has increased sharply in recent decades. In particular, the general field of law and religion has expanded well beyond its traditional concerns with state constitutions, the freedom of religion, and varieties of religious law (Beckford and Richardson 2007; Doe 2011; Sandberg 2011). The complex matrix of overlapping factors driving this expansion includes the juridification – in Western Europe predominantly – of equality and non-discrimination in relation to religion and belief, the intensification of concern with questions about human rights and religion, the acceleration of labour migration between countries with different religious 'complexions', and the globalization and glocalization of religious movements. All these factors shape the social, political, legal and cultural contexts within which religious diversity is recognized, represented, accommodated, encouraged, restricted and regulated.[8]

Sophisticated and in-depth studies of law and religion – with implications for aspects of religious diversity – are already available (Greenawalt 2006, 2008; Sullivan 2005a, b, 2010a, b; Doe 2011; Sandberg 2011). But there is scope for further investigations of secondary legislation and administrative regulations that may have an impact on the recognition or repudiation of religious diversity. For example, social settings such as schools, universities, hospitals, prisons and the military operate their own rules regarding what counts as religion, what is permitted in the name of religion, how the practice of permitted religions is controlled, and – in some places – facilitated. Researchers have tended to emphasise the legal and administrative <u>restrictions</u> imposed on religion, but encouragement and facilitation are the other side of the coin. For example, taxation regimes, concessions to religious charitable organisations, broadcasting opportunities, education syllabuses, exemptions from certain laws on non-discrimination, 'interpellation' to enter into partnerships with agencies of the state (Beckford 2011, 2012), and representation on state bodies and at state ceremonies can all create opportunities for the promotion of the interests of particular religions. And the contribution of inter-faith organisations towards establishing the ground rules for interactions in the public realm between members of different faith communities should not be overlooked (Weller 2008, 2009). In other words, 'Religious pluralism must be understood in its broadest sense – as a normative system that is socially created and maintained. Such

---

[7] See Todd (2010) for a vivid account of the 'politics of religious pluralism' which reduced New York City's diversity of religions to Protestant, Catholic and Jewish participation in the Temple of Religion at New York's World's Fair in 1939–1940.

[8] See, for example, Beckford (1999), Bréchon and Willaime (2000), Ahmed (2005), Poole and Richardson (2006), and Clark (2007).

a normative system does not arise without human effort: it must be envisioned, cultivated, shared, and practiced' (Roof 2007: 8).

In short, the focus on recognition and regulation in the study of religious pluralism highlights the contexts that shape, manage and control the diversity of religious expressions in the public domain. It is not directly concerned with religion 'as such' but is focused on the political, cultural and social forces that push and pull the public expression of religions in various directions. The 'politics of cultural recognition' (Tully 1995) is a common feature of legislatures and courts of law, although the criteria by which claims are made for the official recognition of religious identities may not be fully understood (Eisenberg 2009). But there is even less understanding of the ways in which these claims to, and assertions of, religious identity are negotiated in everyday life. That is the focus of my final category of religious pluralism.

(d) *Everyday interactions in settings of religious diversity*
Instead of being concerned with mapping such things as the extent of religious diversity, the force of normative theories or the impact of regulatory frameworks, the focus of my fourth category of religious pluralism is on the representations, attitudes, negotiations and social interactions that occur in mundane or everyday settings where religious diversity is recognised or denied, challenged or extended. It concerns the skirmishes that take place along the line of 'settled' or 'acceptable' diversity when attempts to extend it are either welcomed or rejected. In the spirit of William Connolly's (1995) sense of 'pluralization', it is about the process of testing the limits of acceptable or reasonable forms of diversity. This involves investigating the outer limits of the diversity that is conventionally celebrated by self-identified pluralists and the criteria that they use for resisting further extensions of acceptable diversity. The crucial question at the heart of such negotiations is why any partic-ular group or identity should be treated differently from 'us'. And, if it is to be treated differently, does it have to conform to the norms governing the existing state of diversity which includes people like 'us'? As Lori Beaman has argued, the social construction of difference necessarily underlies assumptions about 'reasonable accommodation', but 'the language of reasonable accommodation reifies the boundary between "us" and "them" and displaces equality as a framework for negotiation' (Beaman 2012: 208).

In effect, this category of religious pluralism separates out, for analytical pur-poses, the interactive level of social life – without forgetting that social interaction takes place not only against a background of normative ideas about pluralism and regulatory frameworks but also in the presence of uncertainty and ambiguity about religious identities and boundaries. This is not about the construction and imposi-tion of religious labels and boundaries by the state, by courts of law or by other official agencies. Nor is it about 'everyday religion' (Ammerman 2007). It is about social interactions in everyday life that may have a bearing on perceptions of religious differences and/or the state of religious diversity in the eyes of at least some participants.

My main reason for constructing this category is to draw attention to situations in which people use or confront ideas about religious diversity in their everyday life – not only in clearly religious settings. The range of such settings is unlimited, but I shall select just a few in order to illustrate the value of studying religious diversity at the interactive level.

Beginning with the least formal settings, religious diversity can be a feature of personal attitudes (Wuthnow 2005), casual meetings between strangers, of relationships in families containing members of different religions (Arweck and Nesbitt 2010), and of friendship networks.

At a more formal level, relationships between colleagues, associates and fellow-workers in places of employment can be inflected by differences of religion. Other public settings with varying degrees of formality where religious diversity and its associated claims about identity (Eisenberg 2009) is expressed and experienced include: childcare centres, schools (Francis 2011), police forces (Armitage 2006), healthcare centres, youth groups (Valk et al. 2009), higher education institutions (Gilliat-Ray 2000; Tomalin 2007; Mayrl and Oeur 2009), voluntary associations (Harris and Young 2010), major public exhibitions and millennium celebrations (Gilliat-Ray 2004, 2006), the Olympic Games (Watson et al. 2005), sites of humanitarian aid delivery (Hicks 2010) and sports clubs (Taskforce on Religious Diversity 2011) may all be among the places where encounters with religious diversity take place.

Residential settings in which religious diversity may require careful consideration include hospitals (Gilliat-Ray 2001; Cadge et al. 2009), prisons (Beckford and Gilliat 1998; Beckford et al. 2005), welfare facilities (Kelly and Sinclair 2005), and military establishments (Benham Rennick 2009; Hansen 2012).

These studies of social interaction in formal and informal social settings open a window on to religious diversity as a dimension of lived experience and a fact of social life. They raise a number of questions such as: (a) What is at stake when religious diversity becomes part of everyday social interactions? (b) How are religious differences signified, side-stepped or suppressed in social interactions? (c) Does social interaction tend to reify religious identities or liquefy them? (d) Does the prevailing ethos of pluralism favour certain forms of interaction and discourage others? (e) How do appeals to 'secular neutrality' affect claims to religious difference and identity in social interactions?

Conclusions

This chapter makes three main points:

(i) First, it is unhelpful to confuse normative pluralism with empirical diversity. For analytical purposes, they should always be kept separate, although the confusion may be common in everyday discourse. A clear conceptual distinction between the normative and the empirical is a pre-requisite of sound social science.

(ii) Second, debates about religious diversity and religious pluralism are part of much broader discussions of identity and difference in political, legal and cultural contexts. There is no reason to think that religion deserves special treatment in these discussions.

(iii) And, third, there are good reasons for conducting careful analyses of the uses to which religious diversity is put in everyday social settings and interactions. This is a dimension of religious diversity and pluralism which is underdeveloped but essential to the understanding of what is at stake in different social settings.

The spirit in which I have made these three points is not in harmony with Humpty Dumpty's boast that he could make words mean anything he chose. Rather, my aim has been to demonstrate the value of making conceptual distinctions that help to throw light on the range of social contexts in which the varied meanings of religious pluralism are in play either as features of discourse and/or as analytical categories.

References

Ahlin, Lars, Jørn Borup, Marianne Qvortup Fibiger, Lene Kühle, Viggo Mortensen, and René Dybdal Pedersen. 2012. Religious diversity and pluralism: Empirical data and theoretical reflection from the Danish Pluralism Project. *Journal of Contemporary Religion* 27(3): 403–418.

Ahmed, Tahira Sameera. 2005. Reading between the lines: Muslims and the media. In *Muslim Britain. Communities under pressure*, ed. Tahir Abbas, 109–126. London: Zed Books.

Allott, Antony. 1990. Religious pluralism and the law in England and Africa. In *Religious pluralism and unbelief. Studies critical and comparative*, ed. Ian Hamnett, 205–224. London: Routledge.

Ammerman, Nancy Tatom (ed.). 2007. *Everyday religion. Observing modern religious lives.* New York: Oxford University Press.

Armitage, Richard Norris. 2006. Issues of religious diversity affecting visible minority ethnic police personnel in the workplace'. Unpublished Ph.D. thesis, University of Birmingham.

Arweck, Elisabeth, and Eleanor Nesbitt. 2010. Plurality at close quarters: Mixed-faith families in the UK. *Journal of Religion in Europe* 3: 155–182.

Beaman, Lori G. 2012. Conclusion. Alternatives to reasonable accommodation. In *Reasonable accommodation. Managing religious diversity*, ed. Lori G. Beaman, 208–223. Vancouver: UBC Press.

Beckford, James A. 1999. The mass media and new religious movements. In *New religious movements. Challenge and response*, ed. Bryan R. Wilson and Jamie Cresswell, 103–119. London: Routledge.

Beckford, James A. 2003. *Social theory and religion.* Cambridge: Cambridge University Press.

Beckford, James A. 2008. Secularism and coercive freedoms. *British Journal of Sociology* 59(1): 41–45.

Beckford, James A. 2010a. The return of public religion? A critical assessment of a popular claim. *Nordic Journal of Religion and Society* 23(2): 121–136.

Beckford, James A. 2010b. The uses of religion in public institutions: The case of prisons. In *Exploring the postsecular. The religious, the political and the urban*, ed. Arie Molendijk, Justin Beaumont, and Christoph Jedan, 381–401. Leiden: Brill.

Beckford, James A. 2011. Religion in prisons and in partnership with the state. In *Religion and the state. A comparative sociology*, ed. Jack Barbalet, Adam Possamai, and Bryan S. Turner, 43–64. London: Anthem Press.

Beckford, James A. 2012. Public religions and the post-secular: Critical reflections. *Journal for the Scientific Study of Religion* 51(2): 1–19.

Beckford, James A., and Sophie Gilliat. 1998. *Religion in prison. Equal rites in a multi-faith society*. Cambridge: Cambridge University Press.

Beckford, James A., and James T. Richardson. 2007. Religion and regulation. In *The SAGE handbook of the sociology of religion*, ed. James A. Beckford and N.J. Demerath III, 396–418. London: Sage.

Beckford, James A., Danièle Joly, and Farhad Khosrokhavar. 2005. *Muslims in prison: Challenge and change in Britain and France*. Basingstoke: Palgrave Macmillan.

Bender, Courtney, and Pamela E. Klassen (eds.). 2010. *After pluralism. Reimagining religious engagement*. New York: Columbia University Press.

Benham Rennick, Joanne. 2009. Religion in the Canadian military: Adapting to an increasingly pluralistic society. *Horizons* 10(2): 40–43.

Bouma, Gary, and Rod Ling. 2009. Religious diversity. In *The Oxford handbook of the sociology of religion*, ed. Peter B. Clarke, 507–522. Oxford: Oxford University Press.

Bramadat, Paul, and Matthias Koenig (eds.). 2009. *International migration and the governance of religious diversity*. Montreal/Kingston: McGill-Queen's University Press.

Bréchon, Pierre, and Jean-Paul Willaime (eds.). 2000. *Médias et Religion en Miroir*. Paris: PUF.

Butler, Judith. 2008. Sexual politics, torture, and secular time. *British Journal of Sociology* 59(1): 1–23.

Cadge, Wendy, Elaine Howard Ecklund, and Nicholas Short. 2009. Religion and spirituality: A barrier and a bridge in the everyday professional work of pediatric physicians. *Social Problems* 56(4): 702–721.

Cant, Sarah, and Ursula Sharma. 1998. *A new medical pluralism?: Complementary medicine, doctors, patients and the state*. London: Routledge.

Carmel, Emma, and Jenny Harlock. 2008. Instituting the 'third sector' as a governable terrain: Partnership, procurement and performance in the UK. *Policy & Politics* 36(2): 155–171.

Carroll, Lewis. 1871. *Through the looking glass, and what Alice found there*. London: Macmillan & Co.

Clark, Lynn Schofield. 2007. Religion, twice removed: Exploring the role of media in religious understandings among 'secular' young people. In *Everyday religion*, ed. Nancy Tatom Ammerman, 69–81. New York: Oxford University Press.

Connolly, William E. 1995. *The ethos of pluralization*. Minneapolis: University of Minnesota Press.

Dahl, Robert A. 1967. *Pluralist democracy in the United States: Conflict and consent*. Chicago: Rand McNally.

Dahl, Robert A. 1982. *Dilemmas of pluralist democracy: Autonomy vs. control*. New Haven: Yale University Press.

Deveaux, Monique. 2000. *Cultural pluralism and dilemmas of justice*. Ithaca: Cornell University Press.

Doe, Norman. 2011. *Law and religion in Europe*. Oxford: Oxford University Press.

Douglas, Gillian, Norman Doe, Sophie Gilliat-Ray, Russell Sandberg, and Asma Khan. 2011. *Social cohesion and civil law: Marriage, divorce and religious courts*. Report of a Research Study funded by the AHRC. Cardiff: Centre for Law and Religion.

Eisenberg, Avigail. 2009. *Reasons of identity: A normative guide to the political and legal assessment of identity claims*. Oxford: Oxford University Press.

Figgis, John Neville. 1913. *Churches in the modern state*. London: Longmans, Green and Co.

Francis, Leslie. 2011. *Young people's attitudes to religious diversity*. Research project outline, Warwick University. http://www2.warwick.ac.uk/fac/soc/wie/research/wreru/research/current/ahrc. Accessed 25 Nov 2011.

Furnivall, John Sydenham. 1948. *Colonial policy and practice: A comparative study of Burma and Netherlands India*. Cambridge: Cambridge University Press.

Gilbert, Neil. 2000. Welfare pluralism and social policy. In *The handbook of social policy*, ed. James Midgley, Martin B. Tracy, and Michelle Livermore, 411–420. Thousand Oaks: Sage.

Gilliat-Ray, Sophie. 2000. *Religion in higher education*. Aldershot: Ashgate.

Gilliat-Ray, Sophie. 2001. Sociological perspectives on the pastoral care of minority faiths in hospital. In *Spirituality in health care contexts*, ed. Helen Orchard, 135–146. London: Jessica Kingsley Publishers.

Gilliat-Ray, Sophie. 2004. The trouble with 'inclusion': A case study of the faith zone at the Millennium Dome. *The Sociological Review* 52(4): 459–477.

Gilliat-Ray, Sophie. 2006. From 'chapel' to 'prayer room': The production, use, and politics of sacred space in public institutions. *Culture and Religion* 6(2): 287–308.

Global Centre for Pluralism. 2012. Defining pluralism. *Pluralism Papers No. 1*. Ottawa: Global Centre for Pluralism.

Greenawalt, Kent. 2006. *Religion and the constitution, vol. 1: Free exercise and fairness*. Princeton: Princeton University Press.

Greenawalt, Kent. 2008. *Religion and the constitution, vol. 2: Establishment and fairness*. Princeton: Princeton University Press.

Hansen, Kim Philip. 2012. *Military chaplains and religious diversity*. New York: Palgrave Macmillan.

Harris, Margaret, and Patricia Young. 2010. Building bridges: The third sector responding locally to diversity. *Voluntary Sector Review* 1(1): 41–58.

Hick, John (ed.). 1977. *The myth of god incarnate*. London: SCM Press.

Hicks, Rosemary B. 2010. Saving Darfur. Enacting pluralism in terms of gender, genocide, and militarized human rights. In *After pluralism*, ed. Courtney Bender and Pamela E. Klassen, 252–276. New York: Columbia University Press.

Hirst, P.Q. 1997. *From statism to pluralism*. London: Routledge.

Hirst, Paul Quentin. 2000. J.N. Figgis, the churches and the state. In *Religion and democracy*, ed. David Marquand and Ronald L. Nettler, 104–120. Oxford: Blackwell.

Hunter, James D. 2009. The culture war and the sacred/secular divide: The problem of pluralism and weak hegemony. *Social Research* 76(4): 1307–1322.

Johnson, Norman. 1987. *Welfare state in transition: The theory and practice of welfare pluralism*. Brighton: Harvester Wheatsheaf.

Kazepov, Yuri, and Angela Genova. 2006. From government fragmentation to local governance: Welfare reforms and lost opportunities in Italy. In *Administering welfare reform*, ed. Paul Henman and Menno Fenger, 233–255. Bristol: Policy Press.

Kelly, Berni, and Ruth Sinclair. 2005. Understanding and negotiating identity: Children from cross community families in public care in Northern Ireland. *Child & Family Social Work* 10(4): 331–342.

Lassman, Peter. 2011. *Pluralism*. Cambridge: Polity Press.

Leavelle, Tracy. 2010. The perils of pluralism. Colonization and decolonization in American Indian religious history. In *After pluralism*, ed. Courtney Bender and Pamela E. Klassen, 156–177. New York: Columbia University Press.

Lewis, Jane. 2005. New Labour's approach to the voluntary sector: Independence and the meaning of partnership. *Social Policy & Society* 4(2): 121–131.

Mahmood, Sabah. 2007. Agency, performativity, and the feminist subject. In *Bodily citations. Religion and Judith Butler*, ed. Ellen T. Armour and Susan M. St Ville, 177–221. New York: Columbia University Press.

Marty, Martin. 2007. Pluralisms. *Annals of the American Academy of Political and Social Sciences* 612: 14–25.

Mayrl, Damon, and Freeden Oeur. 2009. Religion and higher education: Current knowledge and directions for future research. *Journal for the Scientific Study of Religion* 48(2): 260–275.

Morris, Paul. 1990. Judaism and pluralism. The price of 'religious' freedom. In *Religious pluralism and unbelief*, ed. Ian Hamnett, 179–201. London: Routledge.

One Law for All. 2010. *Sharia law in Britain: A threat to one law for all & equal rights*. London: One Law for All. http://www.onelawforall.org.uk/wp-content/uploads/New-Report-Sharia-Law-in-Britain.pdf. Accessed 27 Dec 2011.

Poole, Elizabeth, and John E. Richardson (eds.). 2006. *Muslims and the news media*. Oxford: I.B. Tauris.

Roof, Wade Clark. 2007. Introduction. *Annals of the American Academy of Political and Social Science* 612: 6–12.

Runciman, David. 1997. *Pluralism and the personality of the state*. Cambridge: Cambridge University Press.

Sandberg, Russell. 2011. *Law and religion*. Cambridge: Cambridge University Press.

Stand for Peace. 2013. *The interfaith industry*. http://standforpeace.org.uk/wp-content/uploads/2013/11/Interfaith-Industry.pdf. Accessed 18 Nov 2013.

Sullivan, Winnifred Fallers. 2005a. *The impossibility of religious freedom*. Princeton: Princeton University Press.

Sullivan, Winnifred Fallers. 2005b. Normative pluralism: Islam, religion and law in the twenty-first century. *Religion* 35(1): 31–40.

Sullivan, Winnifred Fallers. 2010a. Religion naturalized. The new establishment. In *After pluralism*, ed. Courtney Bender and Pamela E. Klassen, 82–97. New York: Columbia University Press.

Sullivan, Winnifred Fallers. 2010b. Varieties of legal secularism. In *Comparative secularisms in a global age*, ed. Linda Cady and Elizabeth Hurd, 107–120. Basingstoke: Palgrave Macmillan.

Taskforce on Religious Diversity. 2011. *Strengthening religious diversity and harmony in South Australia*. Adelaide: Ministry for Cultural Affairs.

Todd, J. Terry. 2010. The temple of religion and the politics of religious pluralism. Judeo-Christian America at the 1939–1940 New York World's Fair. In *After pluralism*, ed. Courtney Bender and Pamela E. Klassen, 201–222. New York: Columbia University Press.

Tomalin, Emma. 2007. Supporting cultural and religious diversity in higher education: Pedagogy and beyond. *Teaching in Higher Education* 12(5–6): 621–634.

Trigg, Roger. 2007. *Religion in public life: Must faith be privatized?* Oxford: Oxford University Press.

Trigg, Roger. 2010. *Free to believe? Religious freedom in a liberal society*. London: Theos.

Tucker, Adam. 2008. The Archbishop's unsatisfactory legal pluralism. *Public Law* 3: 463–469.

Tully, James. 1995. *Strange multiplicity: Constitutionalism in an age of diversity*. Cambridge: Cambridge University Press.

Valk, Pille, Gerdien Bertram-Troost, Markus Friederici, and Céline Béraud (eds.). 2009. *Teenagers' perspectives on the role of religion in their lives, schools and societies*. Münster: Waxmann.

Watson, Nick J., Stuart Weir, and Stephen Friend. 2005. The development of muscular Christianity in Victorian Britain and beyond. *Journal of Religion and Society* 7, paras 1–45.

Weller, Paul. 2008. *Religious diversity in the UK. Contours and issues*. London: Continuum.

Weller, Paul. 2009. How participation changes things: 'Inter-faith', 'multi-faith' and a new public imaginary. In *Faith in the public realm*, ed. Adam Dinham, Rachel Furbey, and Vivien Lowndes, 63–81. Bristol: Policy Press.

Williams, Rowan. 2008. Civil and religious law in England – A religious perspective. *Ecclesiastical Law Journal* 10(3): 262–282.

Woodhead, Linda. 2008. Secular privilege, religious disadvantage. *British Journal of Sociology* 59(1): 53–58.

Wuthnow, Robert. 2005. *America and the challenges of religious diversity*. Princeton: Princeton University Press.

Zubrzycki, Geneviève. 2010. What is religious pluralism in a 'monocultural' society? Considerations from postcommunist Poland. In *After pluralism*, ed. Courtney Bender and Pamela E. Klassen, 277–295. New York: Columbia University Press.

Religious Diversity, Social Control, and Legal Pluralism: A Socio-Legal Analysis

James T. Richardson

Introduction

Religious diversity is a fact of modern life, even if some leaders of societal institutions deny and regret it. Most societies have a dominant religious tradition, and some of those religions have very strong legal protections and prerogatives; they might even be designated as a "state religion." However, no modern society can claim that there is no religious diversity within its boundaries. Migration patterns caused by political conditions, wars, natural disasters, and economic conditions, facilitated by modern means of travel and communication have guaranteed that various ethnic and religious minorities would develop throughout the nations of the world. Also, new indigenous religious groups have developed within societies in response to conditions experienced by members of those societies, including disquiet about the activities and culture of dominant religions. Some newer movements – referred to as New Religious Movements (NRMs) by scholars – have spread across national boundaries because of deliberate efforts to promote their beliefs and values to others, also contributing to religious diversity.

Given the undeniable fact of religious diversity, questions arise about how societies respond to the increasing variety of religious faiths within their borders. Are religious minorities allowed to function within public space, and if so, how? Are they allowed to operate as legal entities with rights and privileges associated with larger traditional faiths? Or, are minority religions harassed by authorities and attacks on them by others allowed to take place? What rights and privileges are allowed members of minority faiths? Are minority religious groups openly discouraged from building or renting space to function, and are they disallowed from opening banking accounts or owning property? Can they offer religious education classes within public schools, or function as chaplains in the military?

J.T. Richardson (✉)
Judicial Studies Program, University of Nevada, Mail Stop 311, Reno, NV 89557, USA
e-mail: jtr@unr.edu

G. Giordan and E. Pace (eds.), *Religious Pluralism*,
DOI 10.1007/978-3-319-06623-3_3, © Springer International Publishing Switzerland 2014

Continuum of legal social control over minority religions

Operating outside	Operating within legal	Operating outside legal
formal legal structure	structure with varying privileges	structure with approval
but with caution; typically	according to placement in	by authoritiesbut with
Ignored by authorities	hierarchy of accepted religions	some limitations

Fig. 1 Continuum of legal social control over minority religions

Answers to these and related questions will reveal much about the degree of tolerance and religious freedom in a society, and also will indicate to what degree minority religious groups are allowed to exist and function within a society. Modern societies are increasingly governed by formalized legal structures. The ways those structures are built and the degree of flexibility within those structures reveals how open and accommodating societies are when dealing with minority faiths developing within or coming from outside their borders. A continuum can be posited (see Fig. 1) that involves significant differences in the legal status of minority religious groups and the ways different societies manage minority religious groups.

At left end of the continuum are religious groups with no legal status at all, which means they are not formally registered and recognized by the state. Religious groups at this end of the continuum are generally quite small, and therefore usually are viewed as inconsequential by societal authorities unless some action is taken by the group that calls attention to it by authorities. These groups operate outside the bounds of whatever legal structure exists within a society, but are always potentially subject to social control actions by the state in which they exist. Ironically, these groups that operate outside the bounds of societal legal structures can implement their own norms and values to an extent, and thus might be thought of as having a very limited form of legal pluralism. However, these groups must operate carefully in order not to attract the attention of authorities. Such groups may be allowed to exist and function with impunity outside the formal legal structure in many societies, but in others (China being an example) they could be subject to arbitrary and punitive efforts at social control by governmental authorities.

In the middle ranges of the continuum are minority religious and ethnic groups that are allowed some measure of legal status, with attendant rights and privileges that vary greatly by society and by specific group. Many societies have formal or informal hierarchies of religious groups, and institutional structures that enforce the rules associated with the various levels within the hierarchy (Richardson 2001; Durham 1996). Typically these minority religious groups are officially registered through a process the state has established, and they are categorized within the hierarchy of religious groups thus making it clear what the group can and cannot do within the society. There are gradations in the middle ranges of the continuum, which means there are many opportunities for states to exercise social control as they attempt to manage religious diversity within their borders.

At right end of the continuum would be religious groups that have managed to acquire a degree of functional legal autonomy by being allowed to have their own legal enclave in which the group's customs, norms, and rules operate, implemented by their own institutional structures. Such groups are generally larger or geographically isolated so that exercising social control over them would be problematic. Also, a society's history might play a role here, as indigenous peoples might be allowed to retain a degree of autonomy. Societal authorities may simply decide to leave such groups alone as much as possible, and let them govern themselves using their own norms and customs.

The situation to the far right of the continuum would be an example of legal pluralism functioning for a religious group within a society. Legal pluralism is defined as occurring when two or more legal and normative structures are allowed to function with the same geographic space. How the two (or more) legal structures function within the legal structure of a society can vary greatly, of course. Some legal pluralism situations might involve only certain matters, such as domestic affairs, to be handled within the subgroup's confines, whereas different societies might allow other areas of life, such as financial matters, to be governed by norms and rules of the subgroup. So, as in the other two major categories on this continuum, there are gradations and ambiguities present that must be understood and taken into account by minority religious groups, as the privileges associated with allowing some degree of legal pluralism can be withdrawn by leaders of the society.

There is a definite reciprocal relationship and interaction between the presence of minority religious and ethnic groups and the development of legal pluralism in a society (Beckford and Richardson 2007; Richardson 2009). If there is openness and flexibility, with religious diversity actually being promoted by a society, then minority groups may be more prone to come into that society, and indigenous religious groups may also be encouraged to develop. If there is a perception that the society is closed and unwelcoming of religious diversity, this may discourage attempts to develop different religious traditions within the society, which also would mean less legal pluralism. But, the presence of religious and ethnic minorities, especially large and politically strong ones, may in turn encourage the development of legal pluralism within a society as these groups negotiate with the powers that be in a society for rights and privileges that allow more self-governance by the groups. Thus this is an ongoing and even dialectical process that can evolve rapidly as conditions and perceptions change within a society.

Theoretical Considerations

There are a number of relevant theoretical traditions germane to understanding how religious diversity is dealt with within a society, and how religious diversity relates to the development of legal pluralism. Adopting a broad socio-legal perspective focuses attention on the history and culture of a society, but also incorporates theories and methods from the social sciences. Thus this approach is explicitly interdisciplinary, calling on several related areas of scholarship to seek a fuller understanding of the effects of religious diversity on a society, and how the society responds to diversity. I have taken this approach in earlier writings, and will be referring to them in what follows (Richardson 2006b, 2007, 2011b; Richardson and Springer 2013).

Sociology of Religion and the Religious History of a Society

The religious history of a society is, of course, very important in understanding how a society might treat minority faiths. If there is a long history of religious pluralism, then the society's political leaders may have, over time, found ways to accommodate religious differences, even if there is a dominant religion that has more privileges and higher status in the society. Such arrangements are always subject to internal or external events that might disrupt the peaceful co-existence mode that had evolved over time. Events such as the destruction of the World Trade Center or the Madrid train bombing can shift public opinion rapidly about certain minority groups within a society.

However, there are historical examples of societies that have accommodated different religious traditions for periods of time, and done so relatively peacefully, as Jamila Hassan (2011) discusses in the case of Malaysia. The accommodation may derive from a formal legal structure that is established that includes a hierarchical arrangement with attendant privileges by category, as has been developed in Singapore (Hill 2004), or the accommodation could be based on customs of long standing, perhaps even from colonial times. Accommodation mechanisms could include a casual approach that ignores minority faiths as long as they are not perceived to be disruptive of the social order, or accommodation could include an overt effort to manage religious diversity using formal processes and procedures established in law.

In situations where minority faiths have developed more recently or come into a society from outside, problems can arise, and quickly. Dominant religious groups may feel threatened when indigenous religious groups arise from within the tradition or when groups enter the society from outside and begin aggressive proselytizing and criticizing the dominant religious tradition. Dominant religions also may work in concert with political authorities to defend and extend their prerogatives and influence using minority faiths as pawns in such machinations. Indeed, dominant religious traditions may attempt to foment anxiety and concern about minority faiths quite deliberately, as was the case with Russia from the 1990s onward. The Russian Orthodox Church (ROC) was attempting to reestablish itself as the dominant faith of the Russian people and as an organization with political influence (Shterin and Richardson 2000, 2002). ROC leaders courted conservative nationalistic politicians who were quite willing to join forces with the ROC using minority religious groups as a foil in their efforts. Similarly, Chinese authorities seem to have used the Falun Gong as a way of solidifying the authority of the Chinese Communist Party during a time of rapid social change in China (Edelman and Richardson 2005; Tong 2009).

There are other concepts besides religious pluralism from the Sociology of Religion that could be brought to bear concerning social control of minority religions. One that is particularly relevant concerns whether a society defines itself as secular or religious (or somewhere in between), and how it implements the relationship between church and state. If a society defines itself as strictly secular (France and Turkey are examples), then the state apparatus may exert considerable effort to control religious groups of all kinds. If a society defines itself as religious, possessing of a theocratic state (Iran is an example), then even more rigorous efforts might be made to control, or even exterminate rival religions. Most modern states fall somewhere in between these extremes, and have worked out arrangements whereby there is some degree of separation of church and state, and mechanisms for managing religions and religious groups have been developed. How those arrangements are constructed has immense implications for social control of religious groups.

Characteristics of Legal and Judicial System

Legal and judicial systems vary considerably in terms of basic characteristics, and the way they are constructed and function influences how minority religious groups are treated in a given society. In some societies the justice system is completely subservient to the political realm, and those functioning within the system lack *autonomy* (see Finke 2013: 302–303; Finke et al. 2013). In societies operating with low levels of autonomy those who enforce the law and make decisions about conflicts and disputes that end up in court are simply following directions or expectations of other more powerful individuals or institutions. Not to do so can result in loss of their position, if not a worse penalty. China is such a society at present where the judicial system lacks independence, and even lawyers attempting to represent clients such as Falun Gong participants can get arrested for doing so (Edelman and Richardson 2005). In Russia there also are examples of directions being given and followed in major cases involving religious groups, in what is referred to as "telephone justice" (Shterin and Richardson 2002).

Examples of China and Russia are not rare, however, as many nations have relatively weak justice systems that are subservient to military rule (present day Egypt), dominance of a particular religion (Iran), or one particular political party (present day Hungary). In such societies the law and its enforcement becomes a weapon for use by those who dominate the society. This use of law and the justice system as a weapon – rule *by* law – is quite contrary to the modern western concept of the rule *of* law, which means that all citizens should be treated equally under the law, and that the law should be administered in a fair and equitable manner.

Legal systems vary greatly in terms of how *pervasive* they are. Do legal consi-derations affect few aspects of life, or do such considerations impinge on most daily activities of citizens and groups, including those related to their religious? Are societal institutions involved in surveillance and monitoring of minority religious groups (Richardson and Robbins 2010), or are such groups generally left alone? A less pervasive legal system would probably result in less attention being paid to smaller religious groups, such as those at the left end of the continuum posited above. Legal pluralism might also be allowed to flourish with some groups, if societal leaders decided that this would be a more prudent course than attempting to enforce normal rules and laws of the society on a minority religious group. Minority religious groups in the middle ranges of the social control continuum also might see fewer efforts to regulate and manage their activities in a society with a less pervasive and intrusive legal system. However, even in more open societies with guarantees of religious freedom minority religious groups may be subject to monitoring and surveillance, as has been shown in the U.S. with the Branch Davidians (Wright 1995) and the Fundamentalist Latter Day Saints in Texas (Wright and Richardson 2011), as well as other groups in the U.S. and elsewhere (Richardson and Robbins 2010).

Closely related but not completely overlapping with pervasiveness is the vari-able of degree of *centralization* of a legal system. If a society had a highly centralized legal system, including a centralized judicial system, then this could, and usually does, indicate considerable control being exerted over the lives of citizens in the society. Legal systems in western European nations are all, to varying degrees, centralized, with Switzerland being an exception to the usual rule with its Canton system of governance. And Germany grants considerable authority to its internal units (called "lands"). However, when a society such as Germany with its centralized legal system also has a "culture of paternalism" this can result in significant social control being exerted toward minority religious groups, with efforts made through governmental institutions to warn citizens of the dangers of such groups (Beckford 1985; Richardson and van Driel 1994; Seiwert 2004). France with its secular ideology of *laicité* working in concert with its centralized legal system, also has attempted to implement strong measures of social control toward minority faiths (Richardson and Introvigne 2001; Beckford 2004; Duvert 2004; Palmer 2011). And China, a quite centralized state system, certainly engages in monitoring and surveillance of unapproved religious groups, and then takes punitive action based on information gathered (Tong 2009; Edelman and Richard-son 2005; Richardson 2011a).

In societies with a federated approach that allows considerable autonomy to states or territories, such as in the United States or Australia, there is more variety in how legal systems operate, thus allowing more flexibility and opportunity for citizens in such a society. Thus if a minority religion group is harassed by author-ities in one region of a society with less centralized governance structure, it might be able to move to another area where the legal situation and social control apparatus differed in important ways. However, even in federated political systems there is usually an overarching legal system operating through a national constitution and legal structure that places limits on what can occur within the federated units that make up the nation. For example, the Bill of Rights of the United States Constitution with its First Amendment guaranteeing religious freedom and precluding establishment of a state religion must be taken into account by any state or local government as it deals with minority religious groups. However, many nations such as Australia do not have a Bill of Rights, so any guarantees are based more on tradition, possibly allowing more flexibility in dealing with minority faiths (but see Bouma (2011) on Australia's culture of tolerance toward minority religions).

There are important caveats to the statements just made about the effects of centralization and pervasiveness of justice systems. One relates to an earlier discussion (Richardson 2006b) about the role of a "strong state" (which might better be thought of as a "history" variable) in promoting and protecting religious freedom for minority faiths. A strong state would usually have a highly centralized justice system. This could allow the state, if its leaders desired, to act in a punitive manner toward religious groups, and do so with impunity, as is the case with contemporary China (Tong 2009). But, leaders of a strong state could also decide to promote religious freedom, and allow or even encourage minority faiths to flourish within the society. This positive approach to diversity and religious pluralism may be rare, but it is possible, as Beckford notes in his discussion of religious pluralism (Beckford 2003). Arguably the United States can be said to promote religious freedom through its pervasive and overarching centralization of a legal system that incorporates key values found in the Constitution, such as the guarantee of religious freedom. Canada seems to be functioning similar since the development of the Charter of Rights and Freedoms adopted in 1982, which makes it clear that the provinces are subservient to federal rules and norm concerning human and civil rights, including in the area of religion.

A strong state could also decide to allow legal pluralism to develop within a society for some ethnic and religious groups, and even sanction such developments with constitutional provisions and statutes, as is the case with the relatively new South African legal structure (Danchin 2013). This might be done for reasons of convenience and economy – it could be less trouble to allow a legal pluralistic situation to develop than to attempt to force compliance with general laws within in a society. Such a situation of legal pluralism in a "strong state" also could simply be a recognition that a society is religiously diverse, and that the societal governance structure must allow for this fact of life (see discussion above about importance of taking religious history into account). Or such a development might simply derive from actions of societal leaders who value religious diversity and pluralism. Therefore it is not at all the case, just because a society has a pervasive and centralized legal system, that minority religious groups will always be more subject to social control.

Note however that, especially in strong state societies with a dominant religion having many rights and privileges, centralization and pervasiveness would usually be expected to contribute to more stringent efforts at social control of competitive minority faiths. Again, the case of Russia with the growing influence of the ROC comes to mind as an example of this type of historical circumstance. This occurs even though there is some decentralization of the legal system in Russia. However, in Russian hinterlands the westernized notions of individual religious freedom never took root after the fall of communism, lending support to the dramatic change of law in 1997 that allowed much more control of minority religions (Shterin and Richardson 1998).

One additional but crucial consideration is that many modern societies are themselves subject to regional or even international legal and judicial systems. For example, the United Nations International Court of Justice, the European Court of Justice, which is the judicial arm of the European Union, and especially the European Court of Human Rights (ECtHR) which is the court for the 47 nations that are members of the Council of Europe (COE) exercise tremendous authority and influence over member nations and their justice and judicial systems. The ECtHR is especially noteworthy in terms of religious freedom as it has in recent decades taken up the cause of protecting minority religious groups, especially in former Soviet dominated nations but also in nations that were some of the original founders of the COE (Hammer and Emmert 2012; Richardson and Lykes 2012; Richardson 2014b; Richardson and Lee 2014; Lykes and Richardson 2014).

Thus, any analysis of how justice systems work has to take into account whether they are part of larger systems of justice, and the authority and effectiveness with which those larger systems function. As Hammer and Emmert (2012) note in their systematic treatment of former Soviet dominated nations, there is a growing tendency for courts in those nations to cite ECtHR case law and decisions as precedent, and to adhere to those precedents. Sadurski (2009) argues that the ECtHR is becoming more like an overarching "Supreme Court" for the region that is developing a willingness to declare laws "unconventional" (not comporting with the European Convention on Human Rights), and encouraging COE Member States to change their laws to better fit with Convention values. Related to this development is the growing importance of constitutional courts in the COE region. Such courts have, in some newer COE nations, over-ruled decisions of supreme courts, and exerted themselves, sometimes on behalf of minority religions (Sadurski 2006, 2009; Richardson and Shterin 2008; Richardson 2006a).

Another characteristic of legal systems that deserves mention is whether there is an *adversarial* or *inquisitorial* system operating. If the former, this means that those involved with the legal system have the right to have an advocate who represents them within the justice system. In the latter situation no advocate is possible, as judges perform multiple roles and manage cases as they see fit; no personal advocates are allowed. It seems clear that having an advocate for a defendant member of a minority religion or for a religious group itself would greatly strengthen chances for a party in a legal matter to defend themselves and increase the chances that they might ultimately prevail. Thus the chances of exerting social control over the activities of a religious group would seem lower in societies where an adversarial legal system operates, and thus those societies might be more prone to allow forms of legal pluralism to exist with some minority faiths.

Sociology of Law Theories

Two prominent Sociology of Law theorists, William Chambliss and Donald Black, have produced theoretical schemes that are quite different, but also somewhat complementary. And both schemes are useful in understanding how minority religious groups are dealt with by societal authorities attempting to manage and even control such groups and movements. Their theories can help with understanding how legal pluralism might be allowed to develop with certain religious and ethnic group. I have applied ideas from these two theorists in some of the work mentioned earlier (Richardson 2006b, 2007, 2011b; Richardson and Springer 2013). More recently the theoretical scheme of Chambliss has been applied directly to understanding how efforts to extend elements of Islamic Shari'a law are being dealt with in American, Canada, and Australia (Richardson 2014; Also see Turner and Richardson 2013).

Applying Donald Black's Theorizing

Black (1976, 1999) focused more on the question of "who wins" when conflict develops that requires resolution. His quite abstract theorizing encompasses various types of self-help dispute resolution, but also is applicable to what happens when disputes end up in court. Black posits some key variables including *social status and prestige,* and *cultural and personal intimacy* to help explain who usually prevails in disputes that arise in society. He and a former student also have proposed an intriguing concept of *third party partisan* to assist in explaining what happens when an entity unexpectedly prevails in a dispute (Black and Baumgartner 1999).

The applicability of Black's theorizing to the area of social control of minority religions is easy to demonstrate. Sometimes religious groups and individuals acting out their faith find themselves caught up in legal battles as they defend themselves from actions of the state when they are perceived to have violated a law. Such entities or individuals might also find themselves defendants in a civil legal action brought by someone who claimed to have had their interests injured by the group or individual. And in some societies private individuals or groups are allowed to bring legal actions against religious groups working in concert with the state. (France and Russia are two such societies.) When such legal actions occur, Black's theorizing allows predictions about who will prevail – those of higher status and more prestige who share cultural and perhaps even personal intimacy with decision makers will usually prevail. And when a party slated to lose because of being of lower status and prestige and not sharing cultural and personal intimacy with the decisions makers does in fact win, the concept of third party partisan often can help make sense of the outcome. In practical terms, this latter situation means that someone who is of higher status and prestige and who does share cultural and even personal intimacy with the decision makers intervenes and becomes a partisan on behalf of the defendant.

Black's theorizing can assist in understanding what happens with religious groups arrayed along the continuum posited above. Groups to the left end are typically smaller and newer, and, unless they do something to attract attention from authorities, they are typically left alone unless and until something happens that does brings them to the attention of societal authorities. If that happens such groups are greatly disadvantaged, whether it is in dealing with representatives of institutions of society such as child welfare agencies, school authorities, or tax agencies. If irate parents of relatively high status and prestige, upset that their son or daughter has joined such a group, can call attention to the group and succeed in getting authorities and mass media to focus on them through political processes or by filing civil suits, the group also is quite disadvantaged.

In these situations the religious group would usually be expected to lose in whatever confrontation developed, unless some entity of much higher status and prestige intervened on their behalf. Such a third party intervention might involve prominent legal assistance from a well-respected advocate (attorney) who takes on the case (if such is allowed in the society), but it might also involve an organization such as the American Civil Liberties Union or an organization of religious groups seeking to defend religious freedom. Indeed, it is even possible to characterize judges or courts as third party partisans if they value religious freedom and have the authority of constitutional or convention provisions or statutes to support them in their decisions. Recent decisions of the European Court of Human Rights (ECtHR) and the United States Supreme Court demonstrate this last point quite well (Richardson and Lykes 2012; Richardson and Shoemaker 2014; Lykes and Richardson 2014; Richardson 2014b).

Those entities on the far right hand of the continuum might be allowed to develop and enforce their own internal laws and procedures in an example of legal pluralism. Leaders of such groups would clearly have to possess sufficient status and prestige, and perhaps also cultural, if not personal, intimacy with societal leaders to effect such an agreement with authorities. The status and prestige for leaders of a minority group seeking a relatively autonomous legal system might derive from various sources, but clearly one such source could be strength of numbers and an accompanying threat, implicit or explicit, that conflict and even violence might occur if the group was not allowed to develop and implement its own rules and procedures covering at least some areas of life. The minority religious group might garner some support from third parties in the process, as leaders of the political structure in a society might agree to allow some form of legal pluralism to develop for a group for several reasons, including convenience or an ideological belief that the group's cultural values should be allowed expression. The most obvious examples of legal pluralism in contemporary western societies involve indigenous peoples being allowed some self-governance, and the development of some degree of legal pluralism with Jewish, Catholic, and even Muslim groups concerning domestic matters such as divorce, child custody, and inheritance rules.[1] Some of these situations might be sanctioned by law in a given society, while others are allowed to exist without formalization in law.

The middle range of the continuum can offer even more clear application of Black's theories. Groups in the middle ranges are subject to regulation such as being placed in some sort of hierarchical ranking of religious groups that grants different rights and privileges depending on where the group is located in the hierarchy. The placement of groups in the hierarchy is done by officials in a governmental agency which has the task of managing religious groups in the society. In developing a hierarchy of religions those officials implement their own values and the values of those who placed them in their positions. Those religious groups with higher status and prestige, and which promote values shared by those doing the ranking would be expected to be ranked at the top, and those groups having lower status and prestige and whose values are not shared by the decision makers would be placed lower in the ranking scheme, and allowed fewer rights and privileges.

One other relevant aspect of Black's theorizing was developed by another student of his, Mark Cooney, whose groundbreaking work on the social production of evidence is relevant to our focus on religious diversity and legal pluralism (Cooney 1994, Likes and Richardson 2014).[2] Cooney's theorizing can be extended to also incorporate the fact that judges not only make decisions about what evidence to admit, but they also can decide what legal rules to apply to a given case. As developed in Richardson (2000), judges are key decisions makers who usually can exercise

---

[1] Although Jewish and Catholic informal or even formalized tribunals have been allowed in certain areas of life in some societies (clear examples of legal pluralism in operation), recently controversies have erupted when Muslim groups have called for even limited legal pluralism for Muslim groups in some western societies. See Ahdar and Maloney (2010) discussion of controversy caused when the Archbishop of Canterbury urged that Shari'a be granted some recognition in the U.K., Turner and Richardson's discussion of controversy in America (2013), Richardson's (2013) discussion of controversies in Australia, Mcfarlane's coverage of the situation in Canada and America (2013), Aires and Richardson (2014) on controversies in Germany, Possamai et al. (2014) volume focusing on Shari'a in western and non-western nations, and Berger's (2013) on Shari's in western nations.

[2] Cooney did not discuss religion but his ideas are useful in understanding conflicts over religion that become legal and judicial matters. Those involved in a legal case make decisions about how much time and resources to spend gathering and developing evidence, and whether evidence developed can and will be used in court. Cooney points out that this is a social process explicable by knowing the status and prestige of those involved on both sides of a case, and how well they (and their advocates in an adversarial system) share the values of decisions makers. Cooney also allows for intervention in cases by third parties who might take the side of a disadvantaged party in the process. He proposes an intriguing concept of "strange attractor" to draw attention to situations where an otherwise lower status and prestige party attracts someone from a quite different station in life to assist in their defense.

considerable discretion in how they handle a given case, and what variant of law might apply in various matters before them.[3] Particularly in matters of family law, judges in many western states allow norms and customs deriving from religious traditions to be influential if not determinative. This can become quite controversial (see footnote 1), but when this happens it demonstrates that limited forms of legal pluralism are being allowed to operate.

Applying William Chambliss' Theorizing

Chambliss (1964; Chambliss and Zatz 1993) is more interested in how major changes in law occur. He posits a never-ending agency-oriented dialectical process that involves *contradictions, conflicts, dilemmas,* and temporary *resolutions.* Chambliss initially focused on economic conditions and how they can lead to problems in how a society functions. He later expanded his definition somewhat and stated Chambliss and Zatz (1993) that contradictions are situations where "...the working out of the logic of extant political, economic, ideological, and social relations must necessarily destroy some fundamental aspect of existing social relations." In short, Chambliss focuses on situations where following the letter of the extant law will lead to major difficulties in a society. When this occurs it can lead to conflicts between interest groups, which in turn can cause a dilemma for the state. The state must attempt to resolve the conflict so that order can be maintained. Thus a resolution may be adopted that solves the problem in the short term, but which causes other contradictions which can lead to more conflict and dilemmas for the state. Thus a given resolution probably is never final, according to Chambliss, even if it may last for a period of time.

Chambliss' ideas have seldom been applied in the area of religion, but the application of his theorizing in this realm can be useful. There are many contradictions concerning religious and religious groups in contemporary societies, not the least being that many modern societies have constitutional provisions guaranteeing religious freedom, and most societies are signatories to international agreements that state clearly that religious freedom is a basic and important value. However, in many

---

[3] Judges sometimes lower the standards of evidence when an unpopular party is a defendant in a case before them. This has happened in some famous cases involving religious groups or individuals where questionable evidence was admitted, leading to convictions and long prison terms. The "Hilton bombing" case involving the Ananda Marga group and the Lindy Chamberlain case involving the Seventh Day Adventists are examples from Australia of such cases that were eventually overturned and the individuals freed from prison after serving long terms (Richardson 2000). But, there are other examples where judges allowed suspect evidence to be admitted. The "brainwashing" cases in the United States are another example of judges allowing weak evidence to be introduced to considerable effect on the outcome of cases brought by individuals against small religious groups (Anthony 1990; Richardson 1993). Judges can also *disallow* crucial evidence that might be quite dispository of a case's outcome. Again, Cooney's theory derived from Black's theories offers assistance in understanding when decisions might be made to either allow or disallow evidence to be used in a legal matter.

societies those provisions are honored in the breech, and simply ignored. And in other societies that make impressive claims to implementing such provisions it is a modern fact of life that *religious are managed*, and that the ways in which members of a religious group can act out their values is limited, sometimes quite severely. However, sometimes the resolution that is developed as a way of managing religious minorities allows them considerable autonomy, especially in certain areas such as domestic matters. Thus, managing does not necessarily always mean rigorous control, but instead legal pluralism may be allowed to develop.

Recent developments in Russia furnish an excellent example demonstrating the value of Chambliss' theoretical approach. Russia's post-communist Constitution clearly states that religious freedom is a paramount value, and so do statutes adopted in the early 1990s. Those religious freedom guarantees are derived from language used in western oriented constitutions and in the European Convention on Human Rights and Fundamental Freedoms. However, a contradiction was immediately obvious in that the Russian Orthodox Church was attempting to assert itself and be accepted as a state church, and a number of political leaders and ordinary citizens agreed with this effort (Shterin and Richardson 1998, 2000). Potential conflicts quickly arose over the rapid influx of many New Religious Movements (NRMs) and other religious groups from the west into Russia, causing a dilemma for the state. Also, it has become obvious that this situation of western religious groups coming into Russia afforded an opportunity for the ROC and more nationalistic politicians to promote their own values and goals.

Thus a "resolution" was eventually achieved with statutes concerning religion being dramatically changed in 1997, in an effort to limit the access of foreign religious groups to Russia. That law has come under heavy criticism from some elements of Russian society, but also externally because Russia is now a signatory to the European Convention on Human Rights and therefore under the purview of the ECtHR. Efforts to enforce the new law in Russia and refuse reregistration of formerly registered groups have resulted in a number of major losses in cases brought to the ECtHR (Richardson and Lykes 2012). This result has forced recognition that the "resolution" afforded by the 1997 law has itself led to other contractions, given Russia's own constitution as well as its membership in the Council of Europe. How this situation will be resolved remains to be seen, but predictably there will be other "resolutions" in the future,[4] and those newer resolution may need to grant more

---

[4] The Russian case also demonstrates the confluence of the theories of Black and Chambliss, and highlights the key role of the judiciary in developing policy toward religious groups in contemporary western societies. As noted, the Russian Constitutional Court has attempted to defend religious freedom for minority groups by enforcing the constitutional provisions concerning religious freedom even to the extent of declaring provisions of the 1997 law void. The rulings of this Court represent movement in the direction of more legal pluralism in Russia. This "resolution" was, however, unacceptable to the Russian bureaucracy which refused to enforce the judgments, leading to several cases before the ECtHR which Russia lost in a series of unanimous decisions. Whether the Russian state will accept those judgments and implement a new resolution that comports with the European Convention is not clear, however (Richardson and Lykes 2012; Richardson and Lee 2014; Lykes and Richardson 2014).

autonomy to religious groups operating in Russia, which would be movement in the direction of more legal pluralism for such groups.

There are many other examples that might be cited where laws relating to religious values have been dramatically changed as a result of contradictions being found, leading to potential conflict, forcing the state to respond to resolve the dilemma it faces. One such dilemma that is widely felt in newer Member States of the COE concerns the issue of conscientious objection to military service, a basic tenant of the Jehovah's Witness religion. Many states do not allow alternative service, but this has led to problems because enforcing the law can result in incarceration of many individuals, which undercuts claims made about religious freedom and is also quite expensive. For example South Korea currently has about 600 members of the Jehovah's Witnesses in prison because of their refusal to serve in the military (Brumley 2013). This issue has also arisen with a number of former Soviet-dominated states now in the COE. Jehovah's Witnesses members have brought many legal actions to force a resolution, and have won a number of those cases, either through a "friendly settlement" that involves a change of law, or by decisions of the ECtHR (Brumley 2013; Richardson and Lykes 2012; Richardson 2014b). When these nations have agreed to allow alternatives to military service, this can be viewed as allowing alternative values to influence societal legal structures (Beckford and Richardson 2007; Richardson 2009) but also as some recognition of legal pluralism in action.

Conclusions

Religious diversity exists in every modern society, and there are as many ways to deal with that diversity as there are societies attempting to manage the diversity that exists within their borders. Herein I have posited a continuum (see Fig. 1) of efforts at social control of minority faiths that goes from little effort to exert control at all to smaller less visible groups, through many different methods of managing religions that want or require legal status, with attendant rights and privileges. At the far right end of the continuum are religious groups which may be allowed to establish their own form of legal pluralism, at least concerning certain areas of life such as domestic affairs. But on the far left end we also see a form of legal pluralism, as smaller less visible groups may be allowed to self-govern to a considerable extent.

I have then attempted herein to develop theoretical ideas derived from the Sociology of Religion and the Sociology of Law to help explain how and why religious social control is exerted over minority faiths at various locations on the continuum. I have focused attention on situations where religious diversity has contributed to the establishment of various forms of legal pluralism, in an effort to demonstrate that sometimes circumstances may allow for degrees of autonomy to develop that allow religious minorities more flexibility in managing their affairs than is commonly assumed. Space did not allow a full-blown effort to illustrate every possible aspect of these efforts, but hopefully what I have presented will generate further research, and contribute to the fruitful integration of the Sociology of Religion and the Sociology of Law, which together can yield much of value to understanding contemporary efforts to manage religion in the very diverse contemporary societies that have developed.

References

Adhar, Rex, and N. Mahoney. 2010. *Shari'a in the west*. Oxford: Oxford University Press.

Aires, Wolf, and J.T. Richardson. Forthcoming, 2014. Trial and error: Muslims and Shari'a in German context. In *Sociology of Shari'*, ed. A. Possamai, J.T. Richardson, and B. Turner. New York: Springer.

Anthony, Dick. 1990. Religious movements and brainwashing litigation: Evaluating key testimony. In *In Gods we trust*, ed. T. Robbins and D. Anthony, 295–344. New Brunswick: Transaction Books.

Beckford, James A. 1985. *Cult controversies: The societal response to new religious movements*. London: Tavistock.

Beckford, James A. 2003. *Social theory and religion*. Cambridge: Cambridge University Press.

Beckford, James A. 2004. 'Laïcité,' 'dystopia,' and the reaction to new religious movements in France. In *Regulating religion: Case studies from around the globe*, ed. J.T. Richardson, 27–40. New York: Kluwer.

Beckford, James A., and James T. Richardson. 2007. Religion and regulation. In *The Sage handbook of sociology of religion*, ed. J.A. Beckford and N.J. Demerath, 396–418. Los Angeles: Sage Publications.

Berger, Maurits. 2013. *Applying Shari'a in the west*. Leiden: University of Leiden Press.

Black, Donald. 1976. *The behavior of law*. New York: Academic.

Black, Donald. 1999. *The social structure of right and wrong*. New York: Academic.

Black, Donald, and M. Baumgartner. 1999. Toward a theory of the third party. In *The social structure of right and wrong*, ed. Donald Black, 95–124. New York: Academic.

Bouma, Gary. 2011. *Being faithful in diversity*. Adelaide: ATF Press.

Brumley, Philip. 2013. Personal communication, August, 2013. (Brumley is General Council for the Jehovah's Witness world-wide organization, the Watchtower Association.)

Chambliss, William. 1964. A sociological analysis of the law of vagrancy. *Social Problems* 12: 46–67.

Chambliss, William, and Marjorie Zatz. 1993. *Making law: The state, the law, and structural contradictions*. Bloomington: Indiana University Press.

Cooney, Mark. 1994. Evidence as partisanship. *Law and Society Review* 28: 833–858.

Danchin, Peter. 2013. The politics of religious establishment: Recognition of Muslim marriages in South Africa. In *Varieties of religious establishment*, ed. Winnifred Sullivan and Lori Beaman, 165–185. Burlington: Ashgate.

Durham, Cole. 1996. Perspectives on religious liberty: A comparative framework. In *Religious human rights in global perspective: Legal perspectives*, ed. J. van der Vyver and J. Witte, 1–44. The Hague: Kluwer.

Duvert, Cyrille. 2004. Anti-cultism in the French Parliament: Desperate last stand or opportune leap forward? A critical analysis of the 12 June 2001 Act. In *Regulating religion: Case studies from around the globe*, ed. J.T. Richardson, 41–52. New York: Kluwer.

Edelman, Bryan, and James T. Richardson. 2005. Imposed limitations on freedom of religion in China and the margin of appreciation doctrine: A legal analysis of the crackdown on the Falun Gong and other 'evil cults'. *Journal of Church and State* 47(2): 243–267.

Finke, Roger. 2013. Origins and consequences of religious freedom: A global overview. *Sociology of Religion* 74: 297–313.

Finke, Roger, Robert Martin, and Jonathan Fox. 2013. The tyranny of the majority: Why all political frameworks can fail minorities. *Presented at annual meeting of the Association for the Sociology of religion*, New York, August.

Hammer, Leonard, and Frank Emmert. 2012. *The European convention on human rights and fundamental freedoms in central and eastern Europe*. The Hague: Eleven International Publishers.

Hassan, Jamila. 2011. More than on law for all: Legal pluralism in southeast Asia. *Democracy and Security* 7(4): 374–389.

Hill, Michael. 2004. The rehabilitation and regulation of religion in Singapore. In *Regulating religion: Case studies from around the globe*, ed. J.T. Richardson, 343–358. New York: Kluwer.

Lykes, Valarie, and James T. Richardson. 2014. The European court of human rights, minority religions, and new versus original member states. In *Legal cases involving new religious movements and minority faiths*, ed. J.T. Richardson and Francois Bellanger. London: Ashgate. Forthcoming.

Macfarlane, Julie. 2013. *Islamic divorce in North America: A Shari'a path in a secular society*. Oxford: Oxford University Press.

Palmer, Susan. 2011. *The new heretics of France: Minority religions, la Republique, and the Government Sponsored 'War on Sects'*. New York: Oxford University Press.

Possamai, Adam, James T. Richardson, and Bryan S. Turner. Forthcoming, 2014. *The Sociology of Shari'a*. New York: Springer.

Richardson, James T. 1993. A social-psychological critique of 'brainwashing' claims about recruitment to new religions. In *The handbook of cults in America*, ed. D. Bromley and J. Hadden, 75–97. Greenwich: JAI Press.

Richardson, James T. 2000. Discretion and discrimination in legal cases involving controversial religious groups and allegations of ritual abuse. In *Law and religion*, ed. Ahdar Rex, 111–132. Aldershot: Ashgate.

Richardson, James T. 2001. Law, social control, and minority religions. In *Frontier religions in public space*, ed. Pauline Cote, 139–168. Ottawa: University of Ottawa Press.

Richardson, James T. 2006a. Religion, constitutional courts and democracy in former communist countries. *The Annals of the American Academy of Political and Social Science* 603: 129–138.

Richardson, James T. 2006b. The sociology of religious freedom: A structural and socio-legal analysis. *Sociology of Religion* 67: 271–291.

Richardson, James T. 2007. Religion, law, and human rights. In *Religion, globalization, and culture*, ed. P. Beyer and L. Beaman, 407–428. London: Brill.

Richardson, James T. 2009. Religion and the law: An interactionist approach. In *The Oxford handbook of sociology of religion*, ed. Peter Clarke, 418–431. New York: Cambridge University Press.

Richardson, James T. 2011a. Deprogramming: From self-help to government sponsored repression. *Crime, Law and Social Change* 53(4): 321–336.

Richardson, James T. 2011b. The social construction of legal pluralism. *Democracy and Security* 7(4): 390–405.

Richardson, James T. 2013. Minority religious and ethnic groups in Australia: Implications for social cohesion. *Social Compass* 60(4): 579–590.

Richardson, James T. Forthcoming, 2014a. Contradictions, conflicts, dilemmas, and temporary resolutions: A Sociology of Law analysis of Shari'a in selected western societies. In *The sociology of Shari'a*, ed. A. Possamai, J.T. Richardson, and B. Turner. New York: Springer.

Richardson, James T. 2014b. In defense of religious rights: Jehovah's witness legal cases around the world. In *Handbook of global contemporary christianityed*, ed. Stephen Hunt. New York: Brill. Forthcoming.

Richardson, James T., and Massimo Introvigne. 2001. 'Brainwashing' theories in European parliamentary and administrative reports on 'cults' and 'sects'. *Journal for the Scientific Study of Religion* 40(2): 143–168.

Richardson, James T., and Brian Lee. Forthcoming, 2014. The role of the courts in the social construction of religious freedom in Central and Eastern Europe. *Review of Central and East Europe Law.*

Richardson, James T., and Thomas Robbins. 2010. Monitoring and surveillance of religious groups in the United States. In *The Oxford handbook of church and state in the United States*, ed. Derek Davis, 353–369. New York: Oxford University Press.

Richardson, James T., and Jennifer Shoemaker. Forthcoming, 2014. The resurrection of religion in the U.S.? The "tea" cases, the Religious Freedom Restoration Act, and the war on drugs. In *Legal cases, new religious movements and minority faiths*, ed. J.T. Richardson and Francois Bellanger. Aldershot: Ashgate.

Richardson, James T., and Marat Shterin. 2008. Constitutional courts in Postcommunist Russia and Hungary: How do they treat religion? *Religion, State, and Society* 36(3): 251–267.

Richardson, James T., and Barend van Driel. 1994. New religions in Europe: A comparison of developments in England, France, Germany, and the Netherlands. In *Anti-cult movements in cross-cultural perspective*, ed. A. Shupe and D. Bromley, 129–170. New York: Garland Publishing.

Richardson, James T., and Valerie Lykes. 2012. Legal considerations concerning new religious movements in the 'new Europe'. In *Religion, rights, and secular society*, ed. Peter Cumper and Tom Lewis, 293–322. Cheltenham, U.K: Edward Elgar.

Richardson, James T., and Victoria Springer. 2013. Legal pluralism and Shari'a in western societies: Theories and hypotheses. In *Varieties of Religious Establishment*, ed. L. Beaman and W. Sullivan, 201–218. New York: Springer.

Sadurski, Wojciech. 2006. *Rights before the courts: A study of constitutional courts in postcommunist states of central and eastern Europe*. New York: Springer.

Sadurski, Wojciech. 2009. Partnering with Strasbourg: Constitutionalization of the European Court of Human Rights, the accession of Central and Eastern European states to the Council of Europe and the idea of 'pilot judgments'. *Human Rights Law Review* 9: 397–453.

Seiwert, Hubert. 2004. The German Enquete Commission on Sects: Political conflicts and compromises. In *Regulating religion: Case studies from around the globe*, ed. J.T. Richardson and J.T. Richardson, 85–102. New York: Kluwer.

Shterin, Marat, and James T. Richardson. 1998. Local laws on religion in Russia: Precursors of Russia's national law. *Journal of Church and State* 40: 319–341.

Shterin, Marat, and James T. Richardson. 2000. Effects of the western anti-cult movement on development of laws concerning religion in post-communist Russia. *Journal of Church and State* 42(2): 247–271.

Shterin, Marat, and James T. Richardson. 2002. The *Yakunin v. Dworkin* trial and the emerging religious pluralism in Russia. *Religion in Eastern Europe* 22: 1–38.

Tong, James. 2009. *Revenge of the forbidden city: Chinese suppression of the Falungong.* New York: Oxford University Press.

Turner, Bryan, and J.T. Richardson. 2013. United States of America: Islam and the problems of liberal democracy. In *Applying Shari'a in the west*, ed. Berger Maurits, 47–63. Leiden: University of Leiden Press.

Wright, Stuart. 1995. *Armageddon in Waco.* Chicago: University of Chicago Press.

Wright, Stuart, and James T. Richardson. 2011. *Saints under siege: The Texas raid on the fundamentalist latter day saints.* New York: New York University Press.

Oligopoly Is Not Pluralism

Fenggang Yang

Religious Freedom and Pluralism

In the world today, religious diversity is on the rise in all societies. Several megatrends in the modern world make the increase of religious diversity inevitable. The first factor is migration. In the globalizing market economy, more and more people have become migrants in order to chase after investment or employment opportunities. In addition to capital and economic skills, immigrants also bring religions that differ from that of the host society. Although immigrants both expect and are expected to accommodate to life in the new society, for most people religion is not something that they can easily unlearn nor easily acquire. For economic and social reasons, the host society also expects and is expected to accommodate the religious beliefs and practices of immigrants who supply either the capital or the social and economic skills needed by the society.

The second factor is transnationalism. In the era of globalization, facilitated by advanced technologies of transportation and communication, more and more migrants are in fact transnationals who maintain homes in two or more countries and travel back and forth regularly. Even those immigrant settlers who maintain a single home in the immigrant country are now more likely to make frequent visits to their country of origin, and they maintain constant contact with relatives and friends in both societies. These transnational connections make it necessary for migrants to maintain religious as well as social ties to their community of origin, either by upholding their traditional religion or by introducing back into their home communities religious practices learned in the communities they have joined.

The third factor is mass media and the Internet. Without migrating themselves or receiving immigrants from another society, people can easily access information on religions practiced in other times and places through books, magazines,

F. Yang (✉)
Center on Religion and Chinese Society, Purdue University, 700 W. State Street,
West Lafayette, IN 47907, USA
e-mail: fyang@purdue.edu

G. Giordan and E. Pace (eds.), *Religious Pluralism*,
DOI 10.1007/978-3-319-06623-3_4, © Springer International Publishing Switzerland 2014

newspapers, television, and increasingly the Internet. They may also join virtual communities dedicated to various religions or make virtual friends with people residing in other parts of the world and practicing their distinct religions.

Finally, the new migratory and cosmopolitan experiences of life have generated both the spiritual and social needs and the practical possibilities that might encourage immigrants or nonimmigrants to develop new religions, perhaps by choosing elements from various traditions to form a new community with a distinct religion. Religious innovation is a common phenomenon of late modernity.

In short, given the megatrends in the economic and social spheres, it is inevitable that a modern society will have an increasing number of religions.

The secularization theory, as exemplified in Peter Berger's earlier works (1967, 1970), predicted that increased religious diversity would lead to an overall decline in religion because the presence of an increasing number of religions, along with developments in science and education, would erode traditional religious beliefs, thus leading to a decline in religiosity among individuals and a decline in religious communities. That prediction has failed and Berger has rescinded his secularization theory. In the contemporary world, religion persists, resurges, and revives in almost all societies (Berger 1999; Berger et al. 2008). The relationship between religious decline and religious vitality became the focus of a series of paradigmatic debates that have occupied creative thinkers and scholars for the last two to three decades. By now, however, it is clear that the paradigm shift has completed (Warner 1993, 2003), even though there are lingering issues that require more careful examination with more sophisticated methods.

If increasing plurality is inevitable, even if it does not necessarily lead to the decline of religion in general, what challenges will it pose? Obviously it challenges the dominant conventional religion or religions in a given society. In terms of individual choice, as more and more religions become available to individuals in the religious marketplace, either through interactions with neighbors and coworkers in the same physical community or in virtual communities facilitated by the Internet, challenging questions arise: How much freedom may individuals have in choosing a religion, and how much freedom may religious groups have in proselytizing? Should individuals have the freedom to choose whatever religion they like? What about unconvential or cultish religions? Should such religions be allowed to operate in a community on equal terms with its dominant conventional religion or religions? Should the state protect the status and privileges of the traditional religion or religions? In economic terms, should the religious market be equally open to all religions, whether they are new or old, conventional or strange? On the part of individuals who choose religion, more specifically, what should parents, schools, and local and national governments be permitted to do about nonconventional religions? As social scientists, we also need to ask questions pertaining to the social scientific study of religion: How do various people and institutions respond or react to the increasing presence of plural religions in a rapidly globalizing society? What are the dynamics and processes of change in church-state relations? What are the different social and political consequences of various ways of dealing with increasing religious plurality?

Religious freedom has become a modern norm. This is in part due to the United Nations' proclamation of the Universal Declaration of Human Rights, the International Covenant on Civil and Political Rights, and the International Covenant on Economic, Social, and Cultural Rights. However, the ideal of religious freedom has encountered serious obstacles and setbacks in the twenty-first century, as both mainstream news and the frequent reports of the Pew Research Center have shown. There are certainly political and economic factors contributing to such obstacles and setbacks. But the concept of religious freedom may have its weaknesses as well.

It seems to me that the concept of religious freedom itself may have an individualistic bias. It narrowly focuses on individual rights, but excessive individualism has become a concern or worry in many societies that are undergoing rapid modernization. In comparison, religious pluralism is probably a better conceptual tool both for the social scientific study of religion and for the implementation of religious freedom. Religious pluralism is the social arrangement that protects both individual freedom and group equality in religious affairs. We as social scientists of religion may ask the following research questions: Is religious pluralism the destiny of social change in the modern world? What are the social conditions that favor or oppose the change toward religious pluralism? What are the costs and benefits to a society that attains and retains religious pluralism?

Pluralism, Plurality, and Pluralization

First of all, we need to differentiate between pluralism at the social and the individual levels. At the individual level, pluralism is a personal perspective, philosophy, or lifestyle by which one deals with multiple religions within one's own mind and heart. It is a philosophical or theological position different from exclusivism, inclusivism, or relativism (see Hemeyer 2009). At the social level, it is a social configuration for dealing with multiple religions within a given society. Although these two levels are closely related, they are not identical. As Robert Wuthnow put it, "A pluralist is someone who can see and appreciate all points of view, a person who is presumably tolerant, informed, cosmopolitan, and a pluralist society is one in which social arrangements favor the expression of diverse perspectives and lifestyles" (Wuthnow 2004:162–163). In such a society, we can see that a person may favor pluralistic social arrangements without buying into a personal philosophy of pluralism or relativism.

For instance, some fundamentalists in the United States do not adhere to a pluralistic philosophy. They are exclusivists, believing that their religion is the only true religion and all other religions are false. Nonetheless, fundamentalists would fight for a social arrangement that includes religious pluralism so that they could hold on to their right of religious freedom without governmental interference. Worries about a fundamentalist takeover or a new theocracy are based on a confusion of individual pluralism and social pluralism. But in the real world few fundamentalist Christians in the U.S. would relinquish their religious freedom or try to take away others' religious freedom, which is guaranteed by the First Amendment to the Constitution and affirmed by conservative Christians. In other words, Christian fundamentalists may reject theological or philosophical pluralism but will fight to maintain the social arrangements of religious pluralism. Social scientists of religion must not confuse the individual and the social levels of religious pluralism, even though the two levels may interact with each other.[1]

Second, on the social level, we need to differentiate further between the descriptive and the normative dimensions – that is, between plurality and pluralism. Some scholars continue to use the term 'pluralism' in both descriptive and normative senses. Such usage hinders further theoretical development.

For the descriptive dimension, James Beckford and others prefer the word "diversity," whereas I would adopt the word "plurality." According to Beckford (2003), the word "plurality" implies a limited set of options, whereas "diversity" suggests many more choices. Granted that the terms have different connotations, I nonetheless believe "plurality" is a more accurate term for two reasons. First, "plurality" shares its root with the word "pluralism," which provides a consistent terminology for theorizing about a set of inseparable things, as explained below. Second, in reality, a society will only have a limited number of religion. The maximum possibility would be one religion per each person of the population, but that assumption defies the very notion of religion as a group phenomenon, as it was conceptualized by the founder of sociology, Emile Durkheim. It is possible that in a given society there could be hundreds or even thousands of different religions, as Gordon Melton has ably documented in his *Encyclopedia of American Religions* (2009). However, the religious market of most societies is dominated by a few large religions while a number of small religions fill in various niches.

In brief, in the descriptive dimension, plurality describes the *degree* of religious heterogeneity within a society, whereas pluralism refers to the *social arrangement* favorable to a high or higher level of plurality. Obviously, some societies have lower degrees of religious plurality than some other societies, and plurality may increase in a given society. Pluralization is the term for the *process* of increasing plurality in a society.

For the purpose of theoretical construction, it is helpful, to me at least, to use this set of words derived from the same root (Latin *plus*, which means "more"). The three terms – plurality, pluralism, and pluralization – refer to the variety of religions tolerated in a given society, the society's arrangements favorable for plurality, and the process of increasing religious plurality in that society, respectively. The social arrangement of religious pluralism means (1) accepting, affirming, and granting equal protection to plural religions in a society; (2) setting up social institutions and (3) creating favorable social and cultural conditions for the presence of plural

---

[1] Eileen Barker in a 2003 article discussed the impacts of the pluralistic society on individuals' belief, behavior, and belongings.

religions; and (4) granting and protecting the freedom of the individual to choose whatever religion he or she wants, or no religion at all.

Levels of Religious Plurality

In societies throughout the world today, there are four major degrees of religious plurality. The lowest is zero religion. That is, religion is banned. This has indeed happened in human history, but only twice and briefly. A total ban on religion was declared in China and in Albania in the mid-1960s; it lasted for 13 years in China (1966–1979) and a decade longer in Albania. There was zero religious freedom under the religious ban. The next level is religious monopoly. That is, only one religion is protected by the state, which has been the case in many societies from antiquity through the early modern times, and up to the present in some parts of the world. Then there are societies in which the state allows the practice of a few select religions. I call this oligopoly. Finally, in societies where religious plurality is unrestricted, numerous religions operate in a society on equal terms guaranteed by law.

Religious oligopoly is not pluralism. Quantitatively, oligopoly permits a plural number of religions, as opposed to monopoly's solitary creed. Qualitatively, however, monopoly and oligopoly are close cousins. Both have to be maintained by the state through political power. When the power of the state is used to support one or a few religions, it inevitably results in the political restriction and persecution of followers of other religions, religious conflict, or even religious wars. In monopoly and oligopoly, religious organizations compete not only for followers, but also for control of state power. Meanwhile, political forces also compete to control the state religion or religions in order to control state power. In other words, the difference between religious oligopoly and religious pluralism is not simply a matter of the number of religions existing in a given society. It is a matter of how that society's religions are treated by law, either equally or unequally. Monopoly and oligopoly also have different dynamics. While Rodney Stark and Roger Finke (2000) have articulated the dynamics of religious monopoly and pluralism, I have tried to articulate the dynamics of religious oligopoly in the triple-markets theory – the red, black, and gray markets of religion – which is not specific to China, but describes all oligopolies (Yang 2012).

In religious pluralism, in contrast to religious monopoly or oligopoly, the ruling power stays out of the competition among religions. But there is much confusion over this kind of church-state relationship. One source of confusion is that religious pluralism is unregulated. In fact, the state may withdraw entirely from the competition among religions, without inserting itself as a competitor as communist governments did. However, the religious market, just like other kinds of markets, needs regulations to maintain order or ensure orderly competition. Consequently the state, as the body responsible for the public order, may regulate the ways and means of religious competition. In a pluralistic arrangement, the religious market is open to all comers, and any religion may enter the fray and compete on equal grounds. In such a marketplace, rational argument and sentimental persuasion are worth more than anything else in winning and keeping members and followers. The power of the state may be used to ensure that proselytization is noncoercive and that conversion remains voluntary, but it will not be used to prohibit any particular religion or outlaw conversion to a particular religion. This kind of legal arrangement is religious pluralism, which, if implemented in social practice, will inevitably result in greater plurality over the long run, as the number of religions coexisting in a given society grows.

It is important to emphasize that a pluralistic arrangement does not mean that the state has nothing to do with religion, or that the religious market is unregulated. Modern society has become so complex that the social order has to be maintained by regulations, especially through the rule of law. However, the pluralistic regulation of religion does not ban or favor any particular religion; it merely administers specific aspects of religious practice that are applicable to all religions, such as the construction of religious buildings, the performance of animal or human sacrifice, and fiscal concerns such as tax exemption and the financial accountability of religions to their members and to the public.

In short, real religious pluralism treats all religions equally and grants freedom to individuals. Of course, this is the ideal of religious pluralism, and the actual practice may fall short of the ideal. However, if a legal arrangement does not guarantee equal treatment to all religions and freedom of choice to all individuals, it is simply not religious pluralism. It is in this sense that I stress that oligopoly is not pluralism. In oligopoly, as in monopoly, the regulations favor a few religions while other religions are outlawed and suppressed.

The Prevalence of Religious Oligopolies

Using regulations or legal arrangements as a criterion, we find that of the almost 200 countries of the world today, about 20 % are clearly pluralistic and 22 % are clearly monopolistic. The rest of the countries fall somewhere in between, being more or less oligopolistic (see Table 1).

Theoretical studies in the sociology of religion have focused almost exclusively on two of the four types of social arrangements outlined above: monopoly and pluralism. These categories have determined the course of scholarly discussion in Europe and North America, where religious monopoly and pluralism have historically been regarded as the most common arrangements. Without empirical studies of oligopolies and theorizing about oligopolies, the social scientific study of religion will remain parochial or provincial, Euro-centric or Euro-America-centric.

Furthermore, I would argue that many of the so-called pluralistic countries are in fact oligopolistic, such as Great Britain and Italy. Evidently, in many countries, even if the constitution or basic law includes a declaration of religious freedom, other parts of the constitution may contradict it and the existing laws may not

Table 1 Four types of state-religion relations

"To what extent is there a favored (or established) religion in the country?"

Religious Policy/law		Number of countries	Percent
Pluralism	All religious brands are treated the same	40	20.4
	Cultural or historical legacies only	16	8.2
Oligopoly	Some brands have special privileges or government access	56	28.6
	One religious brand has privileges or government access	41	20.9
Monopoly	One single state or official religious brand	43	21.9
Total Ban	*All religions are banned*	*(2)**	
TOTAL		196	100.0

"Cross-National Data: Religion Indexes, Religious Adherents, and Other Data"

(http://www.thearda.com/; Grim and Finke 2006).

Source: Fenggang Yang (2010)

"Cross-National Data: Religion Indexes, Religious Adherents, and Other Data" http://www.thearda.com/; Grim and Finke 2006
[a]These 'zero religion' situations happened in the 1960s–1980s but no longer retain in 2006

support it. On the contrary, they may sabotage religious pluralism, making its practical implementation impossible. China is one such case. For over a century since 1912, the constitution of the Republic of China, in its many versions, has retained a guarantee of religious freedom. However, when the Republic of China withdrew to the island of Taiwan, martial law was imposed and the constitution was suspended. Only after 1987 has the religious freedom become implemented in the Republic of China on Taiwan. In the People's Republic of China under the Communist Party, the first constitution of 1954 and the later versions have always included an article guaranteeing freedom of religious belief, but the constitution has little bearing on political and social life in China. In practice, religions have been restricted, suppressed, and even banned (Yang 2013).

Thus, although most countries in the world today have adopted legislation that supports religious pluralism, the full implementation of religious freedom requires more than legal guarantees on paper. There are at least three factors that must be simultaneously present for the ideal of religious pluralism to take effect in practice:

a culturally grounded conceptual framework that supports the ideal, legal regulation, and civil society.

The Conceptual and Civic Arrangements of Religious Pluralism

How do we explain the fact that most countries have written religious freedom into their constitutions but practice religious oligopoly? As sociologists, we must look for other social factors in addition to the legal arrangement. At least two other kinds of social arrangements play important roles, namely, the cultural and intellectual context and civic society. I believe that "civic and cultural arrangements are foundational to attain and retain the legal arrangement for pluralism" (Yang 2010:196). "Without the intellectual understanding and certain level of consensus that legitimize and justify individual freedom of religion and group equality of religions, without civic organizations in the civil society that keep in check the state agencies and religious organizations, the pluralistic legal structure cannot be implemented or maintained in practice" (Yang 2010:196). When the three kinds of social arrangements are not synchronized or in accord, a de facto monopoly or oligopoly is the result.

Definition Matters

When theorizing about religious pluralism, we encounter a serious problem of definition. Toward the end of his response to my 2010 article on religious oligopoly, James Beckford (2010:221) gently suggested that it was necessary to give "serious consideration to questions about the conceptualization and definition of religion in the everyday contexts of politics, public policy, the media and courts of law," because "surely this is where the challenges facing pluralism are most intense." In other words, a definition of religion is in order.

In countries that maintain oligopoly de jure or de facto, a common strategy used by the dominant powers is to label certain religions as non-religions. The authorities and the cultural elites thus adopt a narrow definition of religion. In some cases, the established religions and the state collude to label the other religions as bad religions, sects, cults, or evil cults, to the extent that people may believe it is morally right and in the public interest to ban them. But the moral arguments for banning cults that are advanced by advocates of the established religions are probably self-serving, sabotaging the principles of fairness and equality in the marketplace. As long as the established religions dominate the public discourse about what religion is and is not, they will be able to maintain the status quo of unfair competition.

We certainly should acknowledge that religion is a term whose meaning is contested by various social forces. The question is whether we scholars of religion, especially the social scientists among us, should offer an expert opinion on the definition of religion. Many brilliant scholars have evaded this task. The most notorious is Max Weber, who began his *Sociology of Religion* by stating that "to define 'religion,' to say what it is, is not possible at the start of a presentation such as this. Definition can be attempted, if at all, only at the conclusion of the study" (Weber 1963:1). In the end, he claimed that he has completed his studies and there was no longer any need to make the attempt. Had Weber lived longer, would he have provided a definition? On the other hand, Emile Durkheim devoted his last book (2001) to defining religion.

In my book *Religion in China: Survival and Revival under Communist Rule* (2012), I offered a definition of religion for the social scientific study of religion. Without this definition, the triple-market theory, the shortage economy theory, and the oligopoly theory would fall apart. In other words, the theoretical discussion of religious pluralism requires a definition of religion, which admittedly may have practical implications as well. Because at present I do not see the need to revise my definition, I quote here the main points from my book:

> *A religion is a unified system of beliefs and practices about life and the world relative to the supernatural that unite the believers or followers into a social organization of moral community.* (36)
>
> This definition includes four essential elements of a religion: (1) a belief in the supernatural, (2) a set of beliefs regarding life and the world, (3) a set of ritual practices manifesting the beliefs, and (4) a distinct social organization of moral community of believers and practitioners. From this definition, we will develop a classification of religious phenomena and closely related social phenomena that compete with religion [which is summarized in Table 2]. (36)
>
> This definition with classification combines substantive and functional definitions of religion and encompasses conventional religions and their competitors in modern society. The competitors, besides conventional religions and semi-religions, also include pseudo-religions that are regarded as substitutes for conventional religions and quasi-religious beliefs and practices that are inseparable from other social institutions. (40)
>
> This definition with classification is a useful tool in the political economy of religion that deals with conventional religions and their active competitors in the same society. In a study focusing on the survival and revival of religions in Communist-ruled China, the distinction between religion and pseudo-religion is especially important. In China, as in other Communist-ruled societies, the pseudo-religion of Communism was forced on the people as a substitute for religion, but many people resorted to some semi-religion that would provide the supernatural element. Because of the lack of formal organizations or the elusive nature of the organizational element in popular religion or folk religion, it is more difficult for authorities to suppress such practices and beliefs. (42–43)

My definition probably falls into the category of "second order" definitions of religion, according to Beckford's distinction (2003:7). It can be placed alongside the "first order" definitions used by the practitioners of various religions. In a modern society, nobody can force others to accept a definition, but in the modern world, I believe in the power of persuasion. As part of the scientific enterprise, I also value the ongoing improvement of the conceptual tools that we use to analyze the

Table 2 A definition of religion with classification

	Supernatural	Beliefs	Practices	Organization	Examples
Full religion	Yes	Yes	Yes	Yes	Christianity, Buddhism, Islam
Semi-religion	Yes	Underdeveloped	Yes	Underdeveloped	Folk or popular religion, magic, spiritualities
Quasi-religion	Yes	Yes	Yes	Diffused	Civil religion, ancestor worship, guild cults
Pseudo-religion	No	Yes	Yes	Yes	Atheism, Communism, fetishism

Source: Fenggang Yang (2012)

world. Therefore this definition is laid on the table, waiting for and welcoming critiques and criticisms.

Conclusion

We have seen an increase of religious plurality in most societies in the world today. However, true religious pluralism remains an ideal that begs to be implemented in practice. On the social level, issues pertinent to religious freedom include three important aspects: a conceptual framework, legal regulation, and civil society. Even though many countries have adopted the legal arrangement of religious pluralism, it is not always grounded in a conceptual framework shared among the political and cultural elites, and social institutions to support its implementation in practice are lacking. To attain and retain religious freedom in a society, it is necessary to make social arrangements that promote religious pluralism. More importantly, the conceptual framework, legal regulation, and civil society must be synchronized. In reality, this synchronization is difficult to achieve and maintain in any given society.

References

Barker, Eileen. 2003. And the wisdom to know the difference? Freedom, control and the sociology of religion. *Sociology of Religion* 64(3): 285–307.

Beckford, James A. 2003. *Social theory and religion*. Cambridge: Cambridge University Press.

Beckford, James A. 2010. Religious pluralism and diversity: Response to Yang and Thériault. *Social Compass* 57(2): 217–223.

Berger, Peter. 1967. *The sacred canopy: Elements of a sociological theory of religion.* Garden City: Doubleday.

Berger, Peter. 1970. *A rumor of angels: Modern society and the rediscovery of the supernatural.* Garden City: Anchor Books.

Berger, Peter (ed.). 1999. *The desecularization of the world: Resurgent religion and world politics.* Grand Rapids: William B. Eerdmans.

Berger, Peter, Grace Davie, and Effie Fokas. 2008. *Religious America, secular Europe? A theme and variations.* Hampshire: Ashgate.

Durkheim, Emile. 2001. *The elementary forms of religious life.* New York: Oxford University Press.

Grim, Brian J., and Roger Finke. 2006. International religion indexes: Government regulation, government favoritism, and social regulation of religion. *Interdisciplinary Journal of Research on Religion* 2(2006): article 1.

Hemeyer, Julia Corbett. 2009. *Religion in America*, 6th ed. Upper Saddle River: Pearson.

Melton, J. Gordon. 2009. *Encyclopedia of American religions*, 8th ed. Detroit: Gale.

Stark, Rodney, and Roger Finke. 2000. *Acts of faith: Explaining the human side of religion.* Berkeley/Los Angeles: University of California Press.

Warner, R. Stephen. 1993. Work in progress toward a new paradigm for the sociological study of religion in the United States. *American Journal of Sociology* 98(1993): 1044–1093.

Warner, R. Stephen. 2003. More progress on the new paradigm. In *Sacred markets, sacred canopies: Essays on religious markets and religious pluralism*, ed. Ted G. Jelen, 1–32. Lanham: Rowman & Littlefield.

Weber, Max. 1963. *The sociology of religion.* Boston: Beacon.

Wuthnow, Robert. 2004. Presidential address 2003: The challenge of diversity. *Journal for the Scientific Study of Religion* 43(2): 159–170.

Yang, Fenggang. 2010. Oligopoly dynamics: Consequences of religious regulation. *Social Compass* 57(2): 194–205.

Yang, Fenggang. 2012. *Religion in China: Survival and revival under communist rule.* New York: Oxford University Press.

Yang, Fenggang. 2013. A research agenda on religious freedom in China. *The Review of Faith and International Affairs* 11(2): 6–17.

Part II
Case Studies in Religious Pluralism

Religious and Philosophical Diversity as a Challenge for the Secularism: A Belgian-French Comparison

Jean-Paul Willaime

Three Different Meanings of Secularism

Regarding '*laïcité*/secularism', one may start with observations on vocabulary and semantics. The French word *laïcité* is difficult to translate, especially in English and German. I am not confident that the English word *secularism*, though ordinarily used in translation, would describe it perfectly. How would one extend it to *laïcisme* in this case, for its inference as an ideology that may be critical of religion, or even hostile towards it? But one finds the notion of *laïcité* in the Latin languages, with the word *laicità* in Italian, and the words *laicismo* and *laicidad* in Spanish (also in the name of the Spanish association *Europa laica*, which is a member of the European Humanist Federation). This difficulty with translation becomes quite apparent in Belgium between the two linguistic communities, the French-speaking Walloons and the Dutch-speaking Flemish. While the Walloons speak of *laïcité* and a secular movement (for example, to describe the *Centre d'Action Laïque*) in the same sense as their French neighbours, the Belgian Flemish use the Dutch term *vrijzinnig*, which in French means freethinker. In Flemish, the *Centre d'Action Laïque* is therefore called the *Centrale Vrijzinnige Raad* (Central Council of Freethinkers) and there exists a *Unie Vrijzinnigen Verenigingen* (Union of Free-thinking Associations) which leading member is the *Humanistisch Verbond* (Humanist Association), an organization which also exists in the Netherlands. Such term as 'humanist' is used in Great Britain with the *British Humanist Association*. Also in Great Britain are the *National Secular Society* and the *Rationalist Association*. In France, secular movements are represented by associations or groups that use the term *laïque* in their appellations (such as the *Union des Familles Laïques*, the *Comité National d'Action Laïque*) as well as by associations like the *Union Rationaliste* or the *Union des Athées*, which, as implied by their names,

J.-P. Willaime (✉)
Groupe Sociétés, Religions, Laïcités Ecole Pratique des Hautes Etudes, Sorbonne, Paris
e-mail: jean-paul.willaime@gsrl.cnrs.fr

G. Giordan and E. Pace (eds.), *Religious Pluralism*,
DOI 10.1007/978-3-319-06623-3_5, © Springer International Publishing Switzerland 2014

clearly designate philosophical beliefs conceived as an alternative to religions. A major organization like the *Ligue de l'Enseignement et de l'Education Permanente* is known as a secularist movement, particularly within the school system. As for the French Constitution, the First Article states that "France is an indivisible, secular, democratic, and social Republic", while specifying that the Republic "respects all beliefs".

This cursory overview of words, their translation, and their varying meanings, promptly leads us to make two observations:

1. The term *laïcité* in French has two attributes. On the political plane, it refers to a general principle of neutrality towards any and all belief systems or 'worldviews' (*Weltanschauungen*). This would include the principle of respective independence between government and religion. On the philosophical plane, it refers to secular, non-religious, worldviews conceived as an alternative to religious beliefs. I leave it to English-speakers to determine whether secularism would include these two dimensions. According to the Oxford English Dictionary in 20 volumes (1989 edition), the term secularism has an activist content. It expresses a conviction, a doctrine, whose general aim is to justify secularization and give it a positive and ethical purpose. Some believe that in English the notion of *secularization* is not as extensive as *laïcité*, whereas *secularism*, depending on nuances, may go further (Wolfs et al. 2007). I would also observe that spheres of influence qualifying themselves as *laïque* traditionally include philosophical currents and organizations whose criticism and denouncement of religion play an important part in their *raison d'être*. Three different meanings of secularism are thus straightaway apparent: (1) secularism as non-sectarian neutrality of the state (Secular State); (2) secularism as a secular worldview alternative to religious beliefs; and (3) secularism as an ideology opposing religion and denouncing its misdeeds and deleterious effects (one speaks of 'laicism' in this case). Let us note that anticlericalism, in its criticism of religious institutional power and its clergy, may find expression in these three versions: (1) as religious anticlericalism; (2) as philosophical or political anticlericalism; and (3) as an anticlerical component of overall religious criticism.

2. The fact that we find the very term *laïcité*, or laicity, more often in Latin languages than in Anglo-saxon and Germanic languages, leads us to question whether the notion of 'laicity' would concern more, as regards Europe at least, countries that are predominantly Catholic than those which are predominantly Protestant or bi-confessional. In any event, laicity as a cause for the emancipation of public institutions and individuals from any religious influence is a notion that appears to be more operative in Catholic countries than in Protestant ones. Laicity, in this case, appears as a movement of emancipation reacting against the control and influence that the Catholic Church once exercized within and over some civil societies. The philosopher Jean-Marc Ferry, professor at the Free University of Brussels (Ferry 2009: 164), in comparing France and Germany, made the following remark: "The secularization (*laïcisation*) of French society is not the secularization (*sécularisation*) of German society. They are two different

processes in the political neutralization of religions: the Catholic or post-Catholic process is effected through separation rather, while the Protestant one proceeds more by interiorizing and absorbing elements [that were] initially religious". The spirit of Enlightenment evolved differently by country and in relation with religious questions. In aiming for the emancipation of individuals and the realization of a righteous society, the emphasis was not placed, as Jean-Marc Ferry points out, on the same 'levers of self-development' (*épanouissement*): "Let us say that French Enlightenment would have centered on the State and the political sphere; Scottish Enlightenment, more so on markets and civil society; Prussian Enlightenment, on scholarship (*Université*) and culture". To speak of '*laïcité*/secularism', after all, is it not to speak of this 'other' relative to which '*laïcité*/secularism' is construed, namely, religion? Conversely, this 'other' relative to religion may not be of relevance to all religious thinking, as it presupposes that religion can be dissociated from what it is not. This not comprehensible for a certain number of cultures.

The France-Belgium Comparison

The comparison between France and Belgium is all the more interesting from the viewpoint of secularism as these two countries perfectly illustrate two dimensions of secularism that are both just as real and as legitimate, namely: (1) secularism as a general principle of relations between the State and religions in pluralistic democracies respecting freedom of conscience, of thought, and of religion, as well as everything that freedom implies; and (2) secularism as a philosophical concept that is free-thinking and agnostic promoting a secular-cum-secularist vision of man and the world, as an alternative to religious worldviews. It is in the manner of considering these two dimensions that our two countries differ. In France, one refers so often to secularism as a general precept that one tends to forget that secular activists represent a particular trend which, however respectable, is no more legitimate as a belief system than religions that respect human rights and democracy. In Belgium, one refers so often to the 'secular pillar' one tends to forget that secularism represents not just a particular philosophical movement but also a general principle of organization of mutual independence between government and religions, advocated and valued by believers and non-believers alike. In fact, to compare France and Belgium on the question of secularism is to reflect on the neutrality of the State and the scope to be given to non-religious worldviews.

The France-Belgium comparison instantly portrays the three dimensions implied by the notion of secularism: (1) secularism as an all-embracing principle of neutrality of the State and government vis-à-vis religions and worldviews; (2) secularism as a worldview alternative to religions; and (3) secularism as criticism of, and activism against, religion. The first two dimensions are have particular illustrations in each country. Whereas the French Republic is secular in the sense that secularism is a part of its Constitutional order, the Belgian monarchy is pluralistic:

secularism, regarded as 'organized secularism', is identified with a particular philo-sophical current that groups individuals affiliated, not along religious lines, but along varying non-religious beliefs – freethinkers, freemasons, marxists, or other. Two leading universities embody this pluralistic model built around pillars in Belgium: the Free University of Belgium on the side of Freethinkers, and the Catholic University of Leuven. As for the third dimension – criticism of religion and its denunciation as alienation – it is equally present in both countries, but in varying degrees and within specific organizations. Tension exists between, on the one hand, a liberal conception of secularism conceived as fair neutrality towards religions and atheistic philosophical convictions, and, on the other hand, a concep-tion of secularism as emancipation from all religious spheres, a combat ideology against religions. I believe that in the case of French secularism this last dimension has never disappeared and resurfaces periodically, as was the case in recent years with the "dérives sectaires" (the expression used for cult-like indoctrination and alienation) and questions relating to Islam (Willaime 2008a). As a result, there has been a resurgence in militant atheisms, even though this development remains fairly limited, all things considered.

The Belgium Case

Whereas the French State does not recognize or fund any religion, the Belgian State recognizes different religions and subsidizes them. While recognizing that "the Belgian system draws a plain and clear distinction between the State and religion" and "sanctions their mutual independence", Rik Torfs (2005), of the Catholic University of Leuven, suggests that the Belgian Sate practices an "active neutrality" towards religions by recognizing certain faiths and funding them. The Flemish Minister Geert Bourgeois recently explained when he opened a university confer-ence in Ghent (Bourgeois 2010: 11): "Neutrality does not mean that public author-ities may not entertain relations with religious or philosophical organizations. It is not opposed to financially supporting Churches and religious or philosophical institutions, any more than it is to subsidize the social activities of Churches and organisations having religious or philosophical vocations". But, of interest to us here is the fact that, besides the six recognized denominations (Catholicism, Protestantism, Anglicanism, the Eastern Orthodox Church, Judaism, and Islam), the Belgian State recognizes by a law of June 21, 2002 "non-confessional philo-sophical communities" as well. This is what in Belgium is designated as 'organized secularism', and what makes the sociologist, Claude Javeau, say that secularism represents the "seventh recognized faith" (Javeau 2005) in Belgium. In prison or the army, one may request a chaplain who is either Catholic, Protestant, Jewish, or Muslim. . . as for a "Humanist" one (non-confessional). The Catholic University of Leuven is a wholly public university, as is the Free University of Brussels influenced by freethought and freemasonry. In other words, in Belgium, secularism is not regarded as a framework embracing all society, it is treated as a non-religious worldview, i.e., a particular philosophical alternative equivalent to a 'religion'. Several have observed that the recognition in an organized form, and subsequent financing, of secularism had the paradoxical effect of consolidating the Belgian system of recognition and funding of religions.

The Belgian Constitution, in Article 24 (on Education), clearly provides for the respect of philosophical or religious conceptions within private and family life in an education system organized by linguistic community (French, Flemish, and German):

> (1) Education is free; any preventative measure is forbidden; the repression of offenses is only governed law or decree.
> The Community offers free choice to parents.
> The Community organizes neutral education. Neutrality implies notably the respect of the philosophical, ideological, or religious conceptions of parents and pupils.
> The schools organized by the public authorities offer, until the end of mandatory schooling, the choice between the teaching of one of the recognized religions and non-denominational moral teaching.
> (2) [...]
> (3) [...] All pupils of school age have the right to moral or religious education at the Community's expense.

Well before the law of June 21, 2002 recognizing secularism alongside religions, official schools in Belgium had provided for the organization of "philosophical teaching" (or the teaching of worldview subjects – *levensbeschouwelijke vakken* – as they say in Dutch-speaking Belgium) allowing pupils and their families to choose between religious teaching in one of the denominations (mainly Catholic, Protestant, Jewish, or Muslim) and "non-denominational moral teaching". In regard to the question of secularism, it is interesting to note at this point the somewhat ambiguous meaning of "non-denominational moral teaching". Does it involve providing pupils with the lowest common denominator of moral teaching in a pluralistic society, a sort of education in citizenship and democracy defining the rights and duties in societies characterized by independence between the State and religions, by human rights, and by individual freedom with respect to worldviews? Or does it involve teaching a particular moral philosophy, that of freethought namely? Although the subject "non-denominational moral teaching" is not termed "secular moral teaching", according to the association *Centre d'Action Laïque*, it refers to *libre examen* (philosophical critical thinking) and is the only "contact between secularism and youth" (Husson 2002: 36). The varying reactions in Wallonia and Flanders are enlightening with respect to requests made by Jehova's Witnesses families for exemptions from "non-denominational moral teaching", as these families, for lack of identification with official denominations, did not wish as a better measure to enroll their children in a non-denominational ethics course. In Wallonia the exemption was refused on the grounds that "non-denominational moral teaching" did not educate children in particular ethics, but in ethics common to all. Flanders on the contrary granted the right to exemption on the grounds that "non-denominational moral teaching" being an ethics course in freethought, the exemption must be granted to enable families to exercise their right of free choice in selecting religious or philosophical teachings in line with their aspirations. Through this example, one also sees how the Belgian system poses without doubt a problem for religious minorities too limited in their numbers to be taken into account by organizing a course dedicated to them (Buddhists, new religious movements...).

Furthermore, it is interesting to note that the different philosophical courses, be they religious or non-confessional, claim to pursue in their separate ways a common set of objectives. Thus one may read, in a brochure published by Belgium's French Community Government entitled *Les cours de morale et de religion - Des lieux d'é ducation* (Class courses in Ethics and Religion – Places of Education) the following statement[1]:

> Whether they refer to a religious experience, to the memory of a people, or to secular culture, human beings are still faced with the same fundamental questions. Birth, life, [and] death, still pose the same great metaphysical questions. Social inequality, denial of democracy, crimes against humanity, demand new exigencies of justice. Advancements in technology, medicine, surgery, [and] genetics, raise new ethical issues.
>
> Whatever values each one of us may evoke to differentiate ourselves, we wish to affirm a few ideals that engage us in the same cause:
>
> • The dynamics of liberation, including liberation of thought, wherever diminishment, pauperization, oppression, or negation, of the human being is manifest
> • The indefatigable pursuit of peace, fraternity, justice, friendship and love
> • The development of democratic commitment through the teaching and learning of dialogue and tolerance with a regard for differences, and mutual respect
> • Education in citizenship through the recognition of, and respect for, human rights and fundamental freedoms.
>
> Schools must be centered on the human being. Class courses in ethics and religion are places of education which, respectful of all particular convictions, promote integration in a pluralistic society. Through proper educational action, they help combat indifference, fanaticism, dogmatism, intolerance, violence, negativism, and other dehumanizing ills of our times.

To conclude on the Belgian case and illustrate all its complexity, let us note that the Buddhist Union of Belgium requested to be recognized in 2006, not as a religion, but as a "non-confessional philosophy of life". If the Buddhists joined the freethinkers, freemasons, and rationalists, in the secular pillar, its purpose in providing an alternative to religions would be progressively diluted. As for class courses in non-confessional ethics, to the extent these are considered to be courses in secular ethics, should one consider Buddhist ethics as secular ethics? The Belgian complexity has the advantage of leading one to raise some good questions regarding secularism. One sees this as well in the area of public funding of 'organized secularism', as demonstrated by Jean-François Husson and Caroline Sägesser (2002: 50). If the State finances recognized beliefs, it should be able to allocate resources to the different beliefs based on numerical importance. This in

---

[1] This brochure provides at the end six contact addresses for moral education in: non-confessional ethics (*Centre d'Action Laïque*), the Catholic religion, the Jewish religion, the Protestant religion, the Islamic religion, and the Christian Orthodox religion.

turn raises the daunting question: how does one count the secular segment? Would this be all persons who identify themselves as being without religion, or solely the declared freethinkers and militant secularists? We will return to this question from a general sociological standpoint.

Secularism as a Non-religious Conception of Man and the World

The question posed is what place should be given to non-religious worldviews, or to secular humanisms, given that a certain form of secular humanism is a common good for all, believers and non-believers alike (i.e., secularism is not exclusive to secular humanists/secularists), and that agnostic and atheist convictions may and should be accounted for if they are socially organized. This may occur via secularist organizations as in Belgium, or through the possibility, as in Germany, for communities holding non-religious conceptions (*Weltanschaungsgemeinschaften*) to incorporate themselves legally (as for religions). The alternatives appear to be either to promote the organization of secular humanisms, to recognize and integrate them alongside religions as *secular* worldviews advocated by *secularist* groups or organizations, or to consider more or less implicitly that *secular* humanism and its *secularist* activists represent a vision more universal and common – in which case religious conceptions would be forcibly denied a universal dimension. At the risk therefore, in the latter case, of considering that *secular* humanism would be the philosophy embracing all society while religious humanisms would represent particular views, whereas it might be argued that secular humanism is also a particular view and that the common and universal humanism which Europe refers to is richly endowed with both 'secular inheritance' and 'religious inheritance'. This is why I suggested using the terms, insofar as the French language is concerned, *humanisme laïque* and *laïcité* to designate the common frame of reference for religious followers and secularists alike, and the framework for harmonious living in a pluralistic Europe. One finds again here two very distinct conceptions of secularism as laicity: laicity as a common good for believers and non-believers alike, and laicity as an alternative to religions, as a *secular* worldview held by organizations and advocates who propone it (rationalist activists, freethinkers, secularists). If both expressions of laicity exist and each has its legitimacy, European laicity can only be all-embracing, integrating all sources of humanism, whether secular or religious. In this sense, one may say that European humanism is *more laïque than it is secular*: it is neither the sole prerogative of secularists nor that of the religious, precisely because it integrates both religious humanisms and secular humanisms.[2] From this viewpoint, it is also important to be rigorous and

---

[2] To speak of *humanisme laïque* in French thus has the advantage of encompassing *secular* humanisms and *religious* humanisms by considering that secularist conceptions of man and the

accurate in the manner of wielding statistics on the religious affiliations of Europeans. In surveys, persons who define themselves as "without religion" may not *ipso facto* be regarded as as secular humanists, as if these individuals were secular activists for the very fact that they declared themselves as being "without religion". The tag of 'secular humanist' should therefore, from this standpoint, be reserved for declared atheists or agnostics. But, as Jacqueline Watson (2010: 15) observes, "taking a general approach to secular worldviews leaves the way open to explore a range of non-religious worldviews and the insights of different agnostic and atheistic 'insiders'. While two-thirds of young people in Britain may refer to themselves as non-religious (*Department for Education and Skills* 2004, 10–11), few will be members of the *British Humanist Association* (BHA), yet, in most syllabuses that include secular worldviews, BHA humanism speaks as the authorative voice".[3] Hubert Dethier (1985: 31), in a study on "Freethought, free-masonry and secular movements" in Belgium, notes that "there is a great difference between the number of people belonging to no church and the number of those who participate in freethinkers' associations". Being non-religious is not enough to be a freethinker, it is not a zero sum distribution. Persons who declare themselves without religion or without particular philosophical identification should rather be considered as indifferent individuals without any identifiable conviction, neither religious nor philosophical. The question is all the more relevant as the line is fine and porous between "doubting believers" who identify themselves as Catholic, Protestant, Muslim, or from other religions, and "believing doubters" who identify themselves as "without religion" while adhering to varying creeds and being interested in spiritual questions. *Secularism* as a secular philosophical conception alternative to religions may not be taken into account unless it demonstrates itself through an organization and a social base of members.

Towards an European Secularism?

In Europe, secularism incorporating religious recognition prevails. In other words, while it respects the mutual independence of the State and religions, and seeks to safeguard the fundamental principles of freedom and non-discrimination which are implied, European secularism recognizes the social, educational and civic contri-butions of religions and convictions, and integrates them as a result in the public sphere.

---

world represent, along with religions, worldviews among others. It also has the advantage of corresponding with the Anglo-Saxon conception which identifies as *secular humanists* advocates of secular worldviews. Secularism as *laïcité*, I insist, is not and should not be the prerogative of secularists, nor be identified unilaterally with a secular worldview. It is a common good for atheists and believers, it is intrinsically neither anti-religious nor pro-religious.

[3] Jacqueline Watson refers to the Department for Education and Skills Report: *Young people in Britain: The attitudes and experiences of 12 to 19 year olds* (2004).

With respect to secularism/*laïcité*, European integration essentially has two consequences. To begin with, it strengthens the judicial means of recourse (*judiciarisation*) of secularism and its inscription in the register of human rights and fundamental principles of liberal and pluralistic democracies, regardless of legal regimes governing faiths, and religious particularities, by country. It is the success of secularism and its acceptance as a commonplace standard (*banalisation*). The role played by the *European Convention on Human Rights* in this regard is far from negligible. The fundamental principles of secularism have been generally 'consecrated' at the European level, while they remain respectful of varying types of church-state relationships prevailing in each country. Otherwise, in the manner that religions and philosphical convictions are organized opposite European institutions in Brussels, secularism is mostly regarded as a particular philosophical conception (freethought, astheist humanisms) that stands alongside religious worldviews, and not as a higher ideology embracing all religions (along the Belgian-Dutch model resting on pillars where the secular world is established as a particular segment of society next to religious worlds). Non-religious beliefs are represented by the *European Humanist Federation*. By dissociating these two aspects of secularism, the Europeanization process would conceivably marginalize the French model of *laïcité*, if such were ever to remain rigid, which is not at all the case. While it incorporates the French model and widely institutionalizes it via 'judiciarization' and secularization, European construction also contributes to the emergence of recognition of the secular humanist current as a particular alternative, rather, to different religions. In some respects, the Europeanization process reinforces the Belgian conception of secularism as a particular philosophical option. Hence, in some respects, the Belgian model is the one which is spreading at European level. By the same token, despite the periodic revival of a certain current in French laicism particularly mistrustful of religion, notably in reaction to sectarian problems and fanaticism in Islam, French practices are becoming more 'Europeanized' by evolving towards a secularism incorporating social recognition of religions (see Willaime 2005, 2008 and Portier 2003, 2008).

In the ultramodern age of modernity, it is no longer the head-on collision between secular and religious magisterial authorities in society that most defines the situation, but the reconfiguration of religious and political spheres in disenchanted societies. Jürgen Habermas (2001), for his part, speaks of "secularization in a post-secular society". We are thus brought to ask ourselves what is happening both with religion in European "post-Christian societies", and with secular convictions in "post-secular societies". The secular and the religious alike are in motion: it is more necessary than ever to break the illusion of an impenetrable line between the two spheres. 'Hypersecularization' of contemporary society invites us to a reappraise the role and resources of religious convictions, even as we hold the fundamental benefits of secularism to be the common good for believers and non-believers alike. From this perspective, religious and secular worldviews appear as resources of conviction, identity and ethics, whose role in furthering social coexistence (*vivre-ensemble*) should be recognized.

References

Bourgeois, Geert. 2010. Toespraak van Viceminister-president en Vlaams minister van Bestuurszaken, Binnenlands Bestuur, Inburgering, Toerisme en Vlaamse Rand, Gent, dinsdag 9 maart 2010, 11.

Dethier, Hubert. 1985. Libre pensée, franc-maçonnerie et mouvements laïques. In *La Belgique et ses dieux. Eglises, mouvements religieux et laïques*, ed. Voyé Liliane, Dobbelaere Karel, Remy Jean, and Billiet Jaak. Louvain-la-Neuve: Cabay (Recherches sociologiques).

Ferry, Jean-Marc. 2009. Les Lumières: un projet contemporain? *Esprit* 8–9(Août-Septembre): 164.

Habermas, Jürgen. 2001. *Glauben und Wissen* (Friedenspreis des Deutschen Buchhandels 2001). Frankfurt am Main: Suhrkamp.

Husson, Jean-François, and Sägesser Caroline. 2002. *La reconnaissance et le financement de la laïcité (II)*, Centre de recherche et d'information socio-politiques, Courrier hebdomadaire no. 1760: 36–50.

Javeau, Claude. 2005. La laïcité ecclésialisée en Belgique. In *Des maîtres et des dieux. Ecoles et religions en Europe*, ed. Jean-Paul Willaime with the collaboration of Séverine Mathieu, 157–164. Paris: Belin.

Portier, Philippe. 2003. De la séparation à la reconnaissance. L'évolution du régime français de laïcité. In *Les mutations contemporaines du religieux*, ed. Jean-Robert Armogathe and Jean-Paul Willaime, 1–24. Turnhout: Brepols.

Portier, Philippe. 2008. Laïcité: la fin de l'exception française ? In *L'identité nationale*. Paris: La Documentation Française. *Cahiers Français* 342: 53–57.

Torfs, Rik. 2005. Eglise, Etat et laïcité en Belgique. Remarques introductives. In *Le financement des cultes et de la laïcité: comparaison internationale et perspectives*, ed. Husson Jean-François, 16–17. Namur: les éditions namuroises.

Watson, Jacqueline. 2010. Including secular philosophies such as humanism in locally agreed syllabuses for religious education. *British Journal of Religious Education* 32(1): 15.

Willaime, Jean-Paul. 2005. 1905 et la pratique d'une laïcité de reconnaissance sociale des religions. *Archives de Sciences Sociales des Religions* 129: 67–82.

Willaime, Jean-Paul. 2008a. The paradoxes of Laïcité in France. In *The centrality of religion in social life. Essays in honour of James A. Beckford*, ed. Barker Eileen, 41–54. Aldershot: Ashgate.

Willaime, Jean-Paul. 2008b. *Le retour du religieux dans la sphère publique. Vers une laïcité de reconnaissance et de dialogue*. Lyon: Editions Olivétan.

Wolfs, José Luis, Boudamoussi El, Coster Lota de Samira, and Dorothée Baillet. 2007. Comment le concept de "laïcité" est-il compris et interprété en dehors de la francophonie ? In *Education, religion et Laïcité. Tome 1/ Des concepts aux pratiques. Enjeux d'hier et d'aujourd'hui*, Education comparée, vol. 61, ed. Abdel Rahamane Baba-Moussa, 98–113. Paris: Association Francophone d'Education Comparée.

The Diversity of Religious Diversity. Using Census and NCS Methodology in Order to Map and Assess the Religious Diversity of a Whole Country

Christophe Monnot and Jörg Stolz

Introduction

Questions of religious diversity and pluralism are of great importance in Western societies and policies of diversity and pluralism must be based on a thorough empirical knowledge (Beckford 2003; Heelas and Woodhead 2005b). It is therefore no wonder that a large number of diversity and mapping studies have emerged in recent years. These often local, regional and qualitative studies have greatly extended our knowledge about questions of religious diversity and pluralism, but they are also plagued by various problems. They often study only small areas, give limited quantitative information about the religious groups, have limited comparability across religious traditions, treat only certain types of diversity and are mainly descriptive.

This chapter claims that studying religious diversity can be improved by using a combination of census and national congregations study (NCS) methodology. With this methodology, it is possible to study religious diversity in a comprehensive way across all religious traditions and in its organizational, geographic, structural, and cultural dimensions. We exemplify this claim by presenting both the state of the art of mapping studies in Switzerland and the added-value of the results produced by the first study with our research design in Switzerland and – for that matter – in Europe.

C. Monnot (✉) • J. Stolz
Institute of Social Sciences of Religion, University of Lausanne, Anthropole, CH – 1015 Lausanne, Switzerland
e-mail: christophe.monnot@unil.ch; joerg.stolz@unil.ch

G. Giordan and E. Pace (eds.), *Religious Pluralism*,
DOI 10.1007/978-3-319-06623-3_6, © Springer International Publishing Switzerland 2014

In what follows, we first comment on the state of the art and then describe our new methodology in order to present a study using this framework to describe various types of religious diversity in Switzerland.

State of the Art

Terminology: Diversity and Pluralism

We make a distinction between a descriptive and a normative way of dealing with questions of religious diversity (Bouma 1997; Stolz and Baumann 2007).[1] *Religious plurality or diversity* is used when describing a state of affairs in a value-neutral way. This plurality or diversity can be analyzed in organizational, geographic, structural, cultural (or other) dimensions. *Religious pluralism,* on the other hand, refers to normative ideas about the value of religious diversity; frameworks that accommodate and regulate religious diversity; or everyday interactions between individuals and groups in settings of religious diversity (Beckford 1999, 2003). In this chapter, we only look at the various dimensions of religious diversity – leaving the description of religious pluralism to other publications.

Religious Diversity

In what follows, we give a state of the art concerning the different types of studies that can be found on religious diversity in Switzerland (for an overview see Baumann and Stolz 2007; Bochinger 2012). Our goal is to use these studies as a backdrop to the kind of information we may obtain from the methodology we propose in this chapter. While we give the most important literature on Switzerland, we only point to some outstanding international literature on religious diversity.

A *first* type of publications consists of *general overviews of religious diversity.* In such publications, various religious traditions are treated, often in an "egalitarian" manner, describing the religious, cultural, structural and geographic attributes of different religions and religious groups. A Swiss example of such a publication is Baumann and Stolz (2007). This book also includes chapters on the historical development of religious diversity in Switzerland as well as on the relationship between religious diversity and various "societal subsystems". A second example is the book by Bochinger (2012) reviewing the results of National Research Program 58. Books of this kind normally rely on secondary sources; their comparisons, while interesting, are of limited depth. Often, several experts on different religious

---

[1] See for a more general treatment of "diversity": Salzbrunn (2012).

traditions collaborate to publish such a book, leading to a pooled expertise, but also creating specific problems (see below). Well-known international publications of this kind are Eck (2001) for the USA, Bouma et al. (2010) for Asia and Australasia, Ferrari and Pastorelli (2012), Pollack (2008), Vertovec (2007) and Willaime (2004) for European countries.

Second, we find *publications using official statistical data*. Authors of such texts use various official statistical sources in order to describe religious diversity. In Switzerland, Bovay (1997) is such a text, providing information on religious membership since 1900, based on Swiss census data. Husistein (2007) is another example, using official Catholic statistics in order to shed light on internal Catholic diversity.

Third, there are so-called *mapping studies*. Authors of such studies normally work on a limited geographic area, try to locate all the existing places of worship for a single religious tradition or for several or all of the traditions, and visit these places or conduct a qualitative description of the places and communities found. In Switzerland, we find such mapping studies for the city of Zurich (Humbert 2004), the city of Basel (Baumann 2000), and the canton of Ticino (Trisconi di Bernardi 2006). A project at the University of Lucerne continually maps religious diversity in the canton of Lucerne[2] and Rademacher (2007) has mapped spiritual groups and new religious movements in the city of Bern. Such mapping studies are extremely useful in getting a sense of the sheer complexity of groups in a certain area. On an international level, one of the first important studies of this type is that directed by Cnaan in Philadelphia. This contributed to the identification of 2,095 different communities in this city (Cnaan and Boddie 2001). In the United States, other surveys were subsequently conducted, such as the one by the United Way of Delaware, which inventoried 100 communities in Wilmington (Cnaan and Wineburg 2009) or the one made in a county of Michigan: the Kent County Congregations Study (KCCS), which identified 720 groups in this area (Hernández et al. 2008). In Europe, two groundbreaking projects based on congregation mapping must be mentioned. The first was conducted in England at Kendal, a town of fewer than 30,000 inhabitants, by Heelas, Woodhead and their collaborators, who visited the groups that they defined as the "congregational domain" and those of the "holistic milieu" (Heelas and Woodhead 2005a, b; Woodhead et al. 2004). Hero, Krech, and their collaborators conducted another large scale project in Germany to identify the religious communities in the state of West Rhine-Westphalia (Hero et al. 2008). Other surveys have been or are now in process in European cities, such as Turku in Finland (Heino 1997; Martikainen 2004); the Aarhus area in Denmark (Ahlin et al. 2012)[3]; or again in Great Britain in the context of the Community Religion Project.[4]

---

[2] http://www.religionenlu.ch

[3] http://teo.au.dk/en/csr/religionindenmark/

[4] http://arts.leeds.ac.uk/crp/

A *fourth* kind of text analyzes the *evolution of religious diversity concerning specific religious traditions*, often in regards to migration. In Switzerland, we find many such studies. Some examples are the studies by Baumann (2004, 2009) on the Tamil and Hindu diasporas in Switzerland, the texts by Behloul (2012a, b) on Muslims from the former Yugoslavia in Switzerland or the work edited by Monnot (2013a) on the institutionalization of Muslim organizations. Well-known international studies include the survey by Knott (2009) on Hinduism in Great Britain, the book by Kay and Dyer (2011) on European Pentecostalism, and the studies on the transformations and influences of Islam in Europe (Al-Azmeh and Fokas 2007; Frégosi 2008; Göle 2011).

General Problems and Issues

We think that both the Swiss and the international studies mentioned have been very useful and have greatly extended our knowledge of religious diversity. However, there are a certain number of shortcomings in many of them. While the first two types mentioned – general overviews and official statistics – give an overall picture of religious diversity, their comparisons are often very limited and lack a certain depth. This depth is often found in the third and fourth types – the mapping studies and the combination of studies concerning specific traditions – but these studies have at least four other drawbacks:

1. They normally study *a relatively small geographic region*. Emerging from them is an overall picture rather like Google maps: certain areas are very precise, with a wealth of ethnographic data, while other areas are very pixilated. Some cities or neighborhoods are richly documented while others are not investigated at all, thus limiting a general representation of the situation.
2. *Limited quantitative information.* Many mapping studies are inherently qualitative, often relying on participant observation, interviews and documentary analysis. While this is certainly very useful information, many interesting questions about religious diversity require quantitative measures that are consistently applied to all the studied groups.
3. *Limited comparability.* This third point is linked to the second. When different religious groups are investigated with qualitative methods by different researchers, the results are often difficult to compare. They are rarely based on the same definitions of the object of study, which is here the religious community. We also find in quite a few mapping studies that experts on certain religions collaborate, each expert working on "his" or "her" religion. However, the problem then arises that the ways in which the religious traditions are studied vary, because different experts adopt different positions, requiring distinctive methodologies. Of course, this leads – once again – to limited comparability among religious traditions.

4. *Inapplicability to different types of diversity.* It also appears that existing mapping studies often treat only certain types of diversity, while neglecting others. It
is rare that organizational, geographic, structural, and cultural diversity are
investigated systematically across religious traditions.
5. *Inability to lead to theory testing.* Finally, mapping studies are normally purely
descriptive, refraining from an explanation of the regularities observed. This is
due, on the one hand, to the methodological inclinations of the researchers; on
the other hand, however, it is also true that the data gathered from mapping
studies are seldom structured and complete enough to allow for systematic
explanation.

Our claim in this chapter is that a number of problems of all four types of studies
may be overcome – at least in part – with the methodology presented here. We of
course do not suggest that all studies on religious diversity should be abandoned in
order to do national congregations studies. Rather, we think that the study here
presented complements the existing ones very usefully, putting the latter into a
larger context and rendering scattered information comparable.

A New Approach: The NCS Method

To gain an overview with parameters permitting the sociological comparison of
local groups and communities, an important 3-year study was carried out in
Switzerland. Modeled on the survey of the NCS (conducted in the United States
in 1997–1998, and then conducted in a second wave in 2006–2007 under the
direction of Chaves (2004; Chaves and Anderson 2008), a major study has recently
been set up in Switzerland (Stolz et al. 2011). A notable difference with the
American study resides in the fact that, in Switzerland, a mapping of all the active
congregations has been undertaken.

Defining and Operationalizing Congregations

We define the term "congregation" as: "a social institution in which individuals
who are not all religious specialists gather in physical proximity to one another,
frequently and at regularly scheduled intervals, for activities and events with
explicitly religious content and purpose, and in which there is continuity over
time in the individuals who gather, the location of the gathering, and the nature
of the activities and events at each gathering. This distinguishes congregations from
other religious social forms such as monasteries or denominational agencies, which
are constituted mainly, perhaps exclusively, by religious specialists; religious
television and radio productions, whose audiences are not in physical proximity
to one another; seasonal celebrations, holiday gatherings, and other religious

assemblies that may occur at regular but infrequent intervals; rites of passage, corroborees, and other events that occur neither frequently nor at regular intervals; and camp meetings, post-game prayer circles, pilgrimages, religious rock concerts, passion plays, revivals, and other religious social forms that lack continuity across gatherings in participants, location, or content of activities" (Chaves 2004: 1–2). This definition covers the groups historically established in Europe, as well as those in the process of implantation; it does not differentiate groups according to a typology, but as specific organizational units regardless of the denomination, the religious tradition or the cultural history of the group.

But is it really possible to apply the notion of "congregation" to non-Christian religions? Here, it is important to bear in mind the exact definition given above. In our view, Christianity, Judaism and Islam may clearly be seen as congregational in modern societies, but even religious traditions that elsewhere are not organized congregationally, such as Hindu traditions or Buddhism, tend to take this form when they try to survive in the diaspora in Western countries. As Ammerman (2005: 3) noticed: "there are common patterns in how people have chosen to gather". The organization of the diaspora pushes religious expression in a congregational direction. This trend was first called "de facto congregationalism" by Wind and Lewis (1994). In Europe, the specialists have identified the same tendency towards a "congregationalization" or a "templeisation" as an effect of the diasporas. For example, Baumann observes that "Tamil Hindus in Germany and Switzerland have been eager to establish collective places of worship, starting with small sites in basements and private rooms, and gradually moving on to much more spacious halls for worship and social gatherings" (Baumann 2009: 166). Thus, we argue that we find in many religious traditions "local communities" or "congregations" as we have defined them above, and that it is feasible to include them in our comprehensive list, if they conform to the definition.

Conducting a Census

We conducted a census from September 2008 to September 2009, counting all local religious groups in Switzerland. This was done by combining all sources of information we could find, such as:

- existing lists of local religious groups by Churches and Federations
- existing lists (published or not) by scholars of religion
- existing lists appearing on institutional internet sites, directories or databases
- data collected from the terrain with, notably, snowball sampling and indications from informers within the religious milieus.

We combined all this information, finely filtering the types of organizations so as to identify only the local religious groups (congregations). Each entry on the final list was checked by two independent sources of information.

Of course, a certain number of hybrid phenomena exist and, accordingly, we had to develop specific rules of decision for "difficult cases" (Marzi 2008). These rules were based partly on the criteria to distinguish a religious organization described by Jeavons (1998) and the definition of religion given in Stolz (2010: 7).

Conducting a Representative Survey of Congregations

In the second phase of our study, we drew a representative sample of 1,040 religious communities in Switzerland, starting from the census report. The existence of the census data allowed us to stratify our sample and to overrepresent religious minority groups. This is why our data let us compare local religious groups across both majority and minority traditions. For every chosen congregation, one key informant (in most cases the spiritual leader) was interviewed by telephone (CATI) in one of the three national languages. A closed question questionnaire was used that was adapted from the American counterpart (Chaves and Anderson 2008).[5] Special care was taken to adapt the questionnaire to Swiss conditions and the whole range of religious traditions.

In order to avoid well-known types of bias in key informant studies, the approximately 250 questions were centered on concrete and verifiable practices as well as on the tangible characteristics of the organization for which the respondent could provide reliable information (Chaves et al. 1999: 463–465; McPherson and Rotolo 1995: 1114). The various religious federations supported the project by encouraging the local leaders to take part in the inquiry, thus producing a response rate of 71.8 %.[6]

Assessing the Diversity of Religious Diversity: Organizational, Geographic, Structural, and Cultural Comparisons

In what follows, we show that the combination of a census and a NCS is able to capture social/organizational, geographic, and cultural diversity in a comprehensive way, thus avoiding the "Google map problem" of only selective precision. We illustrate these claims with various examples.

---

[5] For the adaptation of the questionnaire, we refer to Behling and Law (2000); Forsyth et al. (2007).

[6] The response rates correspond to RR1 calculated according to the standards defined by the AAPOR (2011).

Organizational Diversity: 5,734 Congregations

Our data allows us to give exact statistical information on the number and percentages of local religious groups in Switzerland, that is, social/organizational diversity (Table 1). From September 2008 to September 2009, we identified 5,734 local religious groups active on the Swiss territory. The census survey lets us first observe Christian diversity. We counted 1,750 Catholic communities (30.5 %) and 1,094 Reformed parishes (19.1 %). 1,423 congregations are Evangelical, representing one-quarter of the local groups. All other Christian traditions have a much smaller percentage of local religious groups. The one big surprise in this list is the very high number of Evangelical congregations. The evangelical milieu in Switzerland makes up only about 2–3 % of the population, but it produces about a quarter of all congregations! The obvious explanation is that Evangelical local groups are all rather small in comparison to, say, Roman Catholic or Reformed groups.

Almost one out of five communities in Switzerland (17 %) has its roots in a tradition that is not Christian. If one-third is linked to Islam (5.5 %),[7] let us highlight the internal diversity of these groups: they include Sunni communities (Hanefites, Malechites, Hanbalites, Shafiites); Sufi communities; Shi'as of various traditions such as the Alevis, the Ismaelians, etc.; and a number of groups considered as dissident by Sunni Islam, such as the Ahmadiyya, who built the first mosque in Switzerland in Zurich, and the Abashes, who have the main mosque in Lausanne (Monnot 2013a: 33).

For the other non-Christian collectivities, the groups are very varied, too. For Buddhism (2.5 %), let us note that the first Tibetan monastery in Europe was founded in Switzerland, at Rikon, then a second near Montreux. Both the traditional Buddhist currents (Theravada, Mahayana, Vajrayana, Zen) and the neo-Buddhist ones are present in communities in Switzerland. The same is true of Hinduism (3.3 %), with both the traditional groups, such as the Tamil temples, and the Neo-Hindu groups, such as Hare Krishna (ISKON, six groups), Yoga (Sahaja, self-realization, etc. 0.5 %), and Transcendental Meditation (0.2 %). We also count groupings of Sikhs (0.8 %), Baha'is (0.7 %), as well as various communities (4.5 %) including esoteric groups (1.1 %), Spiritualism (0,8 %), Scientology (0.5 %), six circles of Grail movement and many more besides.

Geographic Diversity: The Urban-Rural Gap

Our methodology can also describe the geographic religious diversity in Switzerland. Geographical religious diversity is not distributed homogeneously over the national territory; it mainly concerns the cities. This can be seen, first, by looking at common measures of diversity on the basis of the number and size of different

---

[7] For one-half of the regular non-Christian worshipers.

Table 1 Distribution of congregations by religious tradition

Religious tradition	Congregations in Switzerland (2008)	
	N	%
Roman Catholic	1,750	30.5 %
Christ Catholic	35	0.6 %
Reformed	1,094	19.1 %
Evangelical	1,423	24.8 %
Orthodox	58	1.0 %
Other Christian	399	7.0 %
Jewish	33	0.6 %
Muslim	315	5.5 %
Buddhist	142	2.5 %
Hindu	189	3.3 %
Other religions	296	5.2 %
Total	**5,734**	**100.0 %**

Source: NCS, University of Lausanne 2008

traditions. Using the Herfindahl-Hirschman Index, we find that the supply of congregations is "moderately concentrated" with an index at 2035.

Second, we see that cities are also much more diverse in that they have the most non-Christian and non-established groups (Fig. 1). In the cities, we find 31 % of non-Christian groups: Buddhists, Hindus, Jews, Muslims, New Religious Movements and others 11 % of Other Christians (e.g. Lutherans, Anglicans, messianic congregations: Jehovah's Witnesses, Latter Day Saints, New-Apostolics, etc.) and 32 % of Evangelicals – leaving only 26 % to the established Christian groups. In rural areas, on the other hand, we find only relatively small percentages of non-Christians (5 %), other Christians (5 %) and Evangelicals (17 %). 74 % of all the groups belong to the established Churches: Roman Catholics and Reformed.

The rural areas show a traditional profile, with an important supply (in relation to the number of inhabitants) in the two historical denominations. The more urban is the geographic space, the greater is the diversity. In the city, on the one hand, Christianity is fragmented into small groups of different denominations and, on the other, non-Christian communities can find room to become established. Several reasons for these disparities can be cited. Historically in Switzerland, the city was the most suitable place for the Reformation, opening the door to Protestant diversity. More recently, the city has been the favored environment for migration (Wihtol de Wenden 2004). Since the beginnings of the Chicago School with *The City* by Park et al. (1925) or – as far as migration and religious communities are concerned – *The Ghetto* by Wirth (1928), we know that the city plays a central role in the absorption of migration. With our methodology, we can measure the impact on religious diversity and thus better understand the disparities in order to document the different dynamics that stem from it.

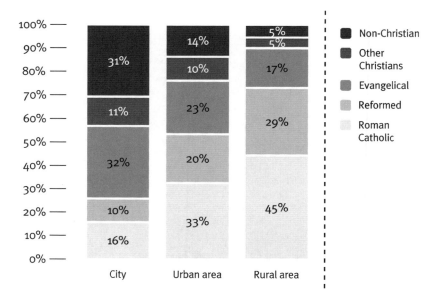

Fig. 1 Types of denominations according to the urban/rural characteristics of the areas (Source: NCS, University of Lausanne 2008)

Structural Diversity: Buildings, Wealth and Staff, Membership

Our methodology also lets us analyze religious diversity in the social/structural dimension. This dimension is often neglected in texts on religious diversity. However, it is of utmost sociological importance. In our study, we were able to reduce the complexity of religious groups to four large profiles: the recognized communities, the non-recognized Christian communities, the non-Christian congregationalist communities and "spiritual" groups organized as networks.

These different profiles were arrived at by inductive analysis of various kinds – but they can best be presented as following from three distinctions (Monnot 2013b) (Fig. 2).

First, we distinguish local religious groups that are established (State recognized) from those that are not established. In the first group, we find Reformed and Catholic churches. They enjoy a public recognition in most cantons (the exact effects of recognition vary)[8] and their local groups enjoy administrative, legal and fiscal advantages that the other groups do not have.

Second, and among the non-established groups, we distinguish those that are Christian and those that belong to other religious traditions. Historically, the associative forms of Western society have influenced the Christian institutions.

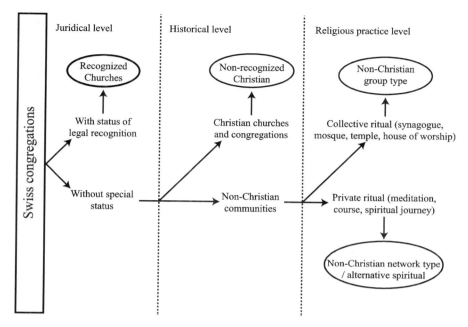

Fig. 2 Four structural profiles (Source: NCS, University of Lausanne 2008)

Third, and among the non-Christian groups, we distinguish on the one hand groups whose religious traditions are based on a collective and organized ritual such as the Jews and the Muslims, the Buddhist temples, the Hindu temples connected with the diaspora (Baumann 2009; Baumann et al. 2003; Knott 2009) and, on the other hand, groups favoring networks and an alternative and individual spirituality, close to that which Heelas and Woodhead (2005a) have named the "holistic milieu".

Together, the three nested distinctions thus lead us to the four profiles that we will now briefly describe. Our claim is that these four profiles make sense of much of the structural diversity of local religious groups in Switzerland. As Table 2 shows, the first is constituted by the *historical, majority and state-recognized Churches*, founded on average before the seventeenth century. The communities of this category meet in dedicated religious buildings that, very often, they own (or have the right to use) and that benefit from historic preservation. These groups have many members; they have a high income and provide their university-educated leader with a comfortable salary, full-time in three-fourths of cases. The worshipers meet in a community close to their homes. The audience there is old and much feminized. An interesting aspect to point out here is the relatively low rate of education/awareness training of the children in the community context. This rate reflects the strong institutionalization of the groups rather than a weak following among the youth. In fact, their status allows them, in more than one-third of cases, to provide religious education within the school system. Moreover, the parishes are

Table 2 Four large institutional profiles

Mean	Recognized Churches	Non-recognized Churches	Non-Christian group type	Non-Christian network type
History and Building				
Founded (year)	1690	1940	1975	1984
Historic preservation of the building	74 %	17 %	20 %	7 %
Religious building	98 %	59 %	35 %	6 %
Rent premises for religious practice	3 %	34 %	46 %	64 %
Wealth and Staff				
Annual income of the congregation (CHF)	850'000	220'000	110'000	13'000
Annual salary of the leader (full-time in CHF)	91'000	42'000	24'000	0
Paid spiritual leader	98 %	62 %	43 %	4 %
Full-time spiritual leader	70 %	45 %	32 %	0 %
Paid staff (part and full-time)	7	2	2	0
University education of the leader	98 %	60 %	63 %	15 %
Age of the leader (years)	51	49	47	54
% of female spiritual leaders	12 %	8 %	9 %	50 %
Members				
Affiliated members (theoretic median[a])	1,400	75	270	16
Regular attendants (median)	90	80	60	15
Female regular attendants	66 %	57 %	42 %	64 %
Regular attendants aged 60 and more	58 %	29 %	22 %	20 %

Source: NCS, University of Lausanne 2008

[a]Estimate of the number of affiliated persons identified in Switzerland (Bovay 2004) calculated from the number of persons having a "link" to a congregation (NCS, University of Lausanne 2008)

interlinked with the Churches that organize or centralize certain services such as catechism.

The *non-recognized Christian congregations* were mostly founded in the nineteenth and twentieth century (mean: 1940). A little more than one-third of the groups rent their premises because they do not possess any. The annual income of the communities is four times lower than that of the recognized Churches. The spiritual leaders work as volunteers in four communities out of ten and a little less than half are employed full-time for a salary of about 42,000 CHF.[9] In six cases out of ten, the leaders have had a university education. In these groups, the median number of regular worshipers corresponds to the number of affiliated persons,

---

[9] CHF: Swiss Francs. The average Swiss salary is 60,000 CHF (FSO 2012: 19).

indicating thereby that a member is almost automatically an active person in the community, which is not the case for members of the recognized congregations. The members must travel a little further to practice, but the majority nevertheless resides less than 10 min away. Contrary to the preceding group, the local community strongly organizes the religious education of the children.

The profile of *non-Christian* groups based on a collective ritual resembles that of the non-recognized Christian communities, since legally they are on the same level. However, the non-Christian congregations are distinguished by a greater instability and recency of the group with a strong foreign presence: only one celebration out of five is given in the language of the linguistic region. Founded on average late in the twentieth century, these communities, in four cases out of ten, do not own premises in which to meet. The average income is circa 110,000 CHF and one-third remunerates a spiritual leader. Another point to bring out is their relative similarity with the recognized Churches regarding the number of affiliated members, very much higher than that of the regular worshipers, since the latter represent about one-fifth of the affiliated. A particularity to note here is the relatively high proportion of men who regularly attend the religious ceremonies. This element depends on traditions and theological elements, in Islam and in Judaism, which strongly differentiate religious practices according to gender.

The final profile assembles *smaller, more recent groups, meeting in premises that are "not religious", sometimes in centers shared by several groups (alternative spirituality).* Their leadership is mainly voluntary since only one group out of ten provides a leader with a salary, and is strongly feminized since a woman directs almost one group out of two. The latter point distinguishes these groups very clearly from the others, since only the recognized Churches and especially the Reformed Church have more than one group out of ten with a female spiritual leader. In groups of the holistic milieu, the number of affiliated members corresponds to that of the regular members, who travel much more than do members of the other groups to get to the place where the main spiritual activities occur. The members, who are mostly adult women, attend these groups in order to experience well-being, develop their personality, and grow spiritually. In this sense, another important point to highlight is that the communities of this category are clearly distinguishable from the others by the absence of the transmission to and education of children. The center of attention is thus the adult member. This category corresponds, at the institutional level, to the "holistic milieu" of Heelas and Woodhead (2005a) or Mayer (1993).

Cultural Diversity: Worship Modalities

Our methodology further lets us compare the groups on the cultural level. Qualitative studies often analyze this type of diversity, but seldom succeed in comparing it across religious traditions; in quantitative studies, cultural diversity is rarely measured.

In the following, we show religious diversity concerning celebrations across religious traditions.

As could have been expected, religious celebrations in Switzerland vary greatly according to religious traditions – our methodology, however, lets us estimate for the first time just *how much* they differ on both a number of general dimensions and very specific attributes.

Take, for example, the length of the religious service. In Fig. 3 we see that Roman Catholics have, on average, the shortest religious services (54 min), while Orthodox groups clearly have the longest services (more than 200 min on average). Other religious traditions fall between these extremes. However, we can compare not only the absolute length of the religious service – but also the relative length of various internal components. Thus, we can see from Fig. 3 that Reformed services are much shorter than Orthodox services – but that they give the same amount of absolute time to the sermon – about 15–16 min. Another way to say this is that the sermon is relatively more important to the Reformed tradition. Again, this is what we would have expected – but here we can (we think for the first time) *estimate the differences.*

Let us go a bit deeper into the description of the four domains of ritual elements that we distinguish in religious services across traditions:

Prayer

Concerning meditation, prayer and liturgical acts, the non-Christian groups distinguish themselves by a major portion for this type of element, which represents more than 50 % of the time of celebration. For the Christians, this element also remains close to one-half of the celebration time. The groups with Protestant roots spend less time on ritual and on prayer, but more on preaching. This is the opposite for the Roman Catholics or the Christian Catholics. For the Orthodox, let us point out further that the priest accomplishes a major part of the ritual by singing, thus blending two elements that remain much more separate in the other denominations.

Music

The portion of music is also very diverse. The Christian groups all spend between 20 and 30 % of the celebration time on music (with the exception of Orthodox worship with more than 60 % of the celebration sung). On the other hand, for the non-Christian communities the time for singing or music is minor, since the groups generally do not sing for more than 10 % of the celebration time, with the exception of the Jewish groups; Hindus, who devote 40 min to music and

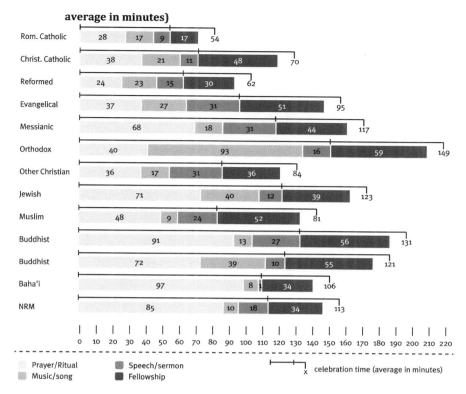

Fig. 3 Time of prayer, music, sermon and fellowship for 13 religious categories (average in minutes) (Source: NCS, University of Lausanne 2008)

singing per celebration; and the Sufi fellowships (included in the Muslim category).[10]

Sermon

The sermon, for all the groups, is the shortest part of their celebration. Two poles emerge, however, with groups where the time for the sermon is marginal and those where it nevertheless represents an important part of the ritual. At one pole, the Baha'i have only a brief address of about 1 min on average; Catholic priests speak for 6 min; Jewish rabbis 12 min, etc. At the other pole are the groups sprung from

---

[10] The Muslims sing from 1 to 2 min in their celebration if we take the call to prayer into account. For many Muslims, the practice of music is forbidden (which is not the case for singing). The average for the denominational category is higher than these few minutes because of the Sufi fellowships.

Protestantism, where preaching takes on a central character and occupies slightly less than one-third of the celebration time.

Fellowship

Concerning fellowship, it is notable that the longer the ceremony is, the more time the worshipers spend together. An Orthodox Christian who has just spent an average of two and a half hours in praise spends another hour with his or her coreligionists in informal discussion. At the other extreme, Catholics who have spent on average 54 min in the celebration spend only slightly more than a quarter of an hour in fellowship. The length of the celebration and that of the time spent informally by the worshipers indicates the type of community. For the groups with a population with a strong immigrant background, the community represents an important center for networking. The celebration is longer, with a greater formal and informal participation of the members. For the others, the celebration is primarily a practice before being a community of fellowship.

Using simple and comparable elements, we can thus analyze and compare – apart from any theological considerations – the cultural production of very diverse religious traditions. In principle – for lack of space we do not go into these questions here – it is also possible to then explain these differences through various cultural, structural, and historical factors.

Conclusion

In this chapter, we have shown that existing problems and issues when studying religious diversity may be tackled with a new methodology that combines a full census and a national congregation study (NCS). Our claim has been that when this method is used, all religious traditions may be compared in a great many dimensions of religious diversity and in an extended geographic region. The data thus gathered may illuminate both diversity and pluralism and allow for both description and explanation of the phenomena observed. The study we have described has analyzed the organizational, geographic, structural, and cultural diversity, as well as aspects of the religious pluralism, of the whole range of religious traditions in Switzerland. This study has led to an entire set of original results, hitherto never observed. Our focus in this chapter has been to present the methodology and some exemplary results. Further publications will present these results in much more depth and will describe various contexts. We hope that other researchers will follow up on this methodology in order to complement all local and regional mapping studies with such national investigations, thus completing our knowledge of the fascinating topic of the diversity of religious diversity.

References

AAPOR (American Association for Public Opinion Research). 2011. *Standard definitions: Final dispositions of case codes and outcome rates for surveys*, 7th ed. Deerfield: AAPOR.

Ahlin, Lars, Jørn Borup, Marianne Qvortrup Fibiger, Lene Kühle, Viggo Mortensen, and René Dybdal Pedersen. 2012. Religious diversity and pluralism: Empirical data and theoretical reflections from the Danish pluralism project. *Journal of Contemporary Religion* 27: 403–418.

Al-Azmeh, Aziz, and Effie Fokas (eds.). 2007. *Islam in Europe. Diversity, identity and influence.* Cambridge: Cambridge University Press.

Ammerman, Nancy T. 2005. *Pillars of faith: American congregations and their partners.* Berkeley: University of California Press.

Baumann, Christoph P. (ed.). 2000. *Religionen in Basel-Stadt und Basel-Landschaft.* Basel: Manava-Verlag.

Baumann, Martin. 2004. Organising Hindu temples in Europe, the case of Tamil migrants from Sri Lanka. In *Unterwegs Neue Pfade in der Religionswissenschaft. Festschrift in honour of Michael Pye on his 65th birthday*, ed. Christoph Kleine, Monika Schrimpf, and Katja Triplett, 379–391. München: Biblion.

Baumann, Martin. 2009. Templeisation: Continuity and change of Hindu traditions in Diaspora. *Journal of Religion in Europe* 2: 149–179.

Baumann, Martin, and Jörg Stolz (eds.). 2007. *Eine Schweiz – viele Religionen: Risiken und Chancen des Zusammenlebens.* Bielefeld: Transcript.

Baumann, Martin, Brigitte Luchesi, and Annette Wilke (eds.). 2003. *Tempel und Tamilen in zweiter Heimat.* Würzburg: Ergon.

Beckford, James A. 1999. The management of religious diversity in England and Wales with special reference to prison chaplaincy. *International Journal on Multicultural Societies* 1: 55–66.

Beckford, James A. 2003. *Social theory and religion.* Cambridge: Cambridge University Press.

Behling, Orlando, and Kenneth S. Law. 2000. *Translating questionnaires and other research instruments: Problems and solutions.* London: Sage Publications.

Behloul, Samuel M. 2012a. Religion or culture? The public relations and self-presentation strategies of Bosnian Muslims in Switzerland compared with other Muslims. In *The Bosnian Diaspora. Integration in transnational communities*, ed. Marko Valenta and Sabrina P. Ramet, 301–318. London: Ashgate.

Behloul, Samuel M. 2012b. Negotiating the 'Genuine' religion: Muslim Diaspora communities in the context of the western understanding of religion. *Journal of Muslims in Europe* 1: 7–26.

Bochinger, Christoph (ed.). 2012. *Religionen, Staat und Gesellschaft. Die Schweiz zwischen Säkularisierung und religiöser Vielfalt.* Zurich: Librio.

Bouma, Gary D. 1997. Religion and cultural plurality in Australia. In *Many religions, all Australian: Religious settlement, identity and cultural diversity*, ed. Gary D. Bouma, 95–108. Kew: The Christian Research Association.

Bouma, Gary D., Rod Ling, and Douglas Pratt. 2010. *Religious diversity in Southeast Asia and the Pacific: National case studies.* Heidelberg: Springer.

Bovay, Claude. 1997. *L'évolution de l'appartenance religieuse et confessionnelle en Suisse Recensement fédéral de la population 1990.* Bern: Federal Statistical Office.

Bovay, Claude. 2004. *Le paysage religieux en Suisse, Recensement fédéral de la population 2000.* Neuchatel: FSO. http://www.bfs.admin.ch/bfs/portal/fr/index/themen/01/22/publ.html?publicationID=1615

Chaves, Mark. 2004. *Congregations in America.* Cambridge: Harvard University Press.

Chaves, Mark, and Shawna L. Anderson. 2008. Continuity and change in American congregations: Introducing the second wave of the National Congregations Study. *Sociology of Religion* 69: 415–440.

Chaves, Mark, Mary E. Konieczny, Beyerlien Kraig, and Emily Barman. 1999. The National Congregations Study: Background, methods and selected results. *Journal for the Scientific Study of Religion* 38: 458–477.

Cnaan, Ram A., and Stephanie Boddie. 2001. Philadelphia census of congregations and their involvement in social service delivery. *Social Service Review* 75: 559–580.

Cnaan, Ram A., and Bob Wineburg. 2009. *The united way of Delaware*. Wilmington: Penn Social Policy and Practice & The University of North Carolina.

Eck, L. Diana. 2001. *A new religious America: How a 'Christian Country' has become the world's most religiously diverse nation*. San Francisco: Harper Collins Publishers.

Ferrari, Silvio, and Sabrina Pastorelli (eds.). 2012. *Religion in public space. A European perspective*. London: Ashgate.

Forsyth, Barbara H., Martha Stapleton Kudela, Kerry Levin, Deirdre Lawrence, and Gordon B. Willis. 2007. Methods for translating an English-language survey questionnaire on tobacco use into Mandarin, Cantonese, Korean, and Vietnamese. *Field Methods* 19: 264–283.

Frégosi, Franck. 2008. *Penser l'islam dans la laïcité : Les musulmans de France et la République*. Paris: Fayard.

FSO (Federal Statistics Office). 2012. *Indicateurs du marché du travail 2012*. Neuchatel: FSO. http://www.bfs.admin.ch/bfs/portal/fr/index/themen/03/22/publ.html?publicationID=4851

Göle, N. 2011. *Islam in Europe: The lure of fundamentalism and the allure of cosmopolitanism*. Princeton: Markus Wiener Publishers.

Heelas, Paul, and Linda Woodhead. 2005a. Kendal, Cumbria : A spiritual laboratory. *CeNtreWoRds* 4: 17–26.

Heelas, Paul, and Linda Woodhead (eds.). 2005b. *The spiritual revolution: Why religion is giving way to spirituality*. London: Blackwell.

Heino, Harri. 1997. *Mihin Suomi Tänään Uskoo*. Porvoo: WSOY.

Hernández, Edwin I., Neil R. Carlson, Nathan Medeiros-Ward, Armanda Steck, and Lori Verspoor (eds.). 2008. *Gatherins of hope. How religious congregations contribute to the quality of life in Kent county*. Grand Rapids: Center for Social Research of Calvin College.

Hero, Markus, Volkhard Krech, and Helmut Zander. 2008. *Religiöse Vielfalt in Nordrhein-Westfalen: Empirische Befunde und Perspektiven der Globalisierung vor Ort*. Paderborn: F. Schöningh.

Humbert, Claude-Alain. 2004. *Religionsführer Zürich: 370 Kirchen, Religiös-spirituelle Gruppierungen, Zentren und Weltanschauliche Bewegungen der Stadt Zürich*. Zurich: Orell Füssli.

Husistein, Roger. 2007. *Katholische Kirche in der Schweiz. Zahlen – Fakten – Entwicklungen 1996–2005*. St-Gallen: SPI.

Jeavons, Thomas H. 1998. Identifying characteristics of 'religious' organizations: An exploratory proposal. In *Sacred companies: Organizational aspects of religion and religious aspects of organizations*, ed. Nicholas J. Demerath, Peter Dobkin Hall, Terry Schmitt, and Rhis H. Williams, 79–94. Oxford: Oxford University Press.

Kay, William K., and Anne E. Dyer (eds.). 2011. *Pentecostalism in Europe*. Leiden: Brill.

Knott, Kim. 2009. Becoming a 'Faith Community': British Hindus, identity, and the politics of representation. *Journal of Religion in Europe* 2: 85–114.

Martikainen, Tuomas. 2004. *Immigrant religions in local society: Historical and contemporary perspectives in the city of Turku*. Åbo: Åbo Akademy University Press.

Marzi, Eva. 2008. *Confrontation d'une théorie au terrain. Le cas de la communauté religieuse* (Bachelor Dissertation). Geneva: Sociology Department, University of Geneva.

Mayer, Jean-François. 1993. *Les nouvelles voies spirituelles. Enquête sur la religiosité parallèle en Suisse, Pluralisme culturel et identité nationale*. Lausanne: L'Age d'homme.

Mcpherson, J. Miller, and Thomas Rotolo. 1995. Measuring the composition of voluntary groups: A multitrait, multimethod analysis. *Social Forces* 73: 1097–1115.

Monnot, Christophe (ed.). 2013a. *La Suisse des mosquées. Derrière le voile de l'unité musulmane*. Geneva: Labor et Fides.

Monnot, Christophe. 2013b. *Croire ensemble. Analyse institutionnelle du paysage religieux en Suisse.* Zurich: Seismo.

NCS (National Congregations Study). 2008. DARIS: Data and Research Information Services. http://forsdata.unil.ch/data/themesearch.asp?lang=e

Pahud de Mortanges, René. 2007. System und Entwicklungstendenzen des Religionsverfassungsrechts der Schweiz und des Fürstentums Liechtenstein. *Zeitschrift für Evangelisches Kirchenrecht* 52: 495–523.

Park, Robert E., Ernest W. Burgess, and Roderick D. Mackenzie. 1925. *The city.* Chicago: University of Chicago Press.

Pollack, Detlef. 2008. Religious change in Europe: Theoretical considerations and empirical findings. *Social Compass* 55: 168–186.

Rademacher, Stefan. 2007. Neue Religiöse Gemeinschaften: Viele Antworten auf ein sich verändernde Welt. In *Eine Schweiz, viele Religionen. Risiken und Chancen des Zusammenlebens*, ed. Martin Baumann and Jörg Stolz, 238–255. Bielefeld: Transcript.

Salzbrunn, Monika. 2012. Vielfalt/Diversity/Diversité. *Soziologische Revue* 35: 375–394.

Stolz, Jörg. 2010. A silent battle. Theorizing the effects of competition between churches and secular institutions. *Review of Religious Research* 51: 253–276.

Stolz, Jörg, and Martin Baumann. 2007. Religiöse Vielfalt: Kulturelle, soziale und individuelle Formen. In *Eine Schweiz, viele Religionen. Risiken und Chancen des Zusammenlebens*, ed. Martin Baumann and Jörg Stolz, 21–38. Bielefeld: Transcript.

Stolz, Jörg, Mark Chaves, Christophe Monnot, and Laurent Amiotte-Suchet. 2011. *Die religiösen Gemeinschaften in der Schweiz: Eigenschaften, Aktivitäten, Entwicklung.* Bern: Swiss National Science Foundation.

Trisconi di Bernardi, Michela. 2006. *Repertorio delle Religioni, Panorama Religioso e Spirituale del Cantone Ticino.* Bellinzona: Dipartimento delle instituzion.

Vertovec, Steven. 2007. Super-diversity and its implications. *Ethnic and Racial Studies* 30: 1024–1054.

Wihtol de Wenden, Catherine. 2004. Ville, religion et immigration. *Les Annales de la recherche urbaine* 96: 115–116.

Willaime, Jean-Paul. 2004. *Europe et religions: les enjeux du XXIe siècle.* Paris: Fayard.

Wind, James P., and James W. Lewis (eds.). 1994. *American congregations volume 1: Portraits of twelve religious communities.* Chicago: University of Chicago Press.

Wirth, L. 1928. *The Ghetto.* Chicago: University of Chicago Press.

Woodhead, Linda, Mathew Guest, and Karin Tusting. 2004. Congregational studies: Taking stock. In *Congregational studies in the UK: Christianity in a post-christian context*, ed. Linda Woodhead, Mathew Guest, and Karin Tusting, 1–23. Aldershot: Ashgate.

Increasing Religious Diversity in a Society Monopolized by Catholicism

Enzo Pace

Introduction

Because of the flow of many people coming from 180 countries around the world, to what extent is the Catholic monopoly in Italy challenged by an increasing degree of religious diversity? Roughly speaking, the question concerns the relation between religion and migration in Europe, in particular in the Southern countries, focusing on the switch from being countries of emigration to becoming countries of immigration. Secondly this process affects the peculiar religious structures of these countries. Many of them, like Greece, Italy, Portugal and Spain (Vilaça et al. 2014; Vilaça and Pace 2010; Perez-Agote 2012), for historical reasons, are countries up to now with a dominant religion: Orthodoxy in Greece, Catholicism in the others. The monopolistic structure of the religious field in any case is challenged by the increasing religious diversity. It means an increase in social complexity and a differentiation of the religious field in relation to and tension with the dominant system of belief.

From a theoretical point of view, it seems to me useful to conceptualize the socio-religious change occurring in the Southern part of Europe according to systems theory. Societies can be studied as systems that interact with environments more complex than the precarious and unstable equilibrium in which each religious system tends to reside. A given society must learn to transfer the external complexity, as represented by the unexpected religious diversity, to an internal differentiation. Religious systems are large organizations that are experts in complexity. The more the social environment in which these organizations operate is differentiated, the greater must be the degree of the expertise of a religious system in order to learn to reduce the complexity of the external environment to avoid the entropy of the system itself (Luhmann 1987, 2012; Pace 2011a, b). The point of view of the

E. Pace (✉)
Dipartimento FISPPA, University of Padua, Via Melchiorre Cesarotti 10/12, 35123 Padua, Italy
e-mail: vincenzo.pace@unipd.it

G. Giordan and E. Pace (eds.), *Religious Pluralism*,
DOI 10.1007/978-3-319-06623-3_7, © Springer International Publishing Switzerland 2014

theory of social systems seems to me particularly useful for analyzing what happens in a society when its environment changes, becoming in many ways not easily amenable to the apparatus of social cohesion and social control (political, ideological, economic and cultural) that could apply to a society relatively more stable and homogeneous. The risk of the entropy both for the society as a whole and for a Catholic institution is even higher when the flow of immigrants coming from a variety of countries around the world is not homogeneous. There is a diversity within the diversity. Not only Islam, but Muslims from different traditions; not only Orthodox Christians, but Romanian, Ukrainian, Serbian, Moldovan, Greek, and Russian Orthodox, each with its own specific religious characteristics; not only people coming from India, but Sikh, Buddhist, Hindu, Christian, Tamil and so on; not only Pentecostals, but African, Latin-American and Chinese Pentecostals, belonging to a plurality of different denominations. If a dominant religion would like to open the dialogue with the new Christian churches and denominations, with whom should it start? How to navigate a field of religious forces that has become so crowded and differentiated? Within the Catholic Church, for instance, there is a Pentecostal movement. Can this movement be a means of communication with the forms of Pentecostal Christianity that come out of Europe? Or could this be a risk for a model of the Catholic church, since Pentecostalism prefers the anarchy of the Holy Spirit's gift? And if I decide to dialogue with Muslims, with which community or group? How can I be sure not to get in front of fundamentalists who interpret my gesture of openness as a sign weaknesses?

Similarly the political system of governance of complex modern societies is questioned by religious diversity. How to find the right balance between the rule of *justice* and the *good* that every religious community intends to follow? How to stay connected to the string of a god, and at the same time, subject to the rules that should apply to all citizens? It was, on closer inspection, the same dilemma that Karl Marx raised in his famous writing on the Jewish question (Marx and Arnold 1844: 42 in the English version):

> The political emancipation of the Jew, the Christian, and, in general, of religious man, is the emancipation of the *state* from Judaism, from Christianity, from religion in general. In its own form, in the manner characteristic of its nature, the state as a state emancipates itself from religion by emancipating itself from the state religion—that is to say, by the state as a state not professing any religion, but, on the contrary, asserting itself as a state. The *political* emancipation from religion is not a religious emancipation that has been carried through to completion and is free from contradiction, because political emancipation is not a form of *human* emancipation which has been carried through to completion and is free from contradiction.

In other words, and focusing on to the Italian case, the political system is called upon to rethink the way the State has traditionally managed the relations on the one hand with the dominant Catholic Church and on the other with the other denominations considered minorities, *admitted* today to enter the legally ruled public space. It means the necessity of an Italian way to manage religious diversity. The peculiar policy of religious pluralism in Italy is an instance, among many, of related conceptual difference introduced by many scholars (Beckford and Demerath 2007; Doe 2011; Finke 2013; Richardson and Bellanger 2014; Wuthnow 2005).

The present discussion is divided into three sections. In a first, using the paradox of Achilles and the tortoise, I intend to specify the contours of the issue of religious diversity and its management policy in Italy. The second section will document with the help of maps of places of worship the spread of major religions that are new to Italy today. In the third and last one I will show how the Catholic Church has responded to the unprecedented religious diversity that challenges its historic monopoly position.

Religion and Immigration: The Social Change

Using the famous paradox of Achilles and the tortoise attributed to the pre-Socratic philosopher Zeno of Elea (fifth century BC), I propose to analyze the social changes taking place in Italy from a particular angle, i.e. the passage from a society under a Catholic monopoly to one characterized by an unprecedented and unexpected religious pluralism. The maps illustrating the presence of a number of different religions from those of a typical Italian's *birth* (Catholicism) show how the country's social and religious geography is changing. Such a change is a major novelty in a country that has always seen itself as Catholic for long-standing historical reasons and also for deeply-rooted and still strong cultural motives.

Despite the religious diversity that is beginning to make itself socially obvious, the Catholic Church continues to have a central role in the public arena but, like Achilles in the metaphor, it is beginning to realize that Italian society (the tortoise in the metaphor) is *moving* on, not only because other religions are striving to gain visibility and public recognition, but also because they are contributing in some cases to making the religious field more variegated.

To better delineate the object of our analysis, if I were asked, "Who does Achilles represent?" in my metaphorical premise, I would answer as follows. According to the Greek myth, Achilles' mother Thetis immersed him as a baby in the waters of the River Styx to make him become invulnerable; to do so, she held him by his heel, which remained the only part of his body liable to harm. Homer's hero symbolizes the Catholic Church and religion in Italy, a system of belief that is still well-organized, permeating every facet of society, custodian of the collective memory and identity of the Italian people, with a complex *potestas indirecta* (Poulat 1974) in the sphere of political decision-making. This is the *majority* system of religious belief, the *religion of Italians' birth*. Albeit with growing difficulty, it has continued to withstand the onslaught of secularization, as an analysis on a representative sample of the population (Garelli 2011) and an ethnographic study (Marzano 2012) have recently confirmed, taking two very different approaches. By comparison with other situations in Europe (Perez-Agote 2012), Italy appears to have become secularized while remaining *faithful* to its image (in collective repre-sentational terms) as a Catholic country, thanks to the Church's organizational strength. It is no longer a Catholic country in terms of many Italian people's practices, but the collective myth of the Italians' Catholic identity still seems to hold (Garelli et al. 2003). So, having explained the role of Achilles, let us see who the tortoise represents. I use the *tortoise* to impersonate the socio-religious shift taking place in Italian society, from a religious single culture to a novel form of religious diversity. This is a slow process that is going largely unnoticed, generating no particular tension or conflict (except for the case of the Muslim places of worship), but it is ultimately producing a change in the country's socio-religious geography. Italian people are no longer born inherently Catholic.

My aim in the following pages is to illustrate and describe this change with the aid of data collected in a study completed in 2012 (Pace 2013), which enable us to go beyond mere generic estimates of the presence of other, non-Catholic religions in Italy to map the different places of worship, by region and by religious confession. In its annual report on immigration, Caritas/Migrantes prepares estimates that measure religious diversity on the basis of a simple (sometimes over-simple) inductive process: if 100 immigrants have arrived from Morocco, for instance, then 99.9 % of them will be Muslims because that is the proportion of people of Muslim faith by birth in their society of origin. Caritas is a Catholic voluntary organization that has the merit of attempting over the years to fill a very obvious gap in the reliable information available on immigration in Italy. Although the number of immigrants reached five million in 2011 (accounting for 7 % of the population), neither the central Italian Statistics Institute (ISTAT) nor the Ministry of the Interior have succeeded in providing a comprehensive picture of the real presence of the various religions in the country, apart from the case of the Muslim places of worship, which are monitored by the police and the intelligence services on behalf of the Ministry of the Interior for reasons of public security. Indeed this source provides a good starting point for examining and further analyzing the situation, as was done recently by Allievi (2010) and Bombardieri (2012).

Be that as it may, the 189 different nationalities of Italy's immigrants make it plain that religious diversity is now part of our lives, at the local market, in our hospital wards, prisons and school rooms, at the offices of our local social services, and so on. Estimates may be a starting point, but they no longer suffice to give an accurate picture of Italy's socio-religious geography, capable of *realistically* illustrating people's experiences and their ways of belonging to a given religion. In other words, estimates cannot answer the question of what people that we formally classify as Muslims, Buddhists, Hindus, Sikhs, Pentecostals, and so on, actually believe in.

We are beginning to gain an idea of the areas where the immigrants' different religions tend to become concentrated, but we have only a very incomplete and imprecise map of their places of worship. These places are still not very obvious to the naked eye—to our cursory gaze, at least: though we are accustomed to recognizing a Catholic church at a glance, we are less well equipped to notice buildings that identify the presence of other, non-Catholic religions. Our eyesight has a role in religions. Our eyes reflect and record an orderly outside world, where we see things that are familiar to us. If, at some future time, we were to see a mosque or a Sikh temple standing alongside our local parish church, the new building might seem like an intrusion, an image that stands out instead of fading into the background. We can learn something from the recent referendum held in Switzerland (in the autumn of 2009) to prevent the building of minarets (not of mosques, note) because the referendum's promoters see them as invasive symbols in a religious landscape characterized and occupied mainly by bell towers.

To begin to really *see* how Italy's socio-religious geography is changing, we must first go a step further, going beyond mere estimates of the different religious realities that have now become well-established in our country. Some religious communities show a marked degree of homogeneity, while others are differentiated even amongst themselves (this is true both of Islam and of the Orthodox Churches that refer to different patriarchal sees or national Churches). It is easy to find information on the homogeneous entities, much more difficult for the heterogeneous (as in the case of the Muslim communities that refer to different associations, some of which represent the world of believers as a whole, while others are based on geographical origin). For some religions, despite some degree of differentiation, we can deal with the problem of obtaining a credible picture of their places of worship by relying on a network (that we have patiently constructed) of witnesses, who have provided addresses and other precious details.

Maps are used for travelling, and combined with a compass, they help us to orient ourselves in an effort to interpret the new situation of religions in Italy. If somebody were to travel through Italy from north to south, and from west to east, they would certainly not be immediately aware of any Sikh temples or mosques, nor would they know how to recognize an Orthodox church (barring a few exceptions in Trieste or Venice, or in Bari or Reggio Calabria in the south, where there are churches that bear witness to the historical presence of flourishing Greek and Albanian Orthodox communities). They would be even less likely to stumble upon evidence of Hindu mandir or Buddhist temples, and would have virtually no chance of noting any African, South American or Chinese neo-Pentecostal Churches. While the African neo-Pentecostal Churches have been the object of a specific investigation (Pace and Butticci 2010), their Latin American and Chinese counterparts have remained in the background. A problem with the new churches, moreover, lies in the fact that it is very difficult to find them because they are often born and survive in very precarious logistic and operating conditions. It is nonetheless common knowledge that some Latin American mega-Churches, and particularly the *Igreja Universal do Reino de Deus* (born in Brazil in 1977) are now widespread in many countries (Corten et al. 2003; Garcia-Ruiz and Michel 2012). This Church has ten locations in Italy (in Rome, Milan, Turin, Genova, Mantova, Verona, Udine, Naples, Florence and Siracusa). Then again, little or nothing is known about the religious habits of the Chinese, with the exception of a study conducted in Turin (Berzano et al. 2010).

Table 1 Places of worship of the new religions in Italy in 2012

Denomination	Places of worship	Immigrant population by religious affiliation (Caritas/Migrantes estimates)
Islam	655	1,645,000
Orthodox Churches	355	1,405,000
African Pentecostal Churches	858	150,000
Sikh	36	120,000
Buddhist	126	80,000
Hindu	2	1,500
Total	**2,032**	**3,265,000**

Source: Pace (2013)

Lento pede. **The Tortoise Is Moving**

Taking a quick look at the map of religions in Italy, we see the following situation for the places of worship (Table 1).

As we can see, the Chinese and Latin American Evangelical Churches are not on the list: the former are difficult to survey; the latter are beginning to spread, but they are of little importance by comparison with the other denominations included in the above table.

There are Islamic places of worship dotted all over the country, with a greater density where the concentration of small and medium enterprises (in the numerous industrial districts of northern and central Italy) has attracted numerous immigrants from countries with a Muslim majority. This means not only the Maghreb countries (Morocco taking first place, with half a million men and women who have now been residing permanently in Italy for 20–25 years), but also Egypt, Pakistan and Bangladesh. The relatively large Iranian and Syrian communities date from further back, having become established at the time of their two countries' political troubles, with the advent of Khomeini's regime in Iran, and Hafez el-Assad's repression of the political opposition in Syria in the 1980s.

The following map gives us an idea of the uneven distribution of the places of worship, which are mainly prayer halls (*musallayat*), sometimes precariously occupying uncomfortable premises. In fact, the number of mosques, in the proper sense, can be counted on the fingers of one hand: there are only three, the most important being the one opened in Rome in 1995 (which can contain 12,000 faithful) (Map 1).

We can see from the above map that the prayer halls are concentrated mainly along the west-east axis, peaking in Lombardy, followed by the Veneto and Emilia-Romagna regions. This distribution also reflects the different components of the Muslim world, recognizable in some of the most important national associations, simply because almost all the places of worship included in the census refer, from the organizational standpoint, to one of these associations. There is the Union of Islamic Communities of Italy (UCOII), which is historically close to the Muslim brotherhood (though it is currently undergoing internal change): this is one of the

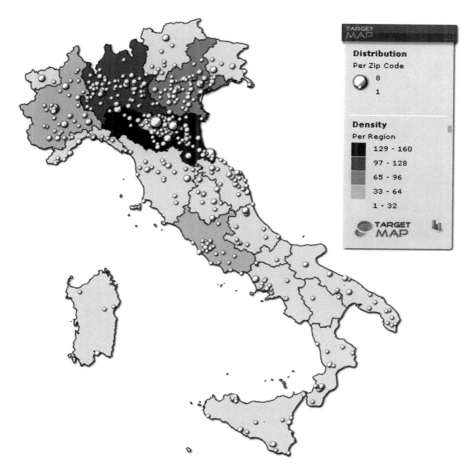

Map 1 The Muslim prayer halls in Italy (data as at 2012, by Province and Region) (Source: Rhazzali 2013)

best-organized associations, which manages 31 % (205) of the prayer halls identi-fied in the census, while another 32 % (209) are part of the new Italian Islamic Confederation, (CII), which mainly enrolls Moroccan immigrants (and their fam-ilies). The other 240 *musallayat* belong to other, smaller associations, at least one of which—called the Islamic Religious Community (COREIS)—was founded by an Italian converted to Islam (through the esoteric tradition that goes back to the figure and thinking of René Guénon); so it is easy to imagine that this is, strictly speaking, an Italian Islam. Although this is numerically a small group, it has a public visibility unlike any of the other, above-mentioned associations.

The presence of the Orthodox Christians appears to be much more stable and well-defined than the still precarious position of the various Muslim communities (also in terms of the often poor, derelict urban locations made available to them as

Table 2 New Orthodox parishes in Italy by reference institution (data as at 2012)

Jurisdiction	Parishes and monasteries
Romanian Orthodox Church (Patriarchate of Romania), Dioceses of Italy	166
Sacred Orthodox Archdiocese of Italy and Malta (Ecumenical Patriarchate of Constantinople)	84
Russian Orthodox Church (Patriarchate of Moscow), Administration of the Churches in Italy	44
Copter Orthodox Church	21
Greek Orthodox Church of the Calendar of the Fathers—Holy Synod in Resistance	9
Archbishopric for the Russian Orthodox Churches of Western Europe (Exarchate of the Ecumenical Patriarchate), Decanate of Italy	7
Ethiopian Orthodox Tewahedo Church	5
Serbian Orthodox Church (Patriarchate of Serbia)	4
Romanian Orthodox Church of the Old Calendar	3
Independent Orthodox Church of Western Europe and the Americas— Metropolia of Milan and Aquileia	3
Bulgarian Orthodox Church (Patriarchate of Bulgaria)	2
Eritrean Orthodox Church	2
Macedonian Orthodox Church	2
Armenian Apostolic Church	1
Russian Orthodox Church of the Ancient Rites (Metropolia of Belokrinitsa)	1
Orthodox Church in Italy	1
Total	**355**

Source: Giordan (2013)

places of worship), since the latter are still waiting to see their legal position confirmed on the strength of an understanding between these Muslim communities and the Italian State, in accordance with the Italian constitution. This difference is not only because one of the Orthodox Churches was recently recognized (in December 2012) by the Italian State, but also because their inclusion in the Italian social and religious fabric has been facilitated, for the Romanian, Moldavian and Ukrainian Orthodox Churches, at least, by the bishops of the Catholic Church. In many a diocese, where there was a visible and pressing demand for places of worship or parishes, the Catholic bishops have authorized Orthodox priests to use small churches left without a priest, or chapels that had remained unused for some time (located on the outskirts of towns). The global picture, accurately reconstructed in a study by Giuseppe Giordan (2013), emerges as follows (Table 2).

The vast majority of the parishes were established after the year 2000, and almost 80 % of them occupy churches that were made available by Catholic bishops; 81 % of the pastors are married and 69 % of them are between 29 and 45 years old. By comparison with the Muslim communities, the Orthodox parishes are more evenly distributed all over Italy, as we can see from the following Map 2.

If we now look at the 36 Sikh temples (*Gurudwara*), their uneven territorial distribution stems from the segments of the job market that immigrants from the Punjab have gradually come to occupy. A sizeable proportion of these workers has

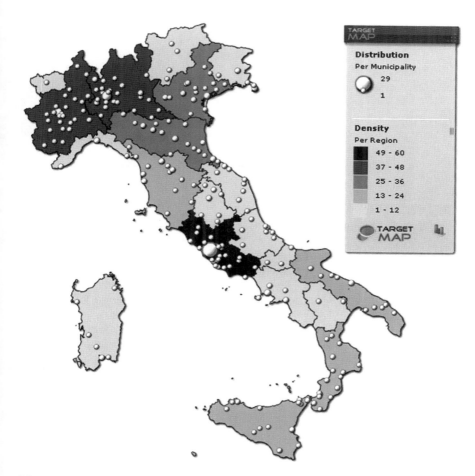

Map 2 Orthodox parishes in Italy (as at 2012 per Municipality and Region) (Source: Giordan 2013)

filled the space abandoned by the Italians throughout the central portions of the North West and North East of Italy, including parts of Emilia, as breeders of cows serving the large dairy industries and pigs for pork meat products: the historical figure of the Italian *bergamini* (as they were called throughout the Po valley) has been replaced by men with a turban, the Sikh. By contract, these migrants have not only benefited from a good salary, they have also been given a home (usually adjacent to the stables so that they could take care of the animals round the clock), and this has made it easier from them to bring their families to Italy—something that is much harder for other communities of migrants to do because they are usually unable to demonstrate that they have a stable home. As a consequence, a generation of Italian Sikhs was soon to develop (either because they arrived at a very young age, or because they were born in Italy).

The Sikh communities now amount to about 80,000, out of the 120,000 immigrants from India. Most of them arrived in Italy around 1984, driven by a combination of factors and severe social problems in the Punjab region because: Great Britain (the country to which these migrants had historically flocked) refused them entry; there was a crisis in the farming sector; and there was political conflict between the independentist Punjabi movement and the government in New Delhi (Denti et al. 2005; Bertolani 2005; Bertolani et al. 2011).

Our map of the *gurudwara* was developed by Barbara Bertolani (2013). First of all, it shows a gradual institutionalization of the Sikh communities, which have proved capable not only of finding the financial resources needed to renovate old industrial sheds and convert them into places of worship, but also of negotiating with the native communities without encountering any particular administrative difficulties or political obstacles (unlike the Muslim communities when they try to set up a prayer hall or mosque). The map also shows the early signs of a differentiation amongst the Sikh: there are two different associations (the Association of the Sikh Religion in Italy and the Italy Sikh Council), to which the various temples refer. There is also a religious minority that mainstream Sikhism considers heterodox, the Ravidasi, followers of a spiritual master named Ravidas Darbar, who appears to have lived between the fourteenth and fifteenth centuries in Punjab; for his wisdom and authority, he was recognized as a new guru and added to the ten that all of the Sikh world venerates. Although some hymns attributed to Ravidas have been included in the Sikh's sacred text (the *Granth Sahib*), most Sikhs deny him the same status as the gurus officially acknowledged by tradition. Ravidas would appear to have come from a *dalit* caste (the tanners, an occupation considered by the Hindu Brahmins to be the very quintessence of impurity) and, although in principle the *way of the Sikh* (which literally translates the expression *sikh-panth*) preaches the abolition of the caste system, there still appears to be a strong resistance to the *dalit* even amongst today's Sikhs (Map 3).

So far, I have chosen just a few of the maps now available to document the slow movement of Italian society towards an unprecedented, unexpected socio-religious configuration that is still, in some aspects, unknown to many Italian people. Just to give an example, in the areas where the Sikhs have settled, for a long time they were mistaken for Arabs with a turban, or Orthodox Christians; few people grasped the differences that exist between them in terms of their different national Churches.

To complete the picture, it is worth taking a look at a few other maps, which reflect changes underway in Italian society that are not due to exogenous phenomena (like the immigration of men and women from other countries). Here again, I have chosen two maps illustrating the growth in the last 10 years of the Jehovah's Witnesses and the various Pentecostal congregations (the most important of which are the Assemblies of God and the Federation of the Pentecostal Churches), both of which have been recruiting new members from among Italian people who were originally Catholics, but have opted to adhere to another form of Christianity.

The Jehovah's Witnesses first came on the scene in 1891; since then, they have grown constantly in number. Today, they are widespread all over Italy (see Map 4), with more than 3,000 congregations, 1,500 kingdom halls, 250,000 evangelizers,

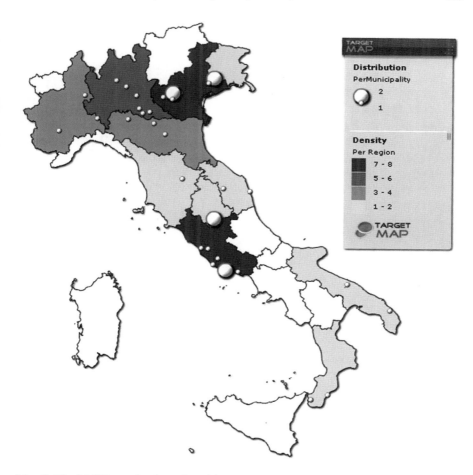

Map 3 The 36 Sikh temples (*gurudwara*) in Italy (as at 2012) (Source: Bertolani 2013)

and a similar number of supporters. They also have a far from negligible number of new conversions drawn from among the Albanian, Romanian, and Chinese immigrants, as well as from the French- and Portuguese-speaking Africans (Naso 2013).

The diffusion of the Pentecostal Churches is even more significant. Most of them come under the heading Assemblies of God, with 1,181 communities dotted all over Italy, with a greater density in certain southern regions (Sicily, Campania, and Calabria, as shown on Map 5), areas that are generally believed to have strong Catholic traditions. The other group, the Federation of Pentecostal Churches, currently has 400 congregations and approximately 50,000 members.

If we combine the Pentecostal communities and Churches with a Protestant matrix with the African, Latin American and Chinese neo-Pentecostal Churches, and then add the movement that has formed within the Catholic Church called Renewal in the Spirit (which now includes approximately 250,000 people in Italy,

Map 4 Pentecostal Churches from Ghana (at 2012 per Province and Region) (Source: Butticci 2013)

with 1,842 communities established in almost every region (Table 3)), we can see that the Church-religion model that Catholicism has developed over the centuries, with its parish-based civilization, is being challenged by an alternative model where the experience (through community rites) of a charism counts for more than a set of dogmas (Map 6).

Above all, the organizational format of these alternative religions no longer preserves the traditional separation between clergy and layman. If the spirit blows where it will, as Pentecostalism (in all its various expressions) becomes more established in Italy's traditionally Catholic society, it could become an element of further differentiation in Italians' choices in the religious sphere.

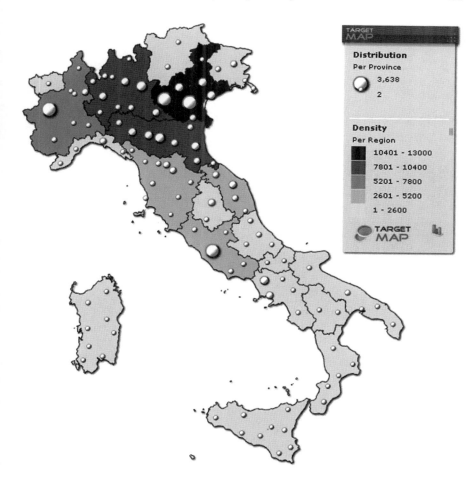

Map 5 The Pentecostal Churches from Nigeria (at 2012, per Province and Region) (Source: Butticci 2013)

If the new type of Pentecostal Christianity challenges Catholicism, Eastern religions represent another alternative that extends the spiritual religious supply in a country of wide and long Catholic tradition.

The Italian society had already met in the 1970s and 1980s of the last century the new face of westernized Buddhism, through the various spiritual movements from India and Japan respectively. The most famous were, among others, in the first case, the Hare Krishna movement and Osho Rajneesh, while in the second, Soka Gakkai. There is, therefore, a long-standing Italian Buddhism. Today it is recognized mainly in an association approved by the State, the Italian Buddhist Union (about 80,000 members). With the arrival of immigrants from Sri Lanka, India, and China a new layer of followers of various schools of Buddhism has formed. It is in fact an innovation that makes even more plural the presence of Buddhism in Italy

Table 3 Communities of the renewal in the spirit (1978–2005) in Italy by region

Region	1978	2005
Abruzzo	9	51
Basilicata	1	27
Calabria	10	97
Campania	13	193
Emilia-Romagna	12	77
Friuli Venezia Giulia	0	23
Lazio	26	100
Liguria	17	46
Lombardia	30	174
Marche	9	83
Molise	6	17
Piemonte	41	176
Puglia	8	114
Sardegna	9	82
Sicilia	22	292
Toscana	9	75
Trentino	0	15
Umbria	4	26
Veneto	42	90
Total	**1,037**	**1,842**

Source: Contiero and Pace (2014)

(Squarcini and Sernesi 2006; Molle 2009, 2013; Macioti 1996, 2001). The distribution of the various meditation centers, as the map shows, clearly documents this (Map 7).

Achilles Travelling at Two Speeds

Italy's socio-religious geography is changing—slowly, but constantly and irreversibly. The above maps and figures also faithfully record a demographic transition, affecting Italian society as a whole, that has been going on for at least 50 years.

The Italian population is continuing to age (nowadays, 20 % of the population is over 65 years old). Meanwhile, the size of Italy's population is not diminishing thanks to a higher birth rate per female (from 1.19 in 2002 to 1.25 in 2012), due to the greater propensity of immigrant families to have children, and more of them, by comparison with Italian couples. Set against this background, it is hardly surprising that the Catholic clergy is constantly ageing too: while there were 42,000 priests in Italy in 1972, this figure is expected to drop to 25,000 by 2023; 48 % of Italian clergymen are now over 65 years old, and the mean age of the clergy as a whole is 62. There is a paucity of vocations, and policies to recruit young Asian and African priests seem unable to fill the gap that is already apparent in the ranks of the Italian clergy (Castegnaro 2012). By comparison, the new pastors of the 355 Orthodox parishes are much younger: 60 % of them are between 30 and 45 years old, and 6 %

Map 6 The Church of Pentecost (at 2012, per Province and Region) (Source: Butticci 2013)

are under 30; the mean age of the Muslim communities' 600 imam is under 35; and the 300 pastors of the African Pentecostal Churches are usually between 28 and 35 years old.

For the Italian Catholic Church, the changes taking place on the religious scene are an absolute historical novelty. Being used to seeing themselves, quite under-standably, as a well-organized salvation organization, with a capillary distribution throughout the country (with 28,000 parishes and a considerable number of mon-asteries, sanctuaries, centers for spiritual retreats, and so on). Though it is still an authoritative actor on the public stage, the Catholic Church—understood here in all its various aspects, from the highest ranks right down to the normal clergyman, from the lay associations to the individual believers and practicing Catholics—Is having to cope with the changes underway. For a good deal of the short history of Italy as a nation, right up to the Second Vatican Council, the Catholic Church had

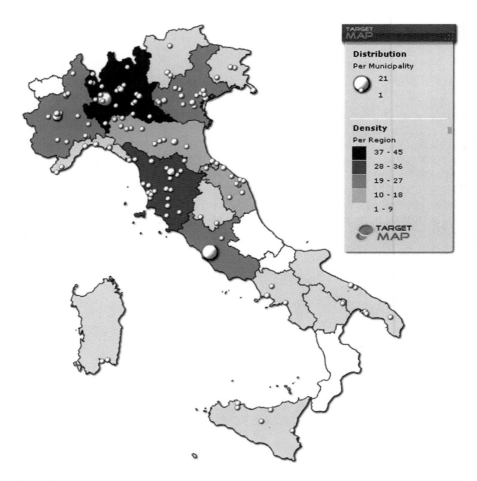

Map 7 Buddhist and Neo-Buddhist Meditation Centers in Italy (at 2012, per municipality and region) (Source: Molle 2013)

maintained a sort of civil disinterest in the country's religious diversity. Then it changed tack, during the years of ecumenical and inter-religious dialogue, becoming more open to exchanges with the Hebrew communities and the Churches of a Protestant matrix. It succeeded in considering the other religious presences established in Italy as potential parties to a dialogue between different faiths, promoted by the Catholic Church with a view to appearing tolerant and open-minded, while emphasizing that it was still the *dominant figure* on the *public stage* in the Italian religious sphere, the *primus inter pares* in regulating public communication on matters of religion. In parallel with official steps taken by popes and bishops, from the Second Vatican Council onwards, the dialogue continued and a number of small spontaneous schemes flourished (associations of Hebrews and Christians; permanent roundtables for Muslims, Christians and Hebrews; and so on). Sociologically speaking, this was an acknowledgement of the existence of other subjects with a religious vocation that were allowed to speak, often for the first time, in a religious arena that had been wholly occupied by a single subject, the Catholic Church (Pace 2011b). The arrival *en masse* of immigrants from various parts of the world completely changed the religious scenario. In addition to differences of faith among Italians, there are other diversities, of language, culture, nationality and customs. What was remote has come closer, and the exotic has become familiar. Instead of just exchanging views with one's neighbors, it is now a matter of acknowledging a profound change in the socio-religious composition of the Italian population.

The Catholic Church, in all its expressions, has not remained indifferent to society's movement; it too has moved, but it two different speeds. It has sought to interpret the phenomenon, calling upon all its material and symbolic internal resources, and taking action as an organized, expert system of religious belief accustomed to operating in a social setting where it had a monopoly of the symbols, and this system is seeking to transfer the unprecedented external complexity into an internal differentiation. The Catholic Church system is striving to incorporate the novel shape and topology of the religious landscape and make sense of it using its own categories, which are broad and narrow at one and the same time, based on open and closed codes. A religious system shows all its power and wisdom (in organizational terms) when it succeeds in functioning as a closed system, capable of defending its symbolic boundaries that identify it as such, in order to remain open towards the outside. If we consider the aspect that can be defined as *Catholic welfare,* managed directly by the Church and its most important supporting associations (from Caritas to the ACLI), the commitment is enormous, as we can see from the map of the centers that provide shelter and (religious) support, set up specifically to serve the material and spiritual needs of many immigrants (see Map 8).

This capillary effort to provide shelter and support has been balanced by a differentiation in the willingness to have a closer exchange with the other religious faiths that have begun to become organized in Italy. Indeed, the Catholic Church has first fine-adjusted its traditional charitable activities, mainly through its *religious* welfare associations, also engaging in openly criticizing the conditions of social injustice and the negative stigma to which immigrants as a whole have been subject, especially when there were center-right governments in office. Secondly, the Italian Catholic Church has tried to reiterate its central role on the public stage, acknowledging the existence of a religious pluralism, but also defending its historically established dominant position. There are two main indicators of this latter tendency, among others that are less pertinent to the present discussion: the first is the Catholic Church's determined defense of the teaching of Catholic religion in all public schools (from kindergarten through secondary school, for an hour a week); the second concerns the different ways in which it communicates with the new religious entities.

Concerning the teaching of Catholic religion at school, the Church's strategy so far has been: from the institutional standpoint, to have the State acknowledge that

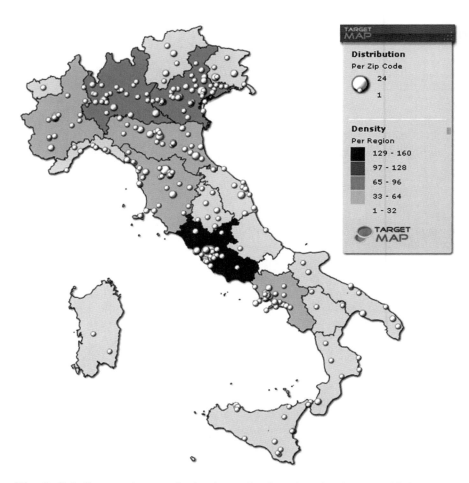

Map 8 Catholic pastoral centers for immigrants by zip code and region (as at 2012) (Source: Chilese and Russo 2013)

teachers of this subject (who are recruited and trained by the Church at institutes of religious sciences run by the bishoprics) have a public role and the same value as teachers of other subjects, and to promote the idea that this lesson on religious culture is not strictly confessional but also presents the other religious faiths.

As for the differentiated willingness to communicate with the other religions, the Catholic Church officially has a soft spot for the Orthodox Churches (which are often granted the use of unused churches and chapels, as mentioned earlier), while it is more cautious in dealing with other religious entities, and particularly with the multicolored world of Islam. While local parish priests and Catholic associations were often willing to exchange views and even provide spaces for prayer in rooms attached to the parishes up until 2001, the attack on the Twin Towers and the growing sentiments of fear and suspicion in its aftermath still make it difficult for practicing Catholics to accept a dialogue with and give credit to Muslims.

Conclusion

From the religious standpoint, the Italian case is a good example of how, and to what extent, a symbolically monopolistic system can be transformed exogenously. The unprecedented, unexpected religious diversity that has begun to emerge in Italy makes it necessary to update the maps of religiosity and secularization that the country's sociologists of religion study to interpret the changes taking place over the years (Naso and Salvarani 2012). In the past, these changes often occurred within Catholicism itself (Cartocci 2011), often involving small percentage displacements in a picture of apparent substantial immobility in terms of the Italians' collective representation of themselves. They saw themselves as Catholic in more than 85 % of cases, though they revealed marked differences (and diversified levels of secularization) in both their attitude to their belief and their behavior (from their religious practices to their moral choices, which were sometimes highly individualized and by no means consistent with the official doctrine of the Catholic Church).

Now, for the first time after years of research, the maps (some of which are illustrated here) show that we need to use a different compass to interpret a rapidly and radically changing social and religious scenario. With time, Catholicism will also experience some degree of internal change. In the debate on pluralism within the Catholic Church, it will no longer be enough to say "bring in the cavalry" to conceal the fact that 5 % of Italy's immigrant population are Catholics, but they come from worlds that are moving away from the theology and the liturgy of the *Roman* Catholic Church. These African, Latin American, Philippine, Chinese, and Korean Catholics will add their own point of view to what being Catholic means, which will not necessarily be consistent with Italian mainstream traditions.

This will give rise to a new area of research that will require new intellectual energies to investigate the real religious experiences of so many people belonging to so many religions, going beyond the ethno-centrism (or Catholic-centrism that has inevitably characterized our research on our predominantly Catholic society). We also have to reflect critically on the concepts and theoretical reference systems needed to deal with the unprecedented religious diversity that has been increasingly characterizing life in Italy.

I can sensibly assume that the change of pace from the Catholic Church may have also reflected on the management policies of pluralism. In particular, with the new Pope Francis. One of his public appearances in July 10, 2013 was in Lampedusa, the island south of Sicily, a place of continual arrivals of immigrants and shipwrecks with thousands of deaths. The last tragedy occurred on July 2013 (see Picture 1 and Picture 2) with 194 deaths. The Pope spoke about the Samaritan "who saw and was moved with compassion"; he addressed the Italian government and politicians, urging them to change policy, rejecting "the globalization of indifference".

In a country where every debate on the granting of citizenship to children of immigrants born in Italy hangs straight to the opposition by center-right parties, it is not easy to predict whether the preaching of Francis will foster new cultural orientations in public opinion and the overcome and even bypass the ideological

Picture 1 The Francis pope at Lampedusa's Mass (Source: Vatican News)

Picture 2 The corpses lined up on the beach of Lampedusa (http://www.mirror.co.uk/news/ world-news/pope-francis-says-lampedusa-migrant)

barriers that have so far prevented a comprehensive policy and liberal religious pluralism in Italy.

References

Allievi, Stefano. 2010. *La guerra delle moschee*. Venezia: Marsilio.

Beckford, James T., and Jay N. Demerath (eds.). 2007. *The Sage handbook of sociology of religion*, 316–348. Los Angeles: Sage.

Bertolani, Barbara. 2005. Gli indiani in Emilia: tra reti di relazioni e specializzazione del mercato del lavoro. In *I Sikh, storia e immigrazione*, ed. D. Denti, M. Ferrari, and F. Perocco, 163–176. Milano: Franco Angeli.

Bertolani, Barbara. 2013. I Sikh. In *Le religioni nell'Italia che cambia*, ed. Enzo Pace, 31–46. Roma: Carocci.

Bertolani, Barbara, Federica Ferraris, and Fabio Perocco. 2011. Mirror games: A Fresco of Sikh settlements among Italian local societies. In *Sikhs in Europe: Migration, identities and translocal practices*, ed. Kristina Myrvold and Knut A. Jacobsen, 133–161. Farnham: Ashgate.

Berzano, Luigi, et al. 2010. *Cinesi a Torino*. Bologna: Il Mulino.

Bombardieri, Maria. 2012. *Moschee d'Italia*. Bologna: EMI.

Butticci, Annalisa. 2013. Le Chiese neopentecostali e carismatiche africane. In *Le religioni nell'Italia che cambia*, ed. Enzo Pace, 85–96. Roma: Carocci.

Cartocci, Roberto. 2011. *Geografia dell'Italia cattolica*. Bologna: Il Mulino.

Castegnaro, Alessandro. 2012. *Nordest. Una società in rapida trasformazione*. Vicenza: Osservatorio Socio-Religioso Triveneto.

Chilese, Monica, and Giovanna Russo. 2013. Cattolici dal mondo in Italia. In *Le religioni nell'Italia che cambia*, ed. Enzo Pace, 215–234. Roma: Carocci.

Contiero, Emanuela, and Enzo Pace. 2014, forthcoming. Movimenti di risveglio religioso cattolico nelle realtà regionali. In *L'Italia e le sue regioni*, ed. Loredana Sciolla and Maria Salvati. Roma: Istituto dell'Enciclopedia Treccani.

Corten, André, Jean-Pierre Dozon, and Ari Pedro Oro (eds.). 2003. *Les nouveaux conquérants de la foi. L'Église du royaume de Dieu*. Paris: Khartala.

Denti, Domenica, Mauro Ferrari, and Fabio Perocco (eds.). 2005. *I sikh, immigrazione e storia*. Milano: Franco Angeli.

Doe, Norman. 2011. *Law and religion in Europe*. Oxford: Oxford University Press.

Finke, Roger. 2013. Origins and consequences of religious restrictions: A global overview. *Sociology of Religion* 74: 1–17.

Garcia-Ruiz, Jesus, and Patrick Michel. 2012. *Et Dieu sous-traita le Salut au marché*. Paris: Armand Colin.

Garelli, Franco. 2011. *Religione all'italiana*. Bologna: Il Mulino.

Garelli, Franco, Gustavo Guizzardi, and Enzo Pace (eds.). 2003. *Un singolare pluralismo*. Bologna: Il Mulino.

Giordan, Giuseppe. 2013. La costellazione delle chiese ortodosse. In *Le religioni nell'Italia che cambia*, ed. Enzo Pace, 97–130. Roma: Carocci.

Luhmann, Niklas. 1987. *Soziale Systeme*. Frankfurt a.M.: Suhrkamp Verlag. (*Social system*. Stanford: Stanford University Press, 1996.)

Luhmann, Niklas. 2012. *Introduction to systems theory*. Cambridge: Polity.

Macioti, Maria Immacolata. 1996. *Il Buddha che è in noi*. Roma: Seam.

Macioti, Maria Immacolata. 2001. *Il Sutra del Loto*. Milano: Guerini e Associati.

Marx, Karl, and Arnold Ruge. 1844. Zur Judenfrage. In *Deutsch-Französische Jahrbrücher*. In *Marx selected essays*, ed. James H. Stenning, 40–97. London/New York: Leonard Parsons.

Marzano, Marco. 2012. *Quel che resta dei cattolici*. Milano: Feltrinelli.

Molle, Andrea. 2009. *I nuovi movimenti religiosi*. Roma: Carocci.

Molle, Andrea. 2013. L'Oriente Italiano. In *Le religioni nell'Italia che cambia*, ed. Enzo Pace, 71–84. Roma: Carocci.

Naso, Paolo. 2013. Il Protestantesimo storico e i suoi nuovi volti. In *Le religioni nell'Italia che cambia*, ed. Enzo Pace, 97–130. Roma: Carocci.

Naso, Paolo, and Brunetto Salvarani. 2012. *Un cantiere senza progetto. Rapporto sul pluralismo religioso in Italia*. Bologna: EMI.

Pace, Enzo. 2011a. Il riconoscimento dell'alterità religiosa. In *Cristiani d'Italia*, ed. Alberto Melloni, 611–616. Roma: Istituto dell'Enciclopedia Treccani.

Pace, Enzo. 2011b. *Religion as communication*. Farnham: Ashgate.

Pace, Enzo (ed.). 2013. *Le religioni nell'Italia che cambia: mappe e bussole*. Roma: Carocci.

Pace, Enzo, and Annalisa Butticci. 2010. *Le religioni pentecostali*. Roma: Carocci.

Perez-Agote, Alfonso (ed.). 2012. *Portraits du catholicisme en Europe*. Rennes: Presses Universitaires de Rennes.

Poulat, Emile. 1974. L'Église romaine, le savoir et le pouvoir. *Archives de Sciences Sociales des Religions* 37: 5–21.

Rhazzali, Khalid. 2013. I musulmani e i loro luoghi di culto. In *Le religioni nell'Italia che cambia*, ed. Enzo Pace, 47–65. Roma: Carocci.

Richardson, James T., and François Bellanger (eds.). 2014. *New religious movements and minority faiths*. Farnham: Ashgate.

Squarcini, Federico, and Marta Sernesi (eds.). 2006. *Il buddhismo contemporaneo. Rappresentazioni, istituzioni, modernità*. Firenze: Società Editrice Fiorentina.

Vilaça, Helena, and Enzo Pace (eds.). 2010. *Religião em movimento: Migrações e comunidades religiosas na Itália e em Portugal*. Porto: Estratégias Criativas.

Vilaça, Helena, Inger Furseth, Enzo Pace, and Per Pettersson. 2014. *The changing soul of Europe*. Farnham: Ashgate.

Wuthnow, Robert. 2005. *America and the challenges of religious diversity*. Princeton: Princeton University Press.

Re-Thinking Religious Diversity: Diversities and Governance of Diversities in "Post-Societies"

Siniša Zrinščak

Introduction

It has become highly problematic to describe modern European societies in terms of religious diversity and religious pluralism. Europe has been religiously diverse for centuries but what we witness today is the acceleration of diversity – in terms of different types of both religious and non-religious and (or) spiritual belonging. However, the meanings and social consequences of this process are far from obvious. The social acceptance of diversity is quite ambiguous and public (state) management of diversity differs highly among countries and has become a topic of heated public debates. There are contradictory processes at play here. On the one hand, diversity is a visible public fact and modern societies describe and understand themselves in pluralistic terms. In the European Union this has been accompanied by anti-discrimination policies, which include the anti-discrimination provision on grounds of religion or belief (as well as racial and ethnic origin, which is relevant when religion is closely intertwined with ethnicity). Acceptance of diversity is also visible in the "disestablishment" process in the Church-state relations, as certain European countries have dissolved their strong ties with the state or national Churches, as well as in the emergence of what is known as the European model of Church and state, partly seen in the protection of religious freedom and rights and neutrality of the state in exclusively religious matters (Robers 2005; Torfs 2007). On the other hand, religious discrimination has been on the rise around the globe and though Western democracies (including Western European states) are still far more tolerant and pluralist in comparison to other world regions, there are also patterns of rising religious discrimination, rising religious regulation, and rising religious legislation (Fox 2007, 2010) in these countries as well. While controversies about Islam are part of this process, this should not be reduced to the question

S. Zrinščak (✉)
Faculty of Law, University of Zagreb, Trg m. Tita 3, 10000 Zagreb, Croatia
e-mail: sinisa.zrinscak@pravo.hr

G. Giordan and E. Pace (eds.), *Religious Pluralism*,
DOI 10.1007/978-3-319-06623-3_8, © Springer International Publishing Switzerland 2014

of the Muslim presence in Europe and how different Islamic traditions are (or are not) in concordance with the European, mostly secular, public spaces, as many European countries continue to discriminate against (or try to highly regulate) non-traditional minority religions, including those which are known as new religious movements (Richardson and Lykes 2012). Fox argued also that "the most common increases in religious discrimination between 1990 and 2008 were new anti-sect laws or policies" in Western democracies (Fox 2012: 174).

Post-communist societies are usually seen as a particular case in regard to the issues of diversity and pluralism. Although there is a general appreciation of high diversity among them in terms of basic religious landscape, post-communist Europe is largely described as a region in which revitalization of religion has been manifested in the post-1989 period, and a region in which controversies about Church and state are particularly high. This is mainly a result of the attempts of traditional Churches to regain the public (and political) influence they had in the pre-communist times, attempts which contradict the position and rights of other (minority and new) religions and which clash with opposing views on the issues of secularity in modern Europe. Yet another, more complicated case concerns the countries with a recent history of violent conflicts (such as wars in post-Yugoslav countries) where religions, as important markers of separate ethnic identities, played a significant social role.

However, the argument here is that a comparative view on the issues of public acceptance of religious diversity and the Church-state relations in Western and Eastern European countries shows that the line of difference does not run between Western countries with a longer democratic history and Eastern countries with a burden of the communist past, but between the countries (both Western and Eastern) which impose a high degree of regulation on minority or new religions and those which seem to be more tolerant of public religious issues. Also, a closer look inside one particular country shows that the issue of regulation of religion is a highly complex reality. This chapter, therefore, draws on a previous work which argues that (1) in regard to the Church-state relations post-communist Europe does not presents a unique case and Europe as a such faces a more general problem of balancing historically shaped Church-state relations that favoured traditional churches with the rising religious and socio-cultural pluralism; (2) that there is no clear connection between the general socio-religious profile of one country and its Church-state relations, i.e. that the countries which are similar in terms of high or low religiosity or high or low religious monopoly are not, at the same time, similar in terms of their Church-state relations; (3) that, in order to understand a basic socio-religious configuration, more attention should be paid to social expectations of people about the public (social) role of Churches; (4) that there is a need to complement studies of the Church-state relations with new understandings of (individual and group) identity construction in contemporary societies (Zrinščak 2011). Drawing on these arguments, this chapter seeks to investigate factors which shape the way religions have been regulated and the way in which this regulation can be understood in relation to diversity and pluralism. In particular, the first and main section of the chapter focuses on the Church-state relations in Croatia, which is usually described as a country with a dominance of collectivistic religions and/or a post-conflict country with a burden of the dominant religion's exclusionary effects on others, but which at the same time maintains public recognition and acceptance, though in different degrees, of a wide range of minority religions. Theoretically, the question is whether the notion of collectivistic religion helps in understanding its way of developing relations to other religions, and what is the role of other social factors in that respect. The next section expands to other post-communist countries and the way they deal with the diverse religious landscape, particularly by examining phases of regulations in different countries. Theoretically, the question is whether the notion of post-communist social space helps in understanding the ways in which different countries deal with their religions. The final, concluding section connects the analysis of Croatia and other post-communist countries with a general discussion on the public recognition of religions in Europe and briefly discusses results of the analysis in the light of future research agenda.

Without going into details, it should be noted that the chapter follows the authors who differentiate between (1) religious diversity as a fact or description of religiously diverse reality (meaning different religions or individuals who are free to build/combine their religious identity), (2) religious corporate pluralism or acceptance/recognition of different religions in the public sphere and (3) (full) religious freedom or religious pluralism as a (positive) value (Dobbelaere and Billiet 2003; Beckford 2003). Although these meanings can be further explored in their different usage, this chapter mainly deals with the recognition of different religions in the public sphere, which is mainly conditioned by the state regulation and by public expectations about their social roles. Thus, it demonstrates further that sociology needs more knowledge about the circumstances and factors influencing ways and forms of the public recognition of different religions in different societies.

Croatia: Religious Diversity in "Post-Yugoslav", "Post-communist" and "Post-conflict" Society

Church and State: Two Phases and Three Tiers

In terms of the Church-state relation, Croatian post-communist history can be divided into two phases. The 1990s are characterized by the transition from the communist to post-communist social order. However, in the case of Croatia this period was marked by the dissolution of the former Yugoslavia and building of an independent Croatian state, the process which was accompanied by its war of independence and by the war in the neighbouring Bosnia and Herzegovina. All of this had considerable effects on the overall social development. Religion was an important part of the overall social processes in the post-communist period. However, this importance comes not only because religion was an important marker of the identity of different nations in the former Yugoslavia (which simply blew up during its downfall), but also because the communist treatment of religions enhanced their political features. Although religion was very much present in everyday lives of the majority of people, religion did not have access to the public scene and though the way it could operate in society was strictly prescribed by the regime, Churches were actually the only social institutions which were not totally controlled by the state and which had a capacity for articulating anti-communist voices. Thus, the immediate post-communist period brought social benefits mainly to the Catholic Church, and was conditioned by restrictions on religion in communism and general support for religion in post-communism, but mainly by the nation- and state-building process which further strengthened the link between the Catholic Church and the Croatian nation. Hence, the Government introduced confessional education in public schools as a non-obligatory subject and in 1996 and 1998 signed four agreements with the Holy See on the position of the Catholic Church, which regulated their numerous rights: from acknowledgement of its full legal entity, co-operation with the state in numerous fields (education, culture, social services, military and police, etc.) to the partial co-funding from the state budget.[1] By regulating the relation with the Catholic Church in such a way and in line with the Constitutional principle of separation of the Church and the state, Croatia positioned itself among the European countries which follow the so-called concordat or co-operation model between the Church and the state (Ferrari 2003a, b; Robers 2005).

During this first phase, other religious communities were free to operate, but their position and rights were not regulated and the issue of their social position was not part of the public agenda. That changed in the early 2000s, when the party in power changed for the first time after 1990. The newly elected left-centre coalition opted for a more democratic development and re-established its relations with the EU with a clear goal to effectively start the process of joining the EU (Stubbs and Zrinščak 2009). Part of this agenda was equality of other religions, vivified in passing the Law on the Legal Position of Religious Communities in 2002, which regulated the procedure of registration by the Ministry of Administration. Moreover, the Law envisaged the possibility of concluding agreements between the Government and respected religious communities on issues of mutual interests which would grant them the rights enjoyed by the Catholic Church on the basis of agreements with the Holy See. Following this Law and further Government's regulation on the criteria for signing the agreements (passed in 2004), the Government concluded a total of seven agreements with 16 (mainly traditional) religious communities, from the Serbian Orthodox Church, the Islamic Community, several Protestant communities, to two Jewish communities which exist in Croatia. The political climate changed after the Law came into force in 2002, which provoked some backlashes in the willingness of the Government to further recognize the rights of smaller religious communities (the backlash came in 2004 when the right-wing party came back to power and indeed did not change when the left-wing party

---

[1] More on that in Zrinščak (2004, 2007).

came back to power in 2011!). Still, the Law had a very positive influence on the position of religious communities and, as religious communities themselves have been very positive about the overall legislative framework in Croatia up to today, the post-2000 period is here treated as one period or as the second phase in terms of the Church-state relations, despite the backlash.

Governmental actions in the first and the second period resulted in the system which is known in many European countries as a three-tier system. The first tier is occupied by the Catholic Church due to international agreements which guarantee its rights but also due to its position and overall social role and influence. In this respect, it is worth highlighting that according to the 2011 Census, 86.28 % of citizens belong to the Catholic Church. The second tier comprises religions that have agreements with the Government in place. The Agreements grant them (at least at the normative level) the same rights enjoyed by the Catholic Church. The third tier comprises all other religious communities which are registered as such and which, on the basis of this registration can operate freely, but as they do not have an agreement with the Government they cannot enjoy additional rights, such as having confessional education in public schools, official (*eo ipso*) recognition of religious marriage, funding from the state budget, etc. This third tier could be even further distinguished into two additional ones. The Law of 2002 introduced differences between the then existing religious communities which were able to perform a simple registration procedure and the new ones, those established after the law had come into force, whose registration was complicated by additional criteria: at least 5 years of existence as citizens association and having at least 500 members – the criteria (particularly the latter) which many of the "old" religious communities do not comply with. Although it is not easy to obtain official (detailed) data and to assess what all this actually brings in respect to the public recognition of smaller religious communities, the fact is that Croatia has a total of 44 registered religious communities – 17 with the agreements and 27 without the agreements with the Government. In relation to further analysis, it should be noted that among the registered religious communities in Croatia there are also those which provoke debates and introduction of restrictions in some other countries, such as Jehovah's Witnesses or the Church of Scientology.

A Puzzle About Public Recognition: Islam vs. Small Protestant Churches

In the same year when the Law on the Legal Position of Religious Communities was adopted by the Croatian Parliament (2002), the Government signed the first agreements with two traditional religious communities, the Serbian Orthodox Church and the Islamic Community. According to the 2001 Census (a year prior to signing of the agreements) these were minority communities (accounting for 4.42 % and 1.28 % respectively) with a history of conflicts or at least tensions, as they also represent different nations, Serbs and Bosniaks. However, due to the fact that these are traditional and old religious communities with a long-standing presence, and due to the wish of the Government to respect their rights thus exemplifying its strong democratic and pro-European stance, these were the first two communities which were able to exercise the rights set out in the 2002 Law.

Thus, the agreement with the Islamic Community regulated a range of rights, from the right to organize confessional education in public schools (based on the number of pupils who were interested in Islamic education), the right to establish their own schools, educational, cultural, and social institutions which were recognized and co-funded by the state, to the official recognition of religious marriage, chaplaincy in military and police forces, the right to be free or not to go to school during religious holidays, etc. As underlined on several occasions and reiterated over the years by the leaders of the Islamic Community in Croatia, this agreement and its observance in everyday life at the national and local levels, places Croatia among a few European countries to have officially recognized Islam (Austria, Belgium, Spain), which is a precondition for the full equality. Moreover, the Islamic Community leaders have been heard to say that Croatia has the best solution for "Islam issues" in Europe and can therefore be a role-model for other countries.[2]

Such a favourable image of respecting religious diversity has a different face when it comes to a few particular religious communities wishing to sign agreements with the Government. The Government firmly declined to do so. Although the Government signed agreements with a few Protestant and other Christian Churches (such as the Evangelical Lutheran Church, the Reformed Christian Church, the Evangelical (Pentecostal) Church, the Christian Adventist Church, the Union of Baptist Churches, etc.), it declined to do so with three small Churches – the Protestant Reformed Christian Church in the Republic of Croatia, the Full Gospel Church and the Word of Life Church. The argument was that they did not comply with the criteria for signing the agreements that the Government passed under the Governmental Conclusion in December 2004. It has to be noted that this Conclusion established additional criteria not envisaged by the Law itself and, moreover, the Government itself did not observe them in the case of some other religious communities with which it signed agreements in the following years. After the case had not been settled in Croatia and after the Constitutional Court had declared it had no jurisdiction over passing such a decision, in December 2010 the case was brought before the European Court of Human Rights, which ruled in favour of these communities. However, the ruling has not been implemented so far (late 2013) and, what is more, this issue has not been high on the public agenda in the meantime.[3]

---

[2] Interview by Aziz ef. Hasanović, leader of the Islamic Community in Croatia: http://balkans.aljazeera.net/vijesti/hasanovic-hrvatska-primjer-zemljama-evrope (Accessed 15 September 2013).

[3] More about that in Zrinščak et al. (2014).

What to make of this puzzle: recognition of full rights to some religious communities (or rather to many of them, including those with a history of conflicts and tensions) and denial of the same rights to some others? What places Croatia among a few European countries that fully recognize the Islamic community and why the same is not extended to others? Are the reasons of sociological interest and what are the social consequences?

Collectivistic Religions and Their Capacity for Otherness

In searching for the answer, I will rely on the concept of "collectivistic religions" introduced and extensively analyzed by Slavica Jakelić (2010). In brief, her main thesis is as follows: "the analytic perspective that focuses on choice correctly recognizes one large part of contemporary religiosity, but omits its other major component: the millions of people around the globe who were 'born into' some religious group rather than religiosity 'born again'. They experience their religion as ascribed to them rather than chosen by them as fixed rather than changeable, despite *and* because of the fact that their religious identities are profoundly shaped by the historical and cultural particularities of their social location" (Jakelić 2010: 1). She argues that collectivistic religious traditions are generally viewed with suspicion. The general (dominant) perception is that collectivistic religion is a kind of dying phenomenon which will be replaced by voluntary religious belonging and that Western Europe is both 'secularized' and 'secularizing'. The idea that collectivistic religions are always reduced (or reducible) to something else because they are identity-oriented is, according to her, historically but also theoretically problematic. This is based on an implicit theory of religion, which understands religion to be about beliefs and rituals (i.e. theology) and not about a kind of belonging that shapes communal boundaries (i.e. identity, culture, or politics) (pp. 9–10). On the contrary, the notion of collectivistic religion puts forward threefold claim: "first, that religions have long been and still are a source of collective identity in their own right; second, that religions, when constitutive of collective identities, are highly adaptable to historical changes: and, finally, that collectivistic religions offer viable resources for tolerance of religious Others, despite their role in establishing group differences" (p. 187). Furthermore, in a detailed analysis of the role of (collectivistic) Catholic Church in Croatia, Bosnia and Herzegovina, and Slovenia (extended as well to the study of the role of respective dominant Churches in Greece, Ireland, and Poland), it is shown that the theoretical perspective which reduces collectivistic religions to 'religious nationalism' and portrays them as essentially anti-modern and intolerant is fully wrong. Yes, they produce such results, but they also produce completely opposite ones. It is because the Church is not a monolith unity itself and also because different social circumstances and different social localities shape the way religion produces specific social consequences. Temporal dimension is easily overlooked in that respect, but (collectivistic) religions change over time. Moreover, the religious life is not reducible to the image of a dominant and powerful Church. Quite the contrary, strong institutional religiosity co-exists with individualized, personally shaped religiosity in a country such as Croatia (Nikodem and Zrinščak 2012).

Going back to the issue of the role of Islam in Croatia, several historical facts are of interest. The coming of Islam to the territory of Croatia and particularly neighbouring Bosnia and Herzegovina was connected with the Ottoman invasion. Throughout the centuries, Islam has been perceived as a completely different religion, as a religious other, religion (and culture) which had threatened the essence of Christian Europe. Still, Islam has remained a dominant religion in Bosnia and Herzegovina after the Ottoman Empire collapsed and as such became a part of the Austrian-Hungarian Empire and later the Kingdom of Yugoslavia (1918–1941) and communist Yugoslavia (1945–1991). The public recognition of Islam as a religion with full equal rights goes back to that period. The Croatian Parliament, which existed at that time, although with a limited purview, passed a law on the recognition of Islam as an official religion in 1916, following the same law passed in the Austrian Parliament in 1912 (Potz 2005). Future position of Islam was very much connected with the political turnovers that dominated the territory of Croatia and former Yugoslavia throughout the twentieth century. Besides the communist repression in the post-WWII period, particularly in relation to the public visibility of religions, the issue was the recognition of Bosniak people as a separate ethnic group in line with their separate religious identity (Islam). The separate identity was questioned due to several historical reasons but particularly due to the fact that Bosniaks speak the same or very similar language as Croats and Serbs which are other majority ethnic groups that live in Bosnia and Herzegovina and whose motherlands are neighbouring Croatia and Serbia. This was solved in the 1960s when the communist Government officially recognized Muslim people as a separate nation. The term Muslim was understood to have a secular meaning, but with an obvious implicit recognition that the Ottomans and Islam as the dominant religion created a group which differs from Croats and Serbs in its ethnic dimension. In the post-Yugoslav period Muslims renamed themselves Bosniaks based on their ethnic belonging, while underlining the strong connection between their ethnic (Bosniak) and religious (Islam) identity. Despite the fact that religion has been the main marker of difference between Croats (Catholics), Serbs (Orthodox) and Muslims or later Bosniaks (Islam) and thus an important part of shaping group boundaries, similarities in language, and partly culture, and the long history of co-existence, albeit marked with tensions and conflicts, gave rise to both inclusionary and exclusionary effects of religion towards the Other. Which effects would occur and prevail depended on the complex relations between history and contemporary social processes. This was visible during the war in Bosnia and Herzegovina in the early and mid 1990s. In one period of the war there was an armed conflict between Croats and Bosniaks in Bosnia and Herzegovina, the conflict that disrupted the alliance between Croats and Bosniaks who had jointly faced Serbs' intention to dissolve Bosnia and Herzegovina as one country. As the armed conflict involved ethnic groups with very different religions (Catholicism and Islam), it immediately acquired religious features as well, particularly visible in the use of religious symbols in order to mark and enforce separate identity (Pace 2004; Zrinščak 2002). Interestingly, a part of the Catholic Church supported the conflict, but the other part (the larger one) strongly opposed it both in Bosnia and Herzegovina and in Croatia. The then Archbishop of Zagreb and president of the Croatian Bishop Conference, Cardinal Kuharić, known as the religious leader who firmly supported the independence of Croatia during the break-up of Yugoslavia and underlined the link between the Croatian ethnic identity and religious Catholic belonging, also firmly opposed the conflict between Croats and Bosniaks.

To sum up, both inclusionary and exclusionary effects of Catholicism on other religions can be traced throughout history to the present day. As regards the position of Islam in Croatia, the inclusionary effects prevail due to a number of reasons. Similarities in language and (partly) culture are important factors in this regard, in line with the Europeanization process which was translated into the need to respect others. The issue of similarity is particularly interesting and needs further elaboration, the one that exceeds the scope of this paper. Still, the long history of co-existence and the fact that the Muslims who live in Bosnia and Herzegovina are autochthonous people and that those who live in Croatia today are those who had (mainly) come to Croatia in search of jobs during the Yugoslavian period, have evoked the widespread feeling that the possibility of not recognizing full rights of the Islamic Community is simply out of question. It is also quite interesting that this happened at a time when major configuration of the way Islam was living was going on. The post-communist circumstances, the war in Bosnia and Herzegovina which had some religious features and the support to and influence on Muslims by other countries with the Muslim majority provoked the growth of religiosity in Bosnia but also internal differences in Islam. There is no need to exaggerate, but volunteers and soldiers who came to Bosnia and Herzegovina during the war from other countries brought pluralisation of Islam in Bosnia. At the same time, leaders of the Islamic Communities in Bosnia and Herzegovina have been very eager to underline the European character of Islam in European countries, as visible in the launch of an official document entitled "A Declaration of European Muslims" (2006), issued by the Islamic Community in Bosnia and Herzegovina, but fully endorsed by the Islamic Community in Croatia and officially released in Zagreb, the Croatian capital, not in Sarajevo, the capital of Bosnia and Herzegovina. Mustafa Cerić, the then Grand Mufti of Bosnia and Herzegovina, said that this document could be viewed as an appeal to: (1) the European audience not to make a mistake in generalizing Muslims and not to spread Islamophobia, (2) to the Muslims who live in Europe to take seriously events in New York (September 2001), Madrid (March 2004) and London (July 2005) that may have great consequences for their stay in Europe and their status in Europe, and (3) to the Muslim world at large to help the Muslims in the West, and especially in Europe, to develop a kind of dialogue that would be acceptable to Muslims and to Europeans. This Declaration was prompted, among other things, by the fact that the Muslims with centuries-long presence in Europe differ in cultural, but also in religious terms, from the Muslims in other parts of the world.

As shown, the circumstances which favour public recognition of specific religious communities are complex and include both historical and contemporary factors. Therefore, the capacities of societies to produce tolerance towards and recognition of others are not reducible to a single factor. Social distance, as a usual measurement of attitudes towards others is, as this analysis suggests, just one of the elements in creating a full picture of the social status of a group. Thus, in the Croatian case, there is a mismatch between the results of the social distance towards Muslims and their public recognition. A comprehensive analysis of anti-Muslim prejudice in Europe based on the 1999–2001 European Value Survey data has reported that the social distance towards Muslims (measured as a percentage of those not willing to have Muslims as their neighbours) is in general higher in Eastern Europe than in Western Europe, while in Croatia it is higher than the Eastern European average (Strabac and Listhaug 2008). Also, interestingly, religiosity does not have strong positive effects on prejudice towards Muslims.

While not downplaying the effects of prejudice or denying the social effects that the existing intolerance towards different minorities in the Croatian society may have, this chapter would support the thesis that one set of factors in the relation between Muslim minorities and the majority population are "to a larger degree under national control", as well as that "national attempts to develop harmonious relations between the majority population and Muslim minorities might prove to be an especially challenging endeavour" (Strabac and Listhaug 2008: 283–284). This point underlines that the state capacity for full recognition of others should not be reduced to the religious capacity of developing full respect for different religions/ groups. Although this chapter deals with religions and the way the religious role in shaping group differences influences the position of religious others, it suggests that even when a religion assumes a collectivistic social role, religion is not reducible to such a role, and particularly that a society is much more than the entity produced by religion and ethnic links.

Assuming this is so, then why is full recognition not extended to small Protestant Churches as compared to the Islamic Community and other Protestant Churches (and other Christian and Jewish ones) which have been recognised and enjoy special rights?

The reasons are far from obvious. No single official explanation has been offered during all these years. Even more, the issue has not attracted much public interest, and this fact could indeed be part of the answer. The position of the Catholic Church is an issue which provokes heated public debates. The social position of Muslims, Orthodox Christians or Jews is an issue that attracts public interest. Opinions diverge on both issues, but the public interest and sensitivity is present. For specific reasons (such as those explained here in regard to the Islamic Community) these Churches and communities can provoke public concerns about their rights, though this is not to suggest that the public is unanimously in favour of their full rights. Still, the official standpoint has not questioned the need for their equal treatment and this standpoint has not provoked a single opposition (at least not a public one). Several Protestant and other Christian Churches, such as Lutherans, Baptists, Calvinists, Pentecostals, Adventists, Churches of Christ received the same treatment (recognition of full rights by signing agreements with the Government), but this was not the case with the Churches briefly outlined previously. In general, the public interest in any Protestant Church is hardly noticeable. They simply do not have the capacity to attract the interest of the public in their problems or in resolving problems with the implementation of the Agreements or in the life of those Churches which are registered and can freely operate but cannot enjoy the same rights as others. It should be also noted that these are small communities, not well known and that some of them are generally labelled as small religious communities, or even sects, giving rise to public suspicion. Also, as heard in the public discourse from time to time, particularly during the Parliamentary and public debate on passing the Law on the Legal Position of Religious Communities, the question remains of where to draw the line? There is no general support in favour of the same treatment of all religious communities irrespectively of their history, teachings and particularly their size. This suggests that the social meaning of "equality" and "recognition" is far more complex than usually perceived.

Religious Diversity and "Post-communist" Space

Although the term post-communist has been widely used, the analysis mentioned earlier concerning the Church-state relations in "post-communist" Europe suggests a very limited explorative power of such a term for two main reasons (Zrinščak 2011). The first one is related to a huge diversity of post-communist societies in a number of aspects: history, post-communist transition, social development and prospects, religious composition, level of religiosity and ways in which their Church-state relations have been developing. The second one is related to the numerous similarities in the Church-state relations between Western and Eastern Europe and the same dilemmas they face, though in slightly different degrees and ways.

Religious diversity is a fact of Central and Eastern European countries as the region comprises countries with very different confessional traditions (Catholic, Orthodox, Protestant, Muslim, etc.) with a long-standing existence in the region as a whole. On the other hand, there are countries which are very monolithic, as more than 90 % of their population belongs to one confession ("Catholic" Poland, "Orthodox" Romania), and countries with different confessions, or those with a large share of atheists (Hungary, Czech Republic and Estonia). The important thing is that diversity is a historical fact, and although it was influenced by atheist regimes, it has not changed as such during the twentieth century. However, the post-communist transition brought about profound social transformation, which includes pluralisation of thoughts, life styles, religions and different ideological stances about the social position and role of religions, both traditional and new ones. This means that the diversity experienced in the post-communist period has been significant, but still different from the one experienced by many Western

European countries, as these countries have still not faced immigration from non-European countries.

These aspects of post-communist social transformation have been reflected in two phases of the Church-state relations which, interestingly, partly differ from what has been described in regard to Croatia. On a more abstract level, it is interesting to note that in many countries the immediate post-communist period (the early and mid 1990s) brought about overall liberalization (as a general reaction to the communist times), which included very liberal conditions for the registration of religions, new ones as well. That triggered opposition from dominant Churches as well as from large sections of society and initiated passing of stricter regulation and stricter conditions for obtaining certain rights. Hungary passed a law in 1990 by which requirements for registration of Churches and other religious communities were quite formal, resulting in the most liberal or permissive regime of the Church-state relations in Europe (Schanda 2003, 2005; Uitz 2012).[4] In the meantime there were several attempts to make requirements stricter, particularly in relation to "dubious sects". However, these initiatives have faced opposition, demonstrating that social consensus on such issues is hardly possible. Still, the Law was amended in late 2011 allowing only a limited number out of over 200 religious associations under the 1990 Law to continue enjoying the Church status, while all others remain religious associations with limited privileges (Uitz 2012). The Czech Republic had a different trajectory, but the consequences are similar (Tretera 2005; Moravčikova 2012). According to the 1992 Law the registration was possible for the religious communities with 10,000 members or 500 members if they belonged to the World Council of Churches. The 2002 amendments made the requirements much easier (only 300 members), but the same Law limited the rights of newly registered communities and the rights such as the right to teach religion in public schools, to have pastoral care in prisons and army, etc. are now recognized as "special" and granted only to those communities that have been registered for more than 10 years and have more than 0.1 % of inhabitants as their followers (which is a bit more than 10,000!). Slovakia has a stricter system that was established in 1991 and has not been changed since. Under this system 20,000 adult citizens are necessary in order to meet the registration criteria (Moravčikova 2005, 2012). Poland does not have such a strict system (the basic requirement is that the organization has at least 100 Polish citizens as its members), but nevertheless there are two groups of Churches and religious communities. The first group, which has greater rights, comprises only 14 out of 150 registered Churches and religious communities (Rynkowski 2005). Changes towards much stricter requirements and, moreover, changes towards very limited religious rights occurred in Russia. However, as Russia is, along with some other post-Soviet Union countries, a special case in this regard, it is not covered here under the heading of "post-communist" Europe (Shterin and Richardson 1998, 2000).

---

[4] For an overview of Church-Sate relations in Central and Eastern Europe see also Ferrari and Durham Jr. (2003).

Although countries differ with regard to the phases of the Church-state relations in the post-communist period, changes that occurred in the meantime have, in one way or another, brought them, with some variations, to the cooperationist model, which privileges certain traditional Churches and allows other religious communities to act as such and to be present in the public, but without enjoying specific rights. Therefore, a clear two- or three-tier system has been established. All of this causes tensions and debates, which are indeed very similar to those in the majority of Western European countries. As already pointed out, the question is how to achieve a balance between the historically shaped Church-state relations and emerging diversity, or rather how the diversity and overall pluralisation might be transferred in an acceptable social space for very different religions. This is also reflected in the debates about new religious movements in the immediate post-communist period. Public debates were in turn reflected in the analyses of the scholars as well as in the concerns about the position of different religions and about observance of basic human and religious rights (e.g. Barker 1997; Črnič 2007, etc.). While it became obvious in the meantime that social hysteria over spectacular rise of new religious movements has been exaggerated and while countries were trying to find, more or less successfully, ways to accommodate to the changing social and religious landscape, it has also become obvious that the post-communist countries significantly differ in the way they treat new religions. Findings of the analysis of new religious movements in a number of Western and Eastern European countries points to "uniqueness" and "differences" over any clear pattern: "This brief overview reveals tremendous variance in the legal status of NRMs and other minority faiths in the 'new Europe'. Some nations such as Hungary and the Netherlands have seemed more solicitous of minority faiths, while others, such as France and more recently Russia, seem quite hostile to such entities. Also, the pattern of legal protections and opportunities afforded such groups varies by location and time, with great changes sometimes occurring in a short period, as has been the case with Russia" (Richardson and Lykes 2012: 321) (author's highlights).

Instead of Conclusion: Diversities and the Research Agenda in "Post-secular" Europe

Starting from an empirical fact that public acceptance of religious diversity has become highly problematic and has been provoking heated debates, even at the time when contemporary European societies face the acceleration of diversity in different social fields, this chapter has demonstrated that the concepts usually used to describe the countries of Central-Eastern or South-Eastern Europe, such as the "post-communist", "post-Yugoslav" or "post-conflict", are not of much help in analyzing how these countries regulate the position and rights of different religious communities and social consequences thereof. By focusing principally on Croatia, it has proved that a complex combination of social and cultural factors (both historical and contemporary) is at play in explaining why Croatia, in respect to the rights and privileges that the Islamic Community obtained, can be considered even a role-model for other European countries at the same time when pluralism in general has not been considered as a highly respected value in the Croatian society and when the same rights have not been extended to a few Protestant religious communities. The extension of the analysis to other "post-communist" countries, mainly those Central-European, has shown how they, after having initially embraced religious pluralism, established a two- or three-tier system in which the rights and position of religious communities differ according to their historic and social relevance. Thus, the dominant or national, or in the majority of cases the Catholic Church backed by international agreements with the Holy See, occupied the first tier, followed by other religious communities (usually those historically present) with special privileges and rights, while a range of very different religious communities comes at the end, as they are free to operate but are deprived of enjoying any special privileges. Very interestingly, particularly in view of the consequences for future research agenda in this field, post-communist countries have positioned themselves close to many other Western European countries in which different religious communities have different types of access to the public sphere and can enjoy different types of state support. Moreover, also interesting from the point of view of research agenda is the fact that focusing just on a two- or three-tier system does not help much in explaining the details of how different religious communities are treated in a society and whether some of them face major restrictions in their public appearance. Hence, the multi-tier system which operates in the majority of Western, Central, and Eastern European countries actually hides a huge range of differences in respect to the treatment of different religious communities.

In explaining the particularities of the Croatian situation the chapter relies on the notion of "collectivistic" religions as analyzed by Slavica Jakelić (2010). The use of it was triggered by two main ideas. The first one is that most of the sociological literature describes collectivistic religions as identity-oriented, religions whose main aim is to sustain group boundaries and, consequently, it views them with suspicion because of their alleged consequences (i.e. religious nationalism), but also because it is assumed that collectivistic religions are a dying phenomenon, a phenomenon not pertaining to the modern or post-modern social conditions. Secondly, collectivistic religions are not seen as being capable of producing tolerance towards other religions and other social groups. However, as shown by Jakelić, and as demonstrated in this chapter, collectivistic religions have the capacity for both exclusionary and inclusionary effects towards the Other. Collectivistic religions vary in space and time and the argument is that a detailed ethnographic insight is a precondition for any sociological conclusion about how collectivistic religions influence the regulation of diversity in a specific society.

All that might be of interest for the general research agenda about diversity and particularly on the Church-state relations in Europe. As indicated in the introductory part, religious discrimination has been on the rise around the globe and although Western European countries are still much more tolerant and pluralist as compared with other parts of the world, they are also experiencing rising religious regulation and very heated public debates with uneven consequences for the rights and positions of different religious communities. The issue is not only Islam, but many other particularly smaller religious communities or new religious movements, public recognition of which is opposed by large sections of societies. This should be connected with an observation that the Church-state relations in (Western) Europe are still heavily influenced by the history, particularly by the way religions had been connected with the process of formation of modern nations and states, and that the normative liberal principle of state neutrality clashes with empirical reality of state involvement in religious matters (Madeley 2003a, b). Still, the reality of the Church-state relations and debates about public religions in Europe, and about (non)secularity, suggest that the state involvement in the regulation of religions, and even higher religious discrimination, is just part of the wider story, i.e. part of the fact that collectivistic religions are realities of Europe, though in different ways and degrees. European identities, political and cultural, whether local, national or global, are strongly connected with religions and religions have continued to play a distinctive role in shaping identities in wider Europe. Whether or not we would agree with a rather normative Casanova's statement (2008) that the European anxiety to recognize Christianity as one of the constitutive components of European cultural and political identity is "responsible" for debates about Islam and other minority religions, the fact is that the role of religion in sustaining a separate identity (and the way these identities interact with other social processes) is a crucial step in understanding if and how diversity is recognized, i.e. the diverse recognition of diversities in different societies. Hence, the concept of collectivistic religions or, in general, the concepts of (religious) identity and (religious) memory (Hervieu-Léger 2000) should be employed more systematically in the contemporary sociology of religion.

Finally, although they were not part of the analysis in this chapter, arguments presented suggest also that research agenda should not be very impressed by the concept of "post-secular" Europe. As it has been shown, the focus on post-secular (which in general wrongly describes the continuing role of religion in different European societies) has diverted attention from the questions of involvement of states in shaping and regulating public response to religious diversity (Beckford 2012). Also, the notion of an open public space inside which secular and religious voices/actors meet and discuss have diverted attention from the fact that public space is heavily influenced by interests and discourses of most powerful social groups (Susen 2011). Therefore, the issue here is not the normative statements on liberal and/or secular preconditions for modern societies or how these principles have (have not) been translated into reality, but rather which groups have the power to shape debates. Which groups define what is equality (or neutrality) and in what ways and what do equality (or neutrality) mean in very practical terms of everyday life? The crucial issue here is a continuing link between religion(s) and identity (ies), and the way in which (in terms of spatial and temporal factors) it influences the Other.

References

Barker, Eileen. 1997. But who's going to win? National and minority religions in post-communist society. In *New religious phenomena in Central and Eastern Europe*, ed. Irena Borowik and Grzegorz Babiński, 26–52. Kraków: Nomos.

Beckford, James. 2003. *Social theory & religion*. Cambridge: Cambridge University Press.

Beckford, James. 2012. SSSR Presidential Address. Public religions and the postsecular: Critical reflections. *Journal for the Scientific Study of Religion* 51(1): 1–19.

Casanova, José. 2008. The problem of religion and the anxieties of European secular democracy. In *Religion and democracy in contemporary Europe*, ed. Gabriel Motzkin and Yochi Fischer, 63–74. London: Alliance Publishing Trust.

Črnič, Aleš. 2007. New religions in "new Europe". *A Journal of Church and State* 49(3): 517–551.

Declaration of European Muslims. 2006. http://www.rijaset.ba/index.php?option=com_content& view=article&id=45&Itemid=732. Accessed 15 Sept 2013.

Dobbelaere, Karel, and Jaak Billiet. 2003. Religious toleration in Western and Central European countries. In *Challenging religion: Essays in honour of Eileen Barker*, ed. James A. Beckford and James T. Richardson, 129–143. London/New York: Routledge.

Ferrari, Silvio. 2003a. The legal dimension. In *Muslims in the enlarged Europe: Religion and society*, ed. Brigitte Maréchel, Stefano Allievi, Felice Dasseto, and Jorgen Nilsen, 219–254. Leiden: Brill.

Ferrari, Silvio. 2003b. The European pattern of church and state relations. *Comparative Law* 20: 1–14.

Ferrari, Silvio, and W. Cole Durham Jr. (eds.). 2003. *Law and religion in post-communist Europe*. Leuven/Paris/Dudley: Peeters.

Fox, Jonathan. 2007. Religious discrimination: A world survey. *Journal of International Affairs* 61 (1): 47–67.

Fox, Jonathan. 2010. The future of civilization and state religion policy. *Futures* 42(6): 522–531.

Fox, Jonathan. 2012. The last bastion of secularism? Government religion policy in Western democracies, 1990 to 2008. *Journal of Contemporary European Studies* 20(2): 161–180.

Hervieu-Léger, Danièle. 2000. *Religion as a chain of memory*. Cambridge: Polity Press.

Jakelić, Slavica. 2010. *Collectivistic religions: Religion, choice, and identity in late modernity*. Farnham/Surrey/Burlington: Ashgate Publishing.

Madeley, John T.S. 2003a. European liberal democracies and the principle of state religious neutrality. In *Church and state in contemporary Europe: The chimera of neutrality*, ed. John T.S. Madeley and Zsolt Eneyedi, 1–21. London/Portland: Frank Cass.

Madeley, John, T.S. 2003b. A framework for the comparative analysis of church-state relations in Europe. In *Church and state in contemporary Europe: The chimera of neutrality*, ed. John T.S. Madeley and Zsolt Eneyedi, 22–48. London/Portland: Frank Cass.

Moravčikova, Mihaela. 2005. State and church in the Slovak Republic. In *State and church in the European Union*, ed. Gerhard Robbers, 491–518. Baden-Baden: Nomos Verlagsgesellschaft.

Moravčikova, Mihaela. 2012. Law, religion and belief in Slovakia, Czech Republic and Poland. In *Religion, rights and secular society: European perspectives*, ed. Peter Cumper and Tom Lewis, 215–232. Cheltenham/Northampton: Edward Elgar.

Nikodem, Krunoslav, and Siniša Zrinščak. 2012. Croatia's religious story: The coexistence of institutionalized and individual religiosity. In *The social significance of religion in the enlarged Europe*, ed. Detlef Pollack, Olaf Müller, and Gert Pickel, 207–227. Farnham/Surrey/Burlington: Ashgate Publishing.

Pace, Enzo. 2004. *Perché le religioni scendono in guerra?* Roma-Bari: Gius. Laterza & Figli.

Potz, Renata. 2005. State and church in Austria. In *State and church in the European Union*, ed. Gerhard Robbers, 391–418. Baden-Baden: Nomos Verlagsgesellschaft.

Richardson, James T., and Valerie A. Lykes. 2012. Legal considerations concerning new religious movements in the "new Europe". In *Religion, rights and secular society: European perspectives*, ed. Peter Cumper and Tom Lewis, 293–322. Cheltenham/Northampton: Edward Elgar.

Robers, Gerhard (ed.). 2005. *State and church in the European Union*. Baden-Baden: Nomos Verlagsgesellschaft.

Rynkowski, Michał. 2005. State and church in Poland. In *State and church in the European Union*, ed. Gerhard Robbers, 419–438. Baden-Baden: Nomos Verlagsgesellschaft.

Schanda, Balász. 2003. Religion and state in the candidate countries to the European Union – Issues concerning religion and state in Hungary. *Sociology of Religion* 64(3): 333–348.

Schanda, Balász. 2005. State and church in Hungary. In *State and church in the European Union*, ed. Gerhard Robbers, 323–345. Baden-Baden: Nomos Verlagsgesellschaft.

Shterin, Marat, and James, T. Richardson. 1998. Local laws on religion in Russia: Precursors of Russia's national law. *A Journal of Church and State* 40: 319–341.

Shterin, Marat, and James, T. Richardson. 2000. Effects of the western anti-cult movement on developments of laws concerning religion in post-communist Russia. *Journal of Church and State* 42: 247–272.

Strabac, Zan, and Ola Listhaug. 2008. Anti-Muslim prejudice in Europe: A multilevel analysis of survey data from 30 countries. *Social Science Research* 37: 268–286.

Stubbs, Paul, and Siniša Zrinščak. 2009. Croatian social policy: The legacies of war, state-building and late Europeanization. *Social Policy and Administration* 43(2): 121–135.

Susen, Simon. 2011. Critical notes on Habermas's theory on the public sphere. *Sociological Analysis* 5(1): 37–62.

Torfs, Rik. 2007. Religion and state relationship in Europe. *Religious Studies Review* 1(4): 31–41.

Tretera, Jiří, Rajmund. 2005. State and church in the Czech Republic. In *State and church in the European Union*, ed. Gerhard Robbers, 35–54. Baden-Baden: Nomos Verlagsgesellschaft.

Uitz, Renata. 2012. The pendulum of church-state relations in Hungary. In *Religion, rights and secular society: European perspectives*, ed. Peter Cumper and Tom Lewis, 189–214. Cheltenham/Northampton: Edward Elgar.

Zrinščak, Siniša. 2002. Rôles, attentes et conflits: la religion et les Eglises dans les sociétés en transition. *Social Compass* 49(4): 509–521.

Zrinščak, Siniša. 2004. Religion and society in tension in Croatia: Social and legal status of religious communities. In *Regulating religion: Case studies from around the globe*, ed. James T. Richardson, 299–318. New York: Kluwer Academic/Plenum Publishers.

Zrinščak, Siniša. 2007. Religion and values. In *Democratic transition in Croatia*, ed. Sabrina P. Ramet and Davorka Matić, 137–159. College Station: Texas A&M University Press.

Zrinščak, Siniša. 2011. Church, state and society in post-communist Europe. In *Religion and the state: A comparative sociology*, ed. Jack Barbalet, Adam Possamai, and Brayn S. Turner, 157–182. London: Anthem Press.

Zrinščak, Siniša, Dinka Marinović Jerolimov, Ankica Marinović, and Branko Ančić. 2014. Church and state in Croatia: Legal framework, religious instruction, and social expectations. In *Religion and politics in Central and Southeastern Europe: Challenges since 1989*, ed. Sabrina P. Ramet, 131–154. Basingstoke/New York: Palgrave Macmillan.

Diversity Versus Pluralism? Notes from the American Experience

James V. Spickard

Europe seems newly awash in a discourse of "pluralism". Long seen as a White, Christian continent—ignore Germany's 'Turks', France's *banlieues*, Spain's Moorish heritage, the Jews, and the Roma—Europe seems to have shifted ethnically and religiously in recent decades. The continent that produced the Westphalian state system as a way to institutionalize religious homogeneity (*cuius regio eius religio*) now confronts newcomers who don't fit the old mold. Cross-border migration has made hash of the nineteenth-century nationalist idea that each 'people' has 'one language', 'one history', 'one phenotype', and 'one culture' and thus deserves one state (Anderson 1983). Religious and ethnic diversity is on the rise. How to reconceptualize Europe becomes a crisis of the first order.

The title of this volume gives us some avenues of understanding, most notably "diversity" and "pluralism". These boast many definitions, but we can do worse than begin with a distinction posed by Professor Diana Eck, the Director of Harvard University's "Pluralism Project". That project's website quotes her as follows: "Diversity is just plurality, plain and simple—splendid, colorful, perhaps threatening." "Pluralism", on the other hand, involves an "energetic engagement with diversity". It is more than just tolerance of others, but "the active seeking of understanding across lines of difference". It is, Eck writes, "the encounter of commitments, based on dialogue" (Pluralism Project n.d.: 1). Put more simply, diversity is a brute fact, while pluralism takes work. It is, indeed, an accomplishment: an accomplishment of communication.

Eck points out that diversity and pluralism have different policy implications. "Diversity can and has meant the creation of religious ghettoes with little traffic between or among them" (Pluralism Project n.d.: 2). It has often meant exclusion: deliberate barriers erected against those whose religions or ethnicities differ from the local norm. Europe's Jewish ghettos come immediately to mind, but the

J.V. Spickard (✉)
Department of Sociology and Anthropology, University of Redlands, 30545 Bridlegate Drive, Bulverde, TX, USA 78163
e-mail: Jim_Spickard@redlands.edu

G. Giordan and E. Pace (eds.), *Religious Pluralism*,
DOI 10.1007/978-3-319-06623-3_9, © Springer International Publishing Switzerland 2014

United States has a similar history. The Chinese Exclusion Act of 1882, augmented by the Immigration Act of 1924 served "to preserve the ideal of American homogeneity" (Office of the Historian n.d.) against an imagined onslaught of Chinese, Italians, Jews, Slavs, and so on. The objections were both ethnic and religious. Italians were shunned for their Catholicism, as the Irish had been 60 years earlier. Chinese were seen as a superstitious race, unable to rise to the level of native Protestant virtue (P. Spickard 2007; Nee and Nee 1973). Japanese (Buddhist, Shinto, and Christian) were famously herded into camps during World War II, something not done to America's largely Christian German population. East Asians may now be our "model minority" (Petersen 1966), but they were long shunned.

There are other ways to handle diversity, of course, among them erasing it through assimilation; I shall return to this below. Eck, however, favors the pluralist option. As she described at length in her 2009 Gifford Lectures (Eck 2009),[1] pluralism seeks to turn diversity to humane uses. Rather than shunning or oppressing those unlike ourselves, we seek them out. We try to understand their humanity, in the hope that it will deepen our own. Diversity, says Eck, is inevitable in the contemporary world. The world is full of disparate peoples, now easier to encounter than ever before. We must, she says, let this unite us rather than divide us. We must get to know them, recognize them, appreciate their humanity, and let them touch our lives. This is a fine moral project and a democratic one. It is also a good deal less simple than meets even Eck's experienced eye.

What can we learn about diversity and pluralism from the American religious and ethnic experiment of the last 200 years? That is my topic for this chapter.

A Nation of Immigrants

The United States is a notoriously diverse country, both ethically and religiously. It has never been resoundingly pluralist. We are known as "a nation of immigrants"—the title of a long pamphlet that our future President John F. Kennedy wrote a few years before taking office. Its two key words—"nation" and "immigrants"—imply a unity that has seldom been part of American practice. Our country has always welcomed immigrants but has also always tried to turn them into something other than they thought they were. As Jason DeParle (2011) recently described, the Virginia colony sought workers but turned them into slaves; Massachusetts sought religious believers but punished dissent; Pennsylvania sought citizens but got foreign enclaves—the Amish, Hutterites, and 'Pennsylvania Dutch' whose rural communities now attract tourists in droves.

Here's how our national myth goes. It says that people come to the U.S. from all over the world and assimilate to become "Americans". Never mind that over half of

---

[1] As of October 2013, these lectures have not been published. They are, however, available for viewing on YouTube.

early-twentieth century Italian 'immigrants' returned home after making money—this being the point of their overseas adventure. Most Chinese intended the same, though their return was more hazardous, as was the racism they suffered. The same is true for many contemporary Mexican laborers: one can, for example, build a very nice house in the little town of Gomez Farias, Michoacán, on wages from American field labor. Yes, one has to endure hardship while doing so, but many find the trip to "Gold Mountain"[2] worth the effort. Also never mind two centuries of anti-Catholic bigotry and even violence, broken only (if temporarily) by John Kennedy's election, toward which his own nation-of-immigrants mythologizing was aimed.

In the religious sphere, the myth takes a particular turn. In its vision, migrants start out immersed in the religions of their homelands—Protestant, Catholic, Orthodox, Jewish, Buddhist, animist, or whatever. They move to the United States and gradually, over two or three generations, become American. This assimilation does not require that they give up their native religions. It does, however, ask those religions to become Americanized. Half a century ago, Will Herberg described this process in his famous book Protestant, Catholic, Jew (1955). There, he argued that American religions have become domesticated: torn from their historical and theological roots to become soft identities. To be a Jew in America, he said, or to be an American Catholic, is to affirm a diffuse religious heritage that one may or may not practice in private life but which certainly does not intrude on the public sphere. As President Dwight Eisenhower put it, American public life "makes no sense unless it is founded on a deeply held religious belief—and I don't care what it is" (quoted in Herberg 1955: 84). Religious diversity works so long as religion doesn't matter very much. This is supposedly the secret to America's success.

Of course there are other factors. As Warner and Wittner (1998), Ebaugh and Chafetz (2000), and others have shown, almost all immigrant religions adopt the congregational form pioneered by early American Protestants. Such congregational communities ease the transition to American life. As Ebaugh and Chafetz put it:

> Whether it was the churches and synagogues of the earlier immigrants, or the churches, temples, mosques, gurdwaras, and storefront churches of today, religious centers serve as places where immigrants can worship in their own languages, enjoy the rituals, music, and festivals of their native lands, share stories from their homelands, and pass on their religious and cultural heritage to the next generation. Simultaneously, these religious centers help immigrants adapt to U.S. society by teaching them civic skills, providing economic and social services, providing the social space for networking, and affording status opportunities by creating socially valued religious roles. (p. 141)

This is the famous American "melting pot", which the American Indian activist Vine Deloria described as "a cauldron in which the scum rises to the top and everything on the bottom gets burned".[3] More technically, it is what historian Paul Spickard (2007) calls "the Ellis Island model" of immigration, after the

---

[2] This was the nineteenth century Chinese term for America.

[3] Personal communication, 1975. He probably did not invent the phrase but he is the first whom I heard speak it and he used it a lot. I have not found a better or earlier attribution.

Ellis Island Federal Immigration Station in New York harbor, which processed much of the late-nineteenth and early twentieth century immigration from Europe, including many of my relatives. In this model, Latvians, Poles, Norwegians, Italians, French, Germans, Croatians, and the like all, in time, became Americans, as they discarded their native languages, attitudes, and identities to become one people.

Framing it this way points up the conceptual flaw: Latvians, Poles, Norwegians, etc. didn't just become 'Americans'; they became White Americans. African immigrants never had that option: the Middle Passage and the fire of slavery stripped away the differences between the Yoruba, Fon, Ibo, Ewe, Akan, and so forth, but it made them Black, not White. Chinese exclusion, Japanese internment, and so on kept 'Asians' separate. The fact that Gary Locke, America's first Chinese-American state governor, got multiple death threats during his term of office was not a result of his policies; it was the color of his skin.

Today the problem is supposedly Mexicans. Anti-immigrant agitation has reached great heights in recent years, but it is not directed against those coming across America's northern border: most of them are White. Anti-immigrant feeling faces south. It does not matter that some of those stopped for "Driving While Latino"[4] never crossed the border; instead, the border crossed over their ancestors after the 1846–1848 U.S.-Mexican war. Europe is familiar with such things: the French-German border has crossed over Alsace many times. In our case, the American Southwest's many Hispanos and American Indians are too often treated as foreigners in their own land.

The point is: race matters. The United States is no melting pot because race is still a source of difference and privilege. At best, the United States is a multi-cultural 'salad'. That image, though, implies some unifying dressing that makes us all taste as if we belong at the same meal. Too bad; we haven't got one. Diversity is the best we can do.

Caesura

So: how did we move from religion to race? Aren't they fundamentally different sorts of things? Unless we're Jews, both sociologists and ordinary folk have long treated race as something we're born with but religion as something we can change. Nineteenth- and early-twentieth-century Christians went to the corners of the earth to 'convert heathens', never imagining that they could make them White by doing so. Their scientific contemporaries argued about whether there were three races or five or twelve, whether or not they all had a common origin, and how one should

---

[4] In American parlance, DWI stands for "driving while intoxicated". DWB ("driving while Black") and DWL ("driving while Latino") are spin-offs that highlight the common police practice of pulling over minority group drivers as a means of intimidation.

rank them, but none doubted that race was a biological matter fixed at birth. Only in the late twentieth century did this view begin to change (P. Spickard 1989). By then, cross-border travel showed that racial systems are different in different places. A Pakistani-American, for example, is "White" at home, but was "Black" in 1960s Britain, although he or she would now be labeled "Asian" there. Race is now recognized as a malleable, if still not a matter of choice.

The fourteenth-century Arab historian Ibn Khaldûn (1958) had a clearer view. Best known for his analysis of the conflict between 'civilization' and 'barbarism', Khaldûn actually produced the first sociological analysis of multi-ethnic and multi-religious society. His approach has uses in the present day.

Ibn Khaldûn saw the history of his native Maghreb as a cyclic struggle between barbarism and civilization—'tribes' and 'cities', to use a contemporary shorthand. In his vision, nomads are typified by *"Badâwah"*: "bedouinity" or "desert attitude". They live a rude and savage life, forced by their harsh surroundings to stick together. Individuals cannot survive here, and are thus of no consequence. The tribe works as a unit, especially in response to outside threats. Its group-feeling is particularly strong. Compelled to courage and fortitude, its members support each other against all comers (I: 249–258). *"Hatharah"*—"town-dwelling" or "sedentari-sation"—on the other hand, typifies city peoples, who are civilized, stable, and relatively rich. Agriculture, trading, and such livelihoods let them accumulate wealth. Having what they need to live, they think more of themselves and less of their neighbors, turning to magistrates and rulers to defend them both against their fellow citizens and against hostile outsiders. They depend on laws, not persons. In short, their living weakens their sense of group solidarity, so that they depend on social institutions for support (I: 249–250, 257–260).

Ibn Khaldûn argued that these two social types live in tension with each other. Harsh life makes tribes hang together, which enables them to conquer their softer neighbors. On doing so, they become rulers, who settle down and take on the civilized habits of their subjects. After a couple of generations of sedentary life, they have lost their unity, so they fall to the next barbarian wave.

The first point, for our purposes, is that ethnicity is a source of social solidarity, but not a fixed one: it waxes and wanes. To Ibn Khaldûn, people lose their unity when their *al 'assabiyyah* or "group-feeling" declines. Town-dwellers are fractious and self-centered. They find it hard to act together, which makes them weak. He thought they could be roused to joint sacrifice, but only if the stimulus were great. They might, for example, come to identify themselves with their town or city, as had been the case for the Greek city-states. Citizenship for the Greeks played the role that ethnicity has played in other societies—an absolute necessity, given the nature of Greek warfare. (The hoplite phalanx, though effective, required that everyone live or die together.) In Ibn Khaldûn's view, clan, tribe, ethnicity, citizenship, and so on formed potentially cross-cutting ties, each contributing (or not contributing) to the *al 'assabiyyah* exhibited at a given place and time. The historian or social analyst, he said, had to look at the exact situation on the ground. What ties of group-feeling are strongest? What solidarities are occluded? How have they shifted over time and what factors led them to do so? For him, none of these factors is fixed—just the opposite of nineteenth-century nationalist and racist dogma.

The second point concerns the role of religion. Ibn Khaldûn thought that religion could be one such locus of solidarity. By tying people together, religion could counteract a larger group's divisions, lending it the strength and unity that it needs to triumph (I: 305–306, 319–327). He used this insight to explain the seventh-century Arab conquests, which had been wide-ranging, sudden, and—given his reading of Arab social life—totally unexpected. The early Arabs, to him, were so tribally oriented that they could not unify around anything. It took the emergence of Islam as a strong, missionary religion to weld them into the unified force that conquered (and absorbed) three sides of the Mediterranean world.

This is not the place to explore Ibn Khaldûn's work in any greater depth (see Dhaouadi 1990; J. Spickard 2001, 2013). For us, his approach is the first sociology of a multi-ethnic society—one in which religion played a key but varied role. Khaldûn saw religion as a parallel means of solidarity, alongside kinship, ethnicity, and so on. All were active in both tribes and cities, but in different strengths and combinations. The key element of his sociology, for our purposes, is that it puts ethnic group-feeling and religious group-feeling into the same mix.

Put otherwise: Ibn Khaldûn confronted socio-religious diversity and saw that it could lead to either chaos or unity, depending on the relative strengths of the various *'assabiyyah* involved. He grasped ethnic and religious solidarities with the same set of concepts. We, too, need to make sure that we see ethnic and religious diversities—particularly those caused by immigration—in the same way.

Religious Diversity in the United States

The contributors to this volume are mostly sociologists, so I would be remiss if I failed to present some data. Table 1 reports responses to questions about religious identification on the American Religious Landscape Survey. "N" is over 35,000, which gives us a ±0.6 % margin of error.

The first thing to note is that America has an overwhelmingly Christian population. This is not just true of the 86.8 % of American adults who are native-born; 74 % of foreign-born (immigrant) American adults identify as Christian, though many more of them are Catholic (46 %) than Protestant (24 %); in fact, that is just about the reverse of the native-born figures. About 9 % of the foreign-born are non-Christian, as opposed to 4 % of native-born. This is the source of the 'new religious pluralism' to which Warner, Ebaugh, Eck, and their co-workers refer. Sixteen percent of immigrants are religiously unaffiliated, exactly the same as the population at large. In short, immigration is indeed changing America's religious landscape, but it is not changing it as much as we might think.

Second, the most prominent shift in American religious life is from affiliation to non-affiliation. Just 6.6 % of American adults claimed to have "no religion" on the 1973 General Social Survey; the 2010 figure was 18 % (Berkeley Social Data Archive n.d.). The shift was more pronounced among native-born adults than

Table 1 Major religious traditions in the U.S. (% of Adult Americans)

Christian	**78.4 %**
Protestant	51.3 %
Evangelical churches	26.3 %
Mainline churches	18.1 %
Historically Black churches	6.9 %
Catholic	23.9 %
Other Christian	3.3 %
Mormon	1.7 %
Jehovah's witness	0.7 %
Orthodox *(various kinds)*	0.6 %
Other religions	**4.7 %**
Jewish	1.7 %
Buddhist	0.7 %
Muslim	0.6 %
Hindu	0.4 %
Other	1.2 %
Unaffiliated	**16.1 %**
Atheist	1.6 %
Agnostic	2.4 %
"Nothing in particular"	12.1 %
Secular unaffiliated	6.3 %
Religious unaffiliated	5.8 %
Don't know/Refused to state	**0.8 %**

Pew Forum for Religion and Public Life (2008)

among those born elsewhere, but non-affiliation grew among them, also. If numbers were all that mattered, religious diversity ought to be less of a 'problem' than religious defection. But the size of a social phenomenon does not always dictate its cultural importance.

These numbers are misleading, however, and in two senses. First, there is a lot of diversity within American Christianity, especially Protestantism. For example, the Pew survey divides the Evangelical Protestants into 16 major traditions, each of which is made up of many denominations. Not all of these are on speaking terms, despite doctrinal similarities. My college town, for example, is home to three different Dutch Reformed churches, from separate denominations, who have little to do with each other. There is thus much more diversity than the table leads us to expect. It is just among Christians, not between Christians and other groups.

Second, the 16 % with "no religion" are less atheist and agnostic than they are "nothing in particular". I guess that's how the 2010 General Social Survey can report that 21 % of those claiming "no religion" pray at least daily, half of those more than once (Berkeley Social Data Archive n.d.). Hout and Fischer (2002) traced this to liberal disgust with Evangelical Protestantism's increased engagement in politics; Putnam and Campbell (2010) recently made the same argument with different and more extensive data. Claiming "no religion" is thus not so much a statement about one's beliefs as about one's unwillingness to be identified with religious organizations.

In sum, America is beset by considerable religion and by considerable diversity, albeit most of it Christian. Religion matters here, but the same religion does not matter to everyone.

Dealing with Diversity

How does one unify a country this diverse? Despite the Ellis Island/Melting Pot myth, American immigrants have never all assimilated to the Anglo-Saxon norm: not racially, not culturally, not religiously. Religious tolerance has periodically worked, most recently during Eisenhower's 1950s, when denominational religion ruled, not the sectarians. Yes, there were evangelicals and fundamentalists around, though they kept to themselves. Catholics were finally elected to high office. Still, my childhood Jewish friends had stomachaches all December from the school Christmas festivities and no one noticed—something not possible today. Yet there was relative religious peace.

Times have changed. American politics are now religiously polarized. It is too much to claim that the Evangelical Christian Right has captured the Republican Party, but presidential candidates routinely trumpet their right-wing Christian credentials in primary elections, when that party's most committed voters go to the polls. The Public Religion Research Institute (2012) reported 2 weeks before the 2012 presidential election that 76 % of White Evangelical likely voters supported the Republican candidate, compared to the 73 % of religiously unaffiliated voters who supported the Democrat.[5] Mark Chaves (2011: 95–96) has demonstrated an increasing correlation between church attendance, political conservatism, and Republican Party affiliation—explained almost entirely by the increasing embrace of that party by White Evangelical Protestants.

In brief, American public life has become sectarian—in both the religious and the political senses of that word. Denominational thinkers, like Diana Eck, may wish for "the active seeking of understanding across lines of difference" (Pluralism Project n.d.: 1) but her opponents are not listening. It is worth reminding ourselves that denominationally oriented people like her recognize the legitimacy of other religious views, while sectarians do not (see McGuire 2002: chapt 4). Pluralist dialogue asks all sides to engage in conversation. Not everyone is willing to come to the table.

So: how does one craft a society that encourages social cooperation without stifling the ethnic, religious, and social diversity that are increasingly inevitable? What kinds of social unity do we need? The American experience does have something to say about this, though it is not the part of America that we have seen so far.

---

[5] Catholics and Mainline Protestants were split, in part along racial and ethnic lines. Race mattered in this election more than it had in years when both candidates were White.

There are at least three ways to craft a unified social order. Émile Durkheim (1893) uncovered two of them over a century ago. First, we can make sure that everyone is alike: what he called "mechanical solidarity", in which people stick together because of their similarities. In this kind of society, people are connected by common ideas, common rituals, and the common practices of daily life. Religious and ethnic diversity threatens this. Exclusion tried to recreate it, but so did the original American "melting pot", in the hope that by dissolving away people's foreignness, socio-political unity can emerge. Will Herberg's (1955) picture of American religious life pointed in this direction, as religion (in his view) no longer defined one's core being. Instead, it had become a cloak lightly worn, a matter of personality and style. His American Jews would never be ultra-Orthodox, his Catholics never ultramontane. His portrayal of Protestantism drew from the Mainline, not the Fundamentalists, whom he thought fringe. Little could he see the Evangelical resurgence two decades down the road.

Herberg was not wrong, of course: there is much truth to his idea that religion is different in America and that immigration changes the shape of the faiths transplanted here. Warner and Wittner (1998), Ebaugh and Chafetz (2000), and others have shown how American congregationalism has stamped immigrant religions with an organizational form that they had not previously known. But the underlying issue remains: the melting pot did not produce social unity, neither ethnically nor religiously. Nor should we expect it to do so.

Durkheim called his second route "organic solidarity", by which he referred to the ties that emerge because we all have different jobs, skills, and tastes, and because our complex economy needs these differences to prosper. Our current division of labor stretches across the globe. To take just one example: our shirts are sewn in Haiti or Vietnam from cotton grown in Tajikistan or El Salvador mixed with polyester from Venezuela or Iran; they are shipped on Liberian or Indian freighters with international (skeleton) crews. Only the selling is local and this only sometimes. This "unity" is a matter of function. Durkheim worried that such society would give people too little in common to avoid social breakdown; his book <u>Suicide</u> (1897) is a treatise on just how this can play out in individual lives.

America provides a third model. Robert Bellah (1967) famously described American "civil religion" as a set of concepts, ritual phrases, and ideals that construct a national sense of purpose. "Civil religion" is not henotheism, a term that theologian H. Richard Niebuhr (1960) used to denote worship of the group itself. It is not worship of a society or a nation, and it is certainly not patriotism. It is, instead, an identity crafted from a sense of mission: a sense that America has a set of special tasks to carry out in the world. The American political Left and Right agree about this "American exceptionalism"; they just do not agree about what those tasks are. Right-wingers think America's purpose is to promote capitalism and 'make the world safe for democracy'. Left-wingers choose human rights and individual freedoms. The two sides thus support different interventions: the Right supported America's invasion of Iraq; the Left was more interested in invading Afghanistan to aid suppressed women. We can perhaps trace our recent political discord to these competing civil religions; doing might help us better see how deeply these visions are held.

Bellah rightly noted that all such national callings are prophetic. Indeed, like the Old Testament prophets, American civil religion calls both government and society to account for their misdeeds. "With great power comes great responsibility" [6] was an effective movie line because it resonates so deeply with American culture. To be exceptional, America's national sense of purpose cannot merely be self-serving. To frame this in identity-language, Americans (in this ideology) are the people who are called to serve everyone. The ideals for which America is famous—democracy, freedom, justice—are an as-yet unfinished project. Can a country shape its collective identity around helping everyone attain them?

In this vision, America begins in diversity, but pluralism is not just a matter of diverse people talking civilly with one another. Pluralism is diversity on a mission. The mission binds us together. This kind of unity is eschatological, embedded in national ideals.

Here we reencounter al 'assabiyyah. In this view, religious group-feeling is not just a matter of a shared history, nor is it just a matter of contemporary need. The 'assabiyyah that Ibn Khaldûn saw in Islam stemmed from a shared purpose: to bring about the rule of Allah on earth and to bring all peoples to righteousness. This enabled religion to unify fractious ethnic groups into a purposeful force. As Ibn Khaldûn predicted, that unity soon flagged. The vision dimmed, though perhaps it just turned sweeter: mystical Sufism had its own vision for a just and connected world, one that it succeeded in fostering for centuries.

Sweet or forceful, can a civil religion of ideals bring people together, leaving room for their diversity within a larger mission? Again, this is more than Eck's call to dialogue. Civil religion has a visionary calling at its core.

Qualms

Yet I have qualms. I hope I do not need to remind readers of the gap between my country's ideals and its realities. We proclaim democracy but we support dictators. We avow independent self-government while we practice empire. The long-past war in Vietnam was no outlier; it was part of the main trend. So, I am afraid, is the illegal prison at Guantanamo Bay Naval Base in Cuba—which is itself an imperial imposition on a sovereign neighbor—the atrocities at Abu Ghraib, and undeclared wars without counting. My country has plenty of dirty laundry (see, *inter alia*, Johnson 2004; Zinn 2003). I frequently air it at home—and in doing so I engage in that same prophetic civil religion that Bellah described. I call on my country to live up to its ideals and to end its sinful ways

---

[6] The original is reportedly by Voltaire. It is a key line in the 2002 Spiderman movie from Columbia Pictures.

There, is, however, a second point of worry. American culture has undergone a shift in recent years, away from this quasi-religious national mission to a distinctly economic one. To be blunt about it, America is now the place where people hope to get rich. We are still the land of freedom, but now it is freedom to enjoy our wealth rather than to do good in the world. Former President George W. Bush didn't actually urge Americans to "go shopping" as a response to the 9/11 terrorist attacks; he did, however, identify our vibrant economy as the thing that our enemies envy and he asked Americans to continue participating in it (Murse 2010).[7] However, the fact that so many people believe that Bush did say "go shopping" tells us something culturally important. We joke about our national addiction to shopping malls and about our need for what our comedians call "retail therapy". We even have a clothing chain called "True Religion" that sells very expensive designer jeans. Have economic enrichment and the resulting consumption become the new American national purpose? Durkheim worried about this—not the consumption part, so much, but about the individualism and anomie that he feared would come from treating our economic differentiation as life's main goal. Bellah also worried about this. So do I.

We are, however, in Europe, not in the United States. You have more immigrants than you did before, and more of them come from diverse lands. They bring with them strange skin colors, customs, allegiances, and—yes—religions. Will your "pluralism" be just a matter of talking together? Or will your plurality find its unity in a sense of mission to the world? Put otherwise, can Europe find its own civil religion, beyond the religions of nationalism and of wealth? Can Europe become prophetic, as it maintains its high standard of living? And can you avoid the pitfalls that have entrapped us, on the other side of the pond?

That is an old question. It is also a Christian one—though not just Christian, I hasten to add. Jesus had a few things to say about the difficulty of serving God while still being economically comfortable.

References

Anderson, Benedict. 1983. *Imagined communities: Reflections on the origin and spread of nationalism*. London: Verso.

Bellah, Robert N. 1967. Civil religion in America. *Daedalus* 96(Winter): 1–21.

Berkeley Social Data Archive. n.d. http://sda.berkeley.edu. Accessed 30 Oct 2013.

Chaves, Mark. 2011. *American religion: Contemporary trends*. Princeton: Princeton University Press.

DeParle, Jason. 2011. Favoring Immigration If not the Immigrant. *New York Times*, May 9, C1.

Dhaouadi, M. 1990. Ibn Khaldun: The founding father of Eastern Sociology. *International Sociology* 5(3): 319–335.

Durkheim, Émile. 1893. *The Division of Labor in Society*. Trans. G. Simpson. New York: Free Press, 1964.

---

[7] He actually said: "I ask your continued participation and confidence in the American economy." G.W. Bush, national address, Sept. 20, 2001.

Durkheim, Émile. 1897. *Suicide: A Study in Sociology*. Trans. J.A. Spaulding and G. Simpson, ed. G. Simpson. New York: The Free Press, 1951.

Ebaugh, Helen Rose, and Janet Chafetz (eds.). 2000. *Religion and the new immigrants: Continuities and adaptations in immigrant congregations*, Abridged student edition. Walnut Creek: Altamira Press.

Eck, Diana. 2009. *Gifford lectures: The age of pluralism*. Unpublished, but viewable at http://www.youtube.com/watch?v=M0wDxV4vOqU. Accessed 30 Oct 2013.

Herberg, Will. 1955. *Protestant, Catholic, Jew: An essay in American religious sociology*. Garden City: Doubleday.

Hout, Michael, and Claude S. Fischer. 2002. Why more Americans have no religious preference: Politics and generations. *American Sociological Review* 67(2): 165–190.

Ibn Khaldûn. [1377–1399]. *The Muqaddimah: An introduction to history (in 3 volumes)*, 2nd ed. Trans. F. Rosenthal. Bollingen Series XLIII. Princeton: Princeton University Press, 1958.

Johnson, Chalmers. 2004. *Blowback: The costs and consequences of American empire*. New York: Holt.

McGuire, Meredith B. 2002. *Religion: The social context*, 5th ed. Belmont: Wadsworth.

Murse, Tom. 2010. *Did Bush really tell Americans to 'go shopping' after 9/11?* About.com: http://usgovinfo.about.com/od/thepresidentandcabinet/a/did-bush-say-go-shopping-after-911.htm. Accessed 30 Oct 2013.

Nee, Victor, and Brettde Bary Nee. 1973. *Longtime Californ': A documentary study of an American Chinatown*. Palo Alto: Stanford University Press.

Niebuhr, H. Richard. 1960. *Radical monotheism and Western culture*. New York: Harper & Brothers.

Office of the Historian, U.S. Department of State. n.d. *The Immigration Act of 1924 (The Johnson-Reed Act)*. http://history.state.gov/milestones/1921-1936/ImmigrationAct. Accessed 2 Mar 2013.

Petersen, William. 1966. Success story: Japanese American style. *New York Times Magazine*, January 20, 20ff.

Pew Forum on Religion and Public Life. 2008. *American religious landscape survey*. http://religions.pewforum.org/pdf/report-religious-landscape-study-full.pdf. Survey carried out between 8 May and 13 August, 2007. Accessed 12 Mar 2013.

Pluralism Project at Harvard University. n.d. http://www.pluralism.org. Accessed 2 Mar 2013. Specific quotes come from: http://pluralism.org/pages/pluralism/what_is_pluralism; http://www.pluralism.org/pluralism/essays/from_diversity_to_pluralism.php

Public Religion Research Institute. 2012. *American values survey, 2012*. http://publicreligion.org/research/2012/10/american-values-survey-2012/. Accessed 12 Mar 2013.

Putnam, Robert D., and David E. Campbell. 2010. *American grace: How religion divides and unites us*. New York: Simon & Schuster.

Spickard, James V. 2001. Tribes and cities: Towards an Islamic sociology of religion. *Social Compass* 48(1): 97–110.

Spickard, James V. 2013. Accepting the post-colonial challenge: Theorizing a Khaldûnian approach to the Marian apparition at Medjugorje. *Critical Research on Religion* 1(2): 158–176.

Spickard, Paul R. 1989. *Mixed blood: Intermarriage and ethnic identity in twentieth-century America*. Madison: University of Wisconsin Press.

Spickard, Paul R. 2007. *Almost all aliens: Immigration, race, and colonialism in American history and identity*. New York: Routledge.

Warner, R. Stephen, and Judith G. Wittner (eds.). 1998. *Gatherings in Diaspora: Religious communities and the new immigration*. Philadelphia: Temple University Press.

Zinn, Howard. 2003. *A people's history of the United States*. San Francisco: HarperCollins.

Between No Establishment and Free Exercise: The Dialectic of American Religious Pluralism

William H. Swatos Jr.

It is well known that "religious freedom" is one of the cornerstones of the American political-social order. The very first words of the First Amendment to the Constitution of the United States are "Congress shall make no law respecting an establishment of religion, or prohibiting the free exercise thereof..." It then takes up the issues of freedom of speech, the press, assembly, and petition for redress of grievances. Indeed, "religious freedom" has always been offered as a cornerstone of American democracy to persecuted creeds around the world. Many would consider it the unique "gift" of the "American experiment" to the rest of the world.

At the same time, however, these words in fact address in one breath two different aspects of the privilege. One is that there will be no law respecting the establishment of religion; thus the state may not establish any religion as a state religion. The second clause, however, is much less straightforward in its potential consequences and is where practically all "religious freedom" questions in the United States and beyond have been argued—namely that there shall be no prohibition of "the free exercise" of that religious freedom. While at first blush this might seem to suggest nothing more than the right of a person to "attend the church of his or her choice," in a "no establishment" context it in fact opens a virtual Pandora's box of possibilities. If there is no legal establishment of a religion or religions, then anyone can effectively create a religion on whatever basis she or he pleases. When we look at the history of the cases that have come to court relating to "religious freedom" questions, they almost universally derive from claims and counterclaims regarding "free exercise."[1]

---

[1] The First Amendment was also the source one of the first cases to come before the U.S. Supreme Court with respect to "states rights"—but on that occasion in New England, far away from the Deep South, where the phrase was invoked in the twentieth century. Several New England states claimed that the word "Congress" meant just what it said, the United States Congress, hence *states*

W.H. Swatos Jr. (✉)
Institute for the Study of Religion, Baylor University, 618 SW 2nd Avenue, Galva, IL 61434-1912, USA
e-mail: William_Swatos@baylor.edu

G. Giordan and E. Pace (eds.), *Religious Pluralism*,
DOI 10.1007/978-3-319-06623-3_10, © Springer International Publishing Switzerland 2014

The matter gets further complicated by the Second Amendment, whence another double-barreled salvo sounds forth: "A well-regulated militia being necessary to the security of a free State, the right of the people to keep and bear arms shall not be infringed." Keeping arms is one thing; bearing them is another. The context of the Amendment makes its rationale clear: national self-defense after an historic revolution. The new nation was in no position to create a either a standing army or the military apparatus that for its day would have been the equivalent of the modern Department of Defense. People needed to keep arms to defend both themselves and their properties against potential attack. There was no standing army, hence all people had to be prepared to join in the defense of their persons and property.

The U.S. Constitution thus sets up in itself, from the nation's very beginning, the potential for both religious pluralism and socio-political and socio-religious conflict. Persons of our generation, for the most part, saw the most dramatic explosion of the energies latent in these two double-barreled amendments in the Branch Davidian conflagration, but smaller explosions at the periphery of religious differences have occurred across US history and continue to occur. The Branch Davidian event was "special" only in the sense of the amount of firepower accumulated by the Davidians on the one hand and the fact that it all blew up on morning TV in our living rooms, inasmuch as the Constitution also gives us freedom of the press.

The Davidian conflagration clearly indicates that whether the language of "diversity" or "pluralism" is operative, the issue of the freedom of "the other" to engage in specific *practices* either in the name of or under the auspices of religious freedom needs far more careful negotiation and articulation than was likely in the minds of the framers of these several Constitutional amendments that, with others, form part of the American Bill of Rights. What happened in the Davidian case was a denial of the privileges extended by these first two amendments to the Constitution—viz. the right of free exercise and the right to keep and bear—when put in juxtaposition to each other. Americans apparently have the right to keep and bear arms and the right of freedom of religion, but not the right to keep and bear arms as a part of their religion. Implicit in this peculiar contradiction of what on the face of it the Constitution specifically entitles to Americans is an assumption that by keeping and bearing arms, the Davidian leadership was denying persons the freedom to leave the Davidian compound, hence their freedom to reject the religion of Davidianism, if they so chose, although in fact this was never proved.

Is the Davidian case an exception, such that I should be considered over-reacting to a single event? I don't think so. For example, the context of the mass suicides at

---

could continue to have religious establishments, specifically in the form of taxation to support the established church within the state, as long as they also allowed people to worship wherever they pleased. In other words, citizens would pay taxes to support the state establishment, but were not required to attend the established church or else face fines or imprisonment. Other churches could be built and public worship conducted there, but a state could, if it chose, continue to tax its citizens to support the established church of the state. This was eventually struck down in the 1830s as unconstitutional, and it is on that decision that all subsequent claims to "states rights" have ultimately also been rejected, giving any privilege extended by the United States Constitution full authority at every other level of civil government.

Jonestown at the end of the 1970s has similar overtones. Again, what we find is a religious group of American origin labeled as "extremist" and then a decision on the part of the U.S. government to intervene. The difference was that Jones in a sense "trumped" his opponents by taking control of the situation out of the government's hands and "ending it all" by his own scheme. Although not directly threatened by physical violence, the Church Universal and Triumphant (CUT), another American NRM, was repeatedly harassed by the United States Internal Revenue Service with claims of tax evasion and a temporary revocation of its tax-exempt status as a religious organization. (Ironically, a certainly unintended beneficial consequence for CUT as a result of the outcry raised by the Davidian fiasco was that CUT's tax exempt status was reinstated, although CUT remained under close government scrutiny, and the initial IRS investigation had symbolic effects on its recruitment of new members.) On a much smaller scale, we can examine the various cases, eventually at least quasi-resolved by a relatively recent Supreme Court decision, about animal sacrifice in various Afro-Caribbean and Afro-Brazilian groups in the US. How else do we understand the amount of both personal energy and finances invested in these cases, when hundreds, possibly thousands, of animals are put to death in public pounds daily—not to mention animals intentionally raised for slaughter to feed not only humans themselves, but also their pets in a thriving trade? The supposed logic of this concern boggles the mind, unless one sees that it has *nothing* to do with the animals and everything to do with putatively "strange" religions—practiced in the main by "strange" people.

I raise these cases from the US because I believe that one should begin with a certain amount of self-criticism with respect to one's own society and understand that written guarantees of rights and privileges are set out in specific historical settings that may or may not be considered practical 1, 2, or 300 years later. Consider, for example, the strange American practice, prior to the end of slavery, of counting a slave as 3/5 s of a person for apportionment of members of the US House of Representatives (for whom, of course, they could not vote) as provided until the 13th Amendment to the Constitution repealed the practice. Perhaps there is no sillier phrase ever written into any other Constitution in history, but of course, the point is that without counting the slaves in some way, the slave states would have had inadequate population numbers to maintain the legality of the slave system, inasmuch as membership in the House is determined by population. I raise this example, which has nothing to do with religious organization directly, simply to point out that we make various kinds of adjustments to accommodate, as it were, preconceived practical necessities on the one hand, while on the other, when matters of practical import are insignificant, we can take more inflexible stands. A case in point here, to move us away from the US, is the vote on the Swiss referendum to disallow the building of (further) minarets in the country, especially inasmuch as none of the four existing minarets was used for the (Islamic) call to prayer. Other European countries have taken similar kinds of steps to minimize the perceived threat of Islamification of either the country as a whole or at least some major urban areas. Much of these have nothing to do with the realities "on the ground" at the moment, but rather "perceived" threats of what might happen in one of several potentially envisionable future scenarios of population change and sociocultural dynamics that might occur "in, with, and under" those.

Here we see rather different notions of "establishment" coming into play. In the US case, the establishment of any one religion is prohibited, but any religion may "establish" itself as a religion very easily. It simply has to have people who congregate for religious observances in a regular way and who do not otherwise break the law in the process—for example, by holding their observances in a locale whose zoning does not permit public-access types of activities (usually "high end" residential areas). It certainly helps if the religion has some form of doctrinal manual and has a "corporate" structure that at least has the appearance of assuring continuity. Religions wishing to take advantages of US tax laws must also keep careful financial records and file papers annually with the Internal Revenue Service. Some states also require separate filings. Religious employees are not tax exempt, though in some cases they may have special privileges that may have the effect of reducing their tax obligations. For example, religious practitioners may opt out of our Social Security tax system, but then they must be careful not to invest their funds in other instruments that have a "corporate" character. (Personal bank accounts and bonds are fine, but not mutual funds.)

Good Will

Underlying American religious freedom is the general notion of Kantian good will that was very much in the air at the end of the eighteenth century; that is, the contemporary premise of American democracy that preceded the Constitution and its Amendments was a beneficent deism that bound together the nation's leadership. For the most part, the Constitutional "fathers" embraced the deism of the late eighteenth century regardless of their particular religious denomination. Absent this understanding of good will, religious freedom can obviously turn ugly. This good will ideology of religious freedom persisted at least into the 1960s and underlies the statement ascribed to President Dwight Eisenhower—but unable to be proof-texted today—that "everyone should have a religion, and I don't care what it is." Eisenhower also supported the idea that "America the Beautiful" should replace "The Star Spangled Banner" as the United States' national anthem, and it was during Eisenhower's administration that the words "under God" were inserted into the "Pledge of Allegiance" to the United States' flag. It was also the era of the "gray flannel suit," and of particularly significant activities on the part of the U.S. House of Representatives Committee on Un-American Activities in a peace-time situation. Un-American Activities in this regard were especially associated with persons of ill-will in American society, including sequentially Nazi sympathizers in its earliest years and then Communist sympathizers once the cold war had set in.

These historical ebbs and flows are particularly significant to understanding the present context of religious freedom in the United States, which continues to be "overdetermined" in some respects by the events of September 11, 2001, which were without a doubt acts of ill will, whether or not they were provoked by specific U.S. positions or commitments. I was particularly struck by the extent to which the events of "9/11" were commemorated in the summer of 2011, on the tenth anniversary of the attacks. I confess I had hardly any awareness of the anniversary myself until it hit the media over the weekend that included that date. What became absolutely clear through the media at that time, however, was the enormous bi-partisanship among American political and social figures denouncing religious bigotry and personal ill-will, while at the same time associating religious bigotry and ill-will with the perpetrators of the events of 9/11, through all of which sounded a chorus of religious devotion to good will. President Obama's political capital was undoubtedly further increased with the death of Osama bin-Laden, an act for which he has been straightforward in accepting personal responsibility. The "Axis of Evil" has shifted from godless Communism to militant Islam (or Islamic radicalism). "Free exercise" clearly does not extend to attacks on the putative "American Satan," by Muslims or any other religious group.

How this plays out for "ordinary Muslims" in the United States is difficult to estimate. On the one hand, there have been relatively large communities of both Arab Christians and Arab Muslims in the Detroit area, for example, for many years. Large blocks of Arab and other Eastern Christians have also more recently settled in southern California—in both cases people from Iran, Iraq, and Syria. Muslims from some of the same areas have also fled to the United States—some to avoid sectarian violence, others as a result of repressive political regimes quite apart from religious issues or simply for perceived opportunities for economic advancement. In general, free exercise seems supported for these populations provided there are explicit declarations that make support for no establishment equally clear—participation of a mullah, for example, in his local ministerial association along with general conformity by him and his congregation to American social standards in regard to such things as clothing, manners, civic participation, the role of women, and so on serve as indicators of acceptance of the "separation" norm.

It may indeed be the case that some Christian groups can get away with forms of disruptive behavior more easily than would be allowed Muslims in a similar situation. The anti-gay protests at the funerals of American military service personnel by the Westboro Baptist Church, for example, might be more difficult for a Muslim group to pull off, if they so desired. That the anti-gay protests are themselves signs of ill will is what makes them so reprehensible to the general American population, not least when they occur in connection with the death of a soldier who is perceived to have given his life "on behalf of his country," a setting where American civil religion is also attacked and where the deceased soldier was not himself gay. Now that the Westboro case has been finally adjudicated, however, American civic groups related especially to veterans' concerns have begun to find ways to use other Constitutional privileges to avert Westboro agitation at funeral sites in some locales. Nevertheless, the Westboro example is an important one to keep in mind, inasmuch as it does demonstrate that American Constitutional privileges extended to religious groups have the potential to turn ugly and move in directions that the founding fathers could never have conceived. On the other hand, regardless of one's personal feelings about the Westboro approach, if the content is removed, then in some respects Westboro's tactics do not stand entirely outside the American tradition of taking one's religion into the public arena to effect change. In particular, the Westboro strategy is one that has not taken up arms in its use of freedom of speech. In that sense, its stands firmly within the American Constitutional tradition.

The sit-ins from the late 1950s into the succeeding decade also shared some formal characteristics with the Westboro protesters—particularly in those cases where "freedom riders" from outside the locales where the protests were to occur in effect rode into town as "outlaws" in the eyes of the locals. There can be no question that the majority of freedom riders knew they were going to places to break the laws of those places, which in those places were considered to be legitimately enacted. Put in the most extreme position from the historic Southern side of the day, it constituted *conspiracy* to break the laws of the land. Of course, from the side of the freedom riders, it was the same question turned around, "Whose land is it, anyway?" Religious freedom allowed the freedom riders to be arrested and prosecuted for opposing unjust laws that the freedom riders believed fundamentally violated the rights of all citizens guaranteed by the United States Constitution. Though intended as an expression of unity, the popular song of the era *This Land is Your Land, This Land is My Land* expressed the tension between the two sides as well.

The Globalization Dynamic and American Civil Religion

Looking at the history of religion in the United States, one might be tempted to see current issues regarding Islam as simply a "stage" in a process of integration of new populations into the national fabric. For example, one can point to the fact that in the nineteenth century various firms would simultaneously put up a sign or take out a newspaper advertisement seeking employees and then add "Catholics need not apply." Inasmuch as the Roman Catholic Church in the United States today is the largest single religious body, an argument could be made for letting time "work itself out." On the other hand, the United States has never been at war with Catholic states as Catholic belligerents—that is to say, states that claimed that they had the right to attack the United States or United States citizens because Americans were heretics or infidels. In that sense, from 1979 forward there has been a new dimension added to the "religious freedom" struggle at the global level, itself becoming thereby a dynamic in the globalization process that was not a part of the work of early globalization theorists, who tended to see states like Iran and Egypt in the 1970s as "progressive" regimes and potential "models" for not only the Islamic world, but also other regions where Christianity was not dominant. Japan, of course, had already made the transition, and in the interim China has also become a major global player—even though it may well be that there are "two Chinas" today in a quite different sense from what was meant 50 years ago, with places like contemporary Wenzhou and Hong Kong being quite different from western regions of the country in terms of economic development. It is not without significance that these two areas have the highest percentages of Christians—and predominantly Protestant Christians—in China.

To say that the conflicts that occur today with some predominately Muslim regimes and regime actors is a "new dimension" in our world is new only to those of us whose lives have been lived in the twentieth century. Barbary piracy, including the taking of American hostages, in the early nineteenth century was one of the several forms of international belligerence that brought fame to the United States Marine Corps whose hymn, also written early in the nineteenth century, begins "From the halls of Montezuma to the shores of Tripoli. . .." The specific occasion for the Tripoli reference was the Battle of Derne in 1805, at whose conclusion the United States flag was raised in the "old world" for the first time. The hymn was written relatively shortly thereafter, so much so that it could be *revised* into its present form in 1828.[2]

Globalization, and American Civil Religion: What Is Justice?

The title "God Bless America" reflects not only the most popular slogan of the responses to the events of 9/11 as they appeared across the United States, but also the diffuse quality of American civil religion, which stands alongside and both complements and is complemented by the specific traditions that compose the American religious milieu. "God Bless America" was simultaneously slogan and song. It gave voice to American emotions. It also has a history of association with both national resurgence and the sociological corpus, as part of the research of Robert Merton and colleagues on the World War II war-bond mass radio audience effort stimulated by singer Kate Smith, who had introduced the song to an immediately successful national reception in 1938, on the occasion of the twentieth anniversary of the World War I armistice (Merton et al. 1946). Written by Irving Berlin during his own military service in 1918, the song was rejected for publication at that time, but at the radio voice of Smith it would become a powerful rallying cry in the midst of World War II—nor of course, was the fact that Irving Berlin was Jewish lost in the midst of Nazi anti-Semitism (cf. http://katesmith.org/gba.html).

When examined in a religious rather than sociopolitical context, what is most immediately obvious is that the song actually says almost nothing about God other than a providential personalism. It primarily exults the goodness of the nation even as it affirms the existence of the deity as an ally for her good. Indeed, various commentators, for example, have noted that if the song were theologically authentic the title would be something along the lines of "America Bless God." This

---

[2] The revision had nothing to do with the Tripoli reference.

observation underscores the important theoretical distinction between theological and religious use of language. Inasmuch as more than 95 % of the US population still acknowledges belief in God (in relatively simplistic surveys), an appeal to God in this undefined way is an appeal to a singularly unifying religious symbol of high generality.

It is significant, however, that this song rather than the National Anthem, became the expressive focus of American reaction to 9/11. Within hours of the attacks, when members of Congress sang "God Bless America" on the steps of the Capitol, and certainly by the time of the memorial observance at National Cathedral, the essentially religious character of American nationhood was increasingly articulated. In the popular vein, Lee Greenwood's 1983 song "God Bless the U.S.A." would also be added to this movement—now incorporated into the naturalization ceremony of new US citizens (see Meizel 2006; Swatos 2006). The Puritan "errand into wilderness" to found a "city upon a hill" was reaffirmed: The United States began as a religious project—the product of a search for "freedom." The American Way of religious freedom, in this mythological recreation—which, as Robert Bellah (1999) has pointed out, is actually far more to be associated with the Baptist Roger Williams than the "Pilgrim fathers"—was set over against a "foreign" way of religious tyranny and oppression. Civil religion in America thus is not as entirely diffuse as it seems at first blush, for there is an aura within which it operates, what Catherine Albanese has termed American "public Protestantism"—the characteristic of Americanism that led G. K. Chesterton (and others) to observe that "in the United States even the Catholics are Protestants." Today we add other groups as well—for example, "Protestant Buddhism." Complementing this public Protestantism is the moral code of the Judeo-Christian ethic.

When the moment came for the specifically religious and the civilly religious to interpret in the events of 9/11, a crucial choice had to be made as to who should utter the prophetic word. Neither the liberal female bishop of Washington Episcopalians, nor the one-time leader of the Moral Majority, but a man who would embody for the bulk of Americans the public Protestantism which they had encountered the most throughout their lives: Billy Graham mounted the steps of Washington's National Cathedral. Though technically a Baptist, Graham has always been noted as a public figure, both in the United States and abroad, associated neither with a specific church nor with an ostensibly commercial enterprise. In his sermon, Graham interfaced doctrinally specific religion and civil religion as he has done throughout his career. In calling America to repentance and renewal, Graham also renewed his own cultural capital as the living icon of the public Protestantism that forms the specifically religious interface for diffuse civil religion of America. And did it occur to no one that Billy Graham spent the bulk of his evangelistic ministry conducting *crusades*?

Public Protestantism and American civil religion particularly coalesced because the attacks of 9/11 constituted *moral outrages* inasmuch as they failed to conform to the norms of civil societies in regard to the conduct of public conflicts. By acting outside the norms of structured national conflicts, the perpetrators of these actions were seen to represent persons who had overstepped the bounds of toleration that are inherent in American civil religion. They both violated the norm of "taking religion too seriously," and simultaneously provided evidence of what happens when people take religion "too seriously." Whereas within American civil religion there is a juxtaposition of freedom for and freedom from religion, the latter was outrageously breached on 9/11. The breaching of this norm means that American civil religion itself was attacked. The events of 9/11 did not simply attack America in general, they attacked the American civil-religious principle of *laissez faire*— which is also a political-economic worldview, theoretically *the* American economic worldview. This interplay of laissez faire religion and laissez faire economics allows constant ultimate value reinforcement for practical behavior. The appeal of Billy Graham was always to bring people to make their "own decision" about religious commitment—*Decision* being, in fact, the title of his magazine for supporters. The attacks on the World Trade Center and the Pentagon thus were cast not merely as military offences, but as assaults on core American values including the religious value of freedom for/from. Not surprisingly, American Muslims quickly had to distance themselves from the contrary values enacted by the terrorists.

The renewal of American civil religion thus can be projected to have an ironic consequence; namely, the decline of the influence of right-wing religious extremism in the political sector within the United States, even as there is a more general turn to religious articulation of central values. This became quickly apparent in the days after the events of 9/11, when attempts by Christian Rightists to associate the attacks with such phenomena as gay/lesbian rights and feminism rang hollow and received scant hearing. American civil religion is not the worship of America, but it is an assertion of central values for the separation of religions from politics even as it asserts the religiousness of the core value of the nation as an instrument of divine intent, if not action. Hence 9/11 served to knit together a stronger conservative Judeo-Christian core while paring away the fringes. Issues that once animated the extreme are being addressed within the core in a spirit of a search for reinvigorated central values, albeit in the context of a specific threat that may in fact obscure the root causes of the problems in question. The contradictions of multinational capitalism, for example, continue to be largely off the agenda of American political and religious discourse.

Not as apparent in the experience of 9/11 was the relationship between the attacker's priorities—the destruction of the state of Israel—and American civil religion. Perhaps because the initial military assaults against Israel in the 1960s by the likes of Egypt's Nasser were fully secularist—Nasser being a great foe of Islamicists, as was the Baath party that brought Saddam Hussein to power in Iraq—American policy-makers and military strategists largely missed or misread the buildup of Islamicist politics during the 1970s. The United States backed democratic efforts where they seemed viable while accepting the leadership of "strong men" as long as they did not threaten American "interests"—specifically, oil resources. Human rights issues were clearly secondary priorities. On the surface of it, for example, one might have thought Jimmy Carter and the Ayatollah Khomeini would have been great friends as advocates of moral high ground; instead they became mortal enemies. Because the state of Israel is intertwined with the Promised Land myth of America, on the one hand, and because of the millennial expectations of American Protestants on the other, American leadership failed to understand the extent to which Islamicists view Israel both as a invasion of their sacred space and, more specifically, as an American client state. Americans by and large continue to fail to see that the Israeli presence in Palestine appears to Islamicists as an American "resettlement project" not essentially different from Soviet resettlements among, for example, the Baltic nations after World War II. Though perhaps born of the highest motives, nevertheless the establishment of the state of Israel, the resettlement of Jews in that territory, and the lack of adequate regard for the people already living there represent a Western incursion of unique significance entirely counter to the decolonization that otherwise characterized the post-World War II era. Hence, by its apparent ignorance and arrogance, the United States becomes the final superpower to be undone.

Undergirding these claims and counterclaims are biblical myths of ownership that extend thousands of years into the past, before either Christianity or Islam was ever named. The Promised Land—which is precisely what God is claimed to have given Abraham—was already populated when the children of Israel arrived. Palestinians claim a pre-Israelitic ancestry. The claims of modern Jews, furthermore, are historically corrupted by the fact that, if the term "Semitic" has any genuinely biological concomitants—rather than its fast-and-loose use by anti-Semites—then many, perhaps most, present-day Jews cannot possibly be biological descendants of those who occupied Judea at the time of the Roman destruction of Jerusalem. Hence, the Jewish claim to land rights in historic Israel is a spiritual claim, rooted in religious myth—a myth ironically shared in part with the majority of actual occupants at the time of the creation of the modern state of Israel—i.e., Muslims. Jerusalem thus becomes the epicenter of myths of eternal significance with practical consequences. In this context, the specifically Judeo-Christian roots of American public Protestantism become quite clear. The claim of the "right of the Jewish people to a nation-state of their own" is shot through with specifically modern American Evangelical thinking about the nature of the world order. Neither Catholics nor Muslims in a world-historical context, for example, would think this way. The process by which American history has been thought and taught in the United States is retrospectively applied to a universal world history of eternal significance. "Manifest destiny" is extended as a result of American participation in World War II from a doctrine regarding the development of the Western hemisphere to a universal law based on a specific civil-religious reading, which is also a political-economic reading, of the purpose of the United States as a nation of eternal significance: "In God we trust"—you can read it on all our money.

At the same time, because of the public Protestantism that pervades the United States, the *successes* of the medieval Crusades are often minimized. The Latin Kingdom of Jerusalem, by contrast, can teach important lessons to those who would too quickly dismiss the persistence of Islamicist forces. Depending on how its boundaries are evaluated, it can be said to have lasted from 45 to 200 years. The modern state of Israel only recently celebrated its 50th anniversary: As Americans fight the current war against Islamicist terrorism, a perspective on what Max Weber termed the "warrior ethic" of Islam needs to be laid over against the work ethic that is enshrined within American civil religion (see Swatos 1995). These ethics represent two competing worldviews of "universal historical" significance. The Islamicist worldview presents a challenge to the United States entirely different in kind from that of the Soviet empire, against which American civil religious defenses were primarily constructed over the last half-century. The terrorists who struck on 9/11 could have chosen many different targets. The specific choices they made need to be seen in their symbolic significance, and the importance of the consequences attached to those choices needs to be addressed in a renewed civil religion in America in the era of globalization.

My intent here is not to be jingoistic, but rather to point out that there have been *essential* differences between the pluralistic worldview espoused in American society and culture regarding the place of religion in civil life and that of some Islamic states for over two centuries. The idea, in other words, that "postmodern globalization" is somehow to be held responsible for problems of religious intolerance—that, in a sense, things are "moving too fast" for local systems of action to adjust themselves simultaneously to global demands is belied by the "shores of Tripoli" line. At the same time, can we not see a kind of Weberian irony, hence a larger truth about American society and culture, that it would be not only a Democratic president (as was Jefferson when the shores of Tripoli lines were written), but also the first African-American president and the first president born outside of the continental United States, who would deploy the necessary troops and tactical support again to both Pakistan and Lybia (and beyond) in the cause of fundamental human rights as conceptualized within the Bill of Rights.

Globalization has been going on since the beginning of the sixteenth century and was sufficiently in place by the beginning of the nineteenth for the fledgling United States to understand that if it was going to protect its national interests it had to be able to act internationally, hence simply having a standing army at home was insufficient to protect the liberties it had won. From its very beginnings, then, the American world view had a global dimension whose focus has narrowed or broadened as various circumstances seemed to require, yet in fact, it has been those times when its focus has narrowed that the country has been at its weakest internally as well as externally. American religious pluralism is part of a broader societal pluralism that at its best strives to give the greatest possible opportunity for free exercise while establishing liberty and justice for all. Certainly "the American way" has had its stronger and weaker moments, not least evidenced not merely in our Civil War but even more so, in some respects, by the failure fully and consistently to nurture the fruits of the Union victory. As the world has shrunk, it is the case that we see these more immediately worked out—indeed appearing on our television screens almost as they happen—than may have been the case in past centuries. The picture is not always pleasant, as it was not in Waco, and there are certainly those who now criticize U.S. decisions and actions within the past year in both Pakistan and Libya. On the whole, however, the premises of no establishment and free exercise have weathered changing times surprisingly well, and the United States continues to show weekly attendance at religious services at a higher rate than virtually any other society in the world.

References

Albanese, Catherine L. 1992. *America: Religions and religion*, 2nd ed. Belmont: Wadsworth.

Bellah, Robert N. 1999. Is there a common American culture? Diversity, identity, and morality in American public life. In *The power of religious publics: Staking claims in American society*, ed. William H. Swatos Jr. and James K. Wellman Jr., 53–67. Westport: Praeger.

Beyer, Peter. 1994. *Religion and globalization*. London: Sage.

Christiano, Kevin J., William H. Swatos Jr., and Peter Kivisto. 2008. *Sociology of religion: Contemporary developments*, 2nd ed. Lanham: Rowman & Littlefield.

Davidson, James D. 1991. *Religion among America's elite: Persistence and change in the protestant establishment*. Notre Dame: Cushwa Center for the Study of American Catholicism.

Davidson, James D., Ralph E. Pyle, and David V. Reyes. 1995. Persistence and change in the protestant establishment, 1930–1992. *Social Forces* 74: 157–175.

Duke, James T., and Barry L. Johnson. 1989. Protestantism and the spirit of democracy. In *Religious politics in global and comparative perspective*, ed. William H. Swatos Jr., 131–146. New York: Greenwood Press.

Kimmel, Michael S., and Rahmat Tavakol. 1986. Against Satan. In *Charisma, history, and social structure*, ed. Ronald M. Glassman and William H. Swatos Jr., 101–112. New York: Greenwood.

Meizel, Katherine. 2006. A singing citizenry: Popular music and civil religion in America. *Journal for the Scientific Study of Religion* 45: 497–503.

Merton, Robert K., et al. 1946. *Mass persuasion*. New York: Harper.

Meyer, John W. 1980. The world polity and the authority of the nation-state. In *Studies of the modern world-system*, ed. Albert J. Bergesen, 109–137. New York: Academic.

Parsons, Talcott. 1963. Christianity and modern industrial society. In *Sociological theory, values, and sociocultural change*, ed. Edward A. Tiryakian, 33–70. New York: Free Press.

Robertson, Roland. 1992. *Globalization*. London: Sage.

Swatos Jr., William H. 1995. Islam and capitalism: A Weberian perspective on resurgence. In *Religion and the transformations of capitalism*, ed. Richard H. Roberts, 47–62. London: Routledge & Kegan Paul.

Swatos Jr., William H. 2006. Implicit religious assumptions within the resurgence of religion in the USA since 9/11. *Implicit Religion* 9: 166–179.

Missionary Trans-Border Religions and Defensive Civil Society in Contemporary Japan: Toward a Comparative Institutional Approach to Religious Pluralism

Yoshihide Sakurai

Introduction

Globalization and modernization have been considered major factors that facilitate religious diversity and pluralism. As James Beckford clarified in his work, the concept of pluralism refers to diversity of religion, public acceptance or recognition of transnational religion, and pluralism as value, and these three aspects of pluralism are interconnected (Beckford 2003). Japan since the 1980s provides an example in this regard.

The migrants who were called "new comers" from East and Southeast Asia, Middle East, and South America brought their historic religions such as Catholic, Evangelism and Pentecostalism, and Islam into Japan and thereby established ethnic churches and mosques. It is in contrast with the "old comers" who arrived from the Korean Peninsula in colonial times with their ancestral cults and shamanism that were almost limited to their own ethnic communities (Sakurai and Miki 2012).

In addition, Japan has also received energetic missionaries from Korean and Western churches. They are so active that some pastors in mainline churches raised eyebrows to them and equated them as new religions and/or cults that solicit general public and obtained converts from their churches (Lee and Sakurai 2011). As a result, the increasing religious diversity urged the existing established religions as well as civil society to regard those particular religious activities as the exercise of their civil rights. Hence, religious pluralism that guarantees freedom and cross-cultural tolerance to new-comer religions is established.

Sociologists of religion in Japan tended to ignore the macro theoretical theory that explains religious change, and just consider globalization and trans-nationalism merely as social background. The primary goal of this chapter is to investigate the

Y. Sakurai (✉)
Graduate School of Letters, Hokkaido University, kita 10 nishi 7, Sapporo 060-0810, Japan
e-mail: hax50440@tree.odn.ne.jp; saku@let.hokudai.ac.jp

G. Giordan and E. Pace (eds.), *Religious Pluralism*,
DOI 10.1007/978-3-319-06623-3_11, © Springer International Publishing Switzerland 2014

dynamism and interaction between new comers' religions and civil society from the institutional perspective of religious and social history. Besides, studies on contemporary Japanese religions, whether they are religious, anthropological, or sociological, have focused rather on specific issues so far, typically snapshots of particular religions and Japanese religiosity. To fill this gap, information of various new comers' religions is discussed in details.

Specifically, I examine how globalization has influenced religious diversity and how incidentally foreign religions have challenged the hegemonic religious order in Japan. How many and what kinds of foreign religions have come to Japan and established their churches in order to expand their social capital as well as missionary for Japanese? How have they adapted to Japanese society and been approved by traditional religions and civil society? To what extent can the institutional perspective more coherently explain the Japanese reactions to religious diversity and pluralism-oriented policies that are considered independent of or inconsistent with its own religious and social history? How does the Japanese case contribute to the comparative studies of religious pluralism in other cultural contexts? These are the descriptive and theoretical questions addressed in this study.

Theoretical Perspective to Explain Contemporary Religions

Japanese social scientists acknowledged the significant theoretical literatures through the introduction by leading scholars and their translations into Japanese language. Since the 1970s and 1980s the concept of secularization, which suggests the negative impact of modernity on religion, was widely recognized through the works of Brian Wilson (1976), Tomas Luckmann (1967), Peter Berger et al. (1973), and Karel Dobbellaere (1981). Although sociologists highly appreciated their theoretical implications, religious scholars question about the applicability of secularization thesis on Japanese social and religious change. In Japan, secular warriors were the power of religions since the ancient Yamato Dynasty, hence there was basically no sacred canopy except for the time when Meiji nation states invented the synergetic Shintoism and Tennoism and promoted it as the national ideology of Nihon Empire in the late nineteenth to early twentieth century (Shimazono 2005). Moreover, new religious movements and New Age also flourished in this period.

Counter arguments to the secularization thesis, such as the concept of civil religion (Bellah 1970) and public religion (Casanova 1994), stimulated Japanese scholars to think whether Japanese religious traditions have become social ethics and bear significant roles in public sphere. But the State Shintoism or other religions are no longer expected to be the foundations of morality and justice for Japanese, because liberalization and democratization rejected any legacy of religious values as well as institutions after World War II. Therefore, scholars just followed the academic trend to reevaluate the public role of religions and read the monographs on new religious movements/cults, Pentecostalism and Evangelism that flourished and expanded in many countries.

Although these literatures are important works to controvert secularization, the general theory of religious market and rational choice advocated by Rodney Stark and William Sims Bainbridge (1985, 1987), Laurence Iannaccone (1992) were not acknowledged or translated into Japanese, showing a lack of interest in understanding religion comprehensively in the Japanese academia. This model has the basic premises: (1) meaning of life and world view are necessary for human-being, hence religious-demand is constant; (2) traditional religions and new religions, mainline churches and new denominations competitively provide meanings in religious market; (3) the relaxation of regulations and religious diversity increase religious options so that participation to church services as well as para-churches' social service would also increase. Criticism to autonomous man with rational choice were also raised (Bruce 1999). Here, my arguments focus on the theoretical premises and universality of this model.

My argument to the first premise is that monotheism does formulate sacred canopy and confessional church monopolizes belongingness, while polytheism and/or customary religious practice is just part of our social life and meaning system. Japan is a very good example of the latter. Secondly and generally speaking, religion in any society exists in hierarchy where some are more favored than the others. They do not necessarily compete to attract consumers. But transnational religious movements and multiculturalism began to challenge this hierarchy and they compete vigorously for believers. Market model is becoming popular in any disciplines as global capitalism prevails in the world system. For the third point, religious market can be highly regulated in reality. For example the triple religious market invented by Fenngang Yang consists of an authorized market, suppressed underground market, and in-between gray market. Furthermore, in the shortage economy of religious groups and specialists, peoples' religious demands do not necessarily disappear but rather sustained. Religion has revived once the regulation is loosened and transnational missionary entered into China (Yang 2012).

A more fundamental limitation of religious market model is the time lag between the change of religious demands and supplies. Although secularization may have negative impacts on peoples' religious interest and church attendance, it does not significantly undermine the development of religious institution in a short time. For example in Japan, after the World War II, the ratio of Japanese believing in polytheistic gods, spirits, and ancestral ghosts has gradually declined from 70 % to approximately 20 %. Yet traditional and new religions have not declined in reality. Similarly, the influx of foreign religions has not increased religious demand either. The supply of religious products is also less elastic and responsive to the changing spiritual demands of Japanese. Otherwise, religious institutions would have already been much commercialized to meet peoples' secular demands of merit-making.

In short, the religious economy model can explain those religious situations in which social institutions are largely commercialized. The US is a market oriented state where religious freedom and diversity is high and no regulation by the federal government has been the institution. However, Europe has strong and unique institutions of religious order and social institutions that have lasted for centuries, and they are more robust than market rule. If that is the case, we should focus on the major institutions that guide and regulate religious demand and supply and provide the "take-it-for-granted-ness" for people. The target of analysis is not the market system but institutions.

Considering the institutional transformation of religions in Japan, religious diversity and control of religions through administrative means are crucial factors in our analysis. We will begin with an overview of Japanese religious history.

Japanese Religious Institutions

Japanese indigenous religions include folk religions, such as spiritualism, nature worship, and rites for guardian spirits and ancestors. Such a stable religious world had become diversified by foreign religions such as Buddhism, Confucianism, and Taoism, when the early Yamato Dynasty developed relations with Silla and Baekje in the seventh to eighth century and subsequently Fujiwara aristocracy sent embassies to Tang China in the seventh to ninth century.

Initially Buddhism was a state religion patronized by the Emperor (Tenno) and their denominations were supported by manorialism. Some monks who were sons of aristocrats had wives and passed their monks status to their children. Japanese monks were not required to renounce from the secular world that was very different from Theravada and Mahayana traditions. Furthermore, recently Japanese historians argued that three fourth of monks at that time were actually non-official monks who shaved their head and put on robes just to evade tax and labors (Ito 2008). On the other hand, the religious element of Confucianism entered into Japan as a form of posthumous name tablets worship and gradually mixed with Buddhist memorial (ullambana) services.

Until the twelfth century new Buddhist sects emerged from old denominations. Shinran, the founder of Jodo Shin shu, (Pure land True Buddhism) were persecuted and exiled. But the exile allowed him to further propagate Buddhism among the general public. Monks were supported by believers for the first time. At the same time Taoism and feng shui pervaded into popular beliefs. At that time, religions were the main components of Japanese civilization and culture among Japanese until they encountered with Christianity in the sixteenth century.

Jesuit missionary successfully propagated and attracted feudal lords and their serfs. However, the chief adviser to Tenno and Shogun of Tokugawa were concerned about the threats of western colonization of Japan as it was happening in Southeast Asia at that time. Finally Shogunate suppressed Jesuits as well as Japanese Christian; some of them suffer martyrdom while others were ordered to renounce their faiths and to belong to particular Buddhist denominations. It was the first religious control that prohibited Japanese from believing in foreign religions for almost two and half hundreds years. Buddhist denominations fortunately enjoyed the privilege to make every Japanese Buddhist parishioners; Buddhism became part of the secular order. As a result Japanese families recognized Buddhism not as religious belief but households' religious customs that were passed down from generation to generation.

In 1867 Tokugawa Shogunate returned its power to the Emperor when low-level samurais and their feudal lords built antiforeigner factions that strongly criticized the shogunate's weak-kneed diplomacy to the West. The new government abandoned the policy of seclusion and suppression of Christianity so that new policies such as freedom of religion, equality of all people, and approval for monks to have wife and surname were implemented. Moreover, Meiji government ordered all religions to support militarism and State Shintoism and suppressed new religions whose founders proclaimed their sacredness deriving from other sources other than the living god Tenno. For more than 300 years' of Tokugawa and Meiji-Taisho period, Japanese became accustomed to regulations on religions and regarded religious devotees as fanatic and esoteric, while customary religions are widely accepted.

The defeat of World War II in 1945 was the turning point of religious policies when the US introduced democracy, politico-religious separation, and religious freedom to Japan. After the decline of state patronized Shintoism, Japan entered the "rush hour of the Gods" (McFarland 1967) and those new religious movements earned political power by forming political party and patronage of politicians. Although such cozy relation was criticized by liberal and leftist academics, new religions won over peoples' mind and became too large to ignore.

On the other hand, secularism has governed many aspects of society including public education, jurisdiction, and administration to the extent that 70 % of Japanese proclaimed themselves as non-religious. This tendency was amplified by the Aum incidents, in which Aum cult group scattered sarin nerve gas in Tokyo subway system and killed 13 peoples and injured more than 6,000 peoples in 1995. Cult phobia also damaged credibility of religions. On the contrary, influential authors and intellectuals preferred spirituality and therefore spiritualists, spiritual entrepreneurs, and their followers increased at the same time (Shimazono 2004). Religious preference varied from very religious to anti-religious among Japanese.

At last, we examine the statistics of Japanese Religious Corporation (Table 1). Total religious believers of 200 million people are almost twice as much as the population of Japan. Shinto shrines consider all residents in their communities as their parishioners, and residential groups usually collect membership fee every year for community shrines. And Buddhist temples ask their members to transfer membership to their children. General public does not concern about double affiliation to Shinto and Buddhism. The memberships of Christianity and New Religious Movement (NRM) seem to be overestimated because they include defectors as well as dead members. At any rate approximately 20 % of believers and the rest of practitioners of religious customs comprise of this syncretism of religious institution.

Table 1 Statistics of
Japanese religions in 2010

	Corporations	Teachers	Believers
Shinto	85,145	76,190	102,756,326
Buddhism	77,478	348,662	84,652,539
Christianity	4,468	35,129	2,773,09 6
Others, NRM	14,906	216,560	9,435,317
Total	181,997	676,541	199,617,278

Source: Ministry of Cultural Affairs, Bulletin of Religions 2013: 34–35

New Comers' Religion and Missionary Religion

In 2012 approximately two million Korean entered into Japan as tourists as well as workers, and among them there are hundreds of missionaries who conducted pioneering missions in cities and campus crusade. Every spring season my university students meet Korean students who talked about Korean film stars, pop songs and Bible in trained and fluent Japanese. At the Starbucks in Sapporo young people meet international crusading people who talked in English and broken Japanese. English learners and people who like western style of communication are brought to church gathering.

Missionary Christianity attracted a lot of new members and developed their churches that doubled its size in a few years. Powerful missionaries such as Jesus Life House International Church built their churches with thousands of member in just 10 years. Japanese mainline church pastors wondered if there were any special techniques in those churches, admitting that Japanese churches held the theology of mission but lacked methodology to proselytize.

Missionary and ethnic churches are two major driving forces to diversify Japanese religions after the stagnation of new religious movements in past decades. In the 1980s Japan enjoyed rapid economic growth and received huge migrants with various religious backgrounds. Korean and Chinese new comers came with their ethnic churches and religions. Brazilian and Peruvian migrants, who were descendants of Japanese who left Japan during poverty, came to work in factories and built their ethnic Catholic and Protestant churches. Myanmar refugees built Protestant churches to maintain and cultivate ethnic identity among their second generation. Thai also established tens of Theravada Buddhist temples as well as Tammakaya temples.

In the next section the author discuss Korean churches, Evangelical and Pentecostal churches from other countries, churches that are regarded as heretic, and other foreign religions and spiritual movements.

Table 2 Korean churches in Japan

Name of denomination	Founded year	Num. of branches
The Global Mission Society of the Presbyterian Church in Korea	1995	2
Korean Methodist Church in Japan	1985	2
The Presbyterian Church in Japan	1982	10
Tokyo Central Church	1985	7
Full Gospel Tokyo Church	1980s	71
Balnaba Gospel Church[a]	1968	2
Yohan Tokyo Christ Church	1988	25
Mission of Jesus Disciple	1983	3
Korean Methodist Church	1994	7
Federation of Baptist Church in Japan[a]	1984	7
International Gospel Church[a]	1986	5
Foreign Mission Board from Korea	2000s	9
Independent Church/Jesus Presbyterian Church	1990s	22
Total		172

Source: Lee and Sakurai (2011: 165)
[a]No official English name

Korean Churches

In the 1980s Evangelical and Pentecostal churches in Japan were strongly stimulated by the Third Wave of Holy Spirit movement. David Cho Yonggi, the founder of Yoido Full Gospel Church, world's NO. 1 mega church of 600,000 members, led this movement in Korea and established Full Gospel Tokyo Church in 1985 and expanded its branches throughout Japan. Furthermore, the concept of Mission of Force and Church Growth from Korean churches deeply influenced Japanese churches (Table 2).

As Korean Protestantism grew rapidly to five million members, churches also trained a considerable number of missionary workers. However, Korea became saturated with Protestant growth, which is in contrast with the ongoing growth of Catholic. Therefore, they turned their eyes to foreign mission and systematically trained missionaries to the extent that Korea became the second largest missionary-dispatching nation in the world after the United States. Their biggest out-reaching country was Japan, where Christians remained at the level of 1 % of the total population.

Korean Churches in Japan were divided into two groups. One is Korean Christian Church in Japan. Such ethnic church was established by Korean old comers in colonial times and preserved Korean service. Social capital derived from these churches was just for Korean residents. On the other hand, new comers and missionary Korean churches did not adhere to Korean language and used Japanese or simultaneous interpretation in order to attract Japanese believers. Furthermore, they expanded their membership through study and service in cell groups and discipleship training program, which were the strategies for the rapid growth of Korean church (Lee and Sakurai 2011).

Foreign Missionary

Western Missionary groups have also expanded their membership since 1980s and some groups collaborated with other Japanese denominations. The groups listed (Table 3) are part of foreign missionaries. They are classifies into three types in terms of missionary and church organization. The first is Crusade and Seminar where well-known preachers were invited to teach church development and management. Campus Crusade for Christ provoked excessive mission problem in Japanese universities. The second is missionary churches from the US and Australia that used music mission to attract young seekers. The third group used Tent-making strategy, by which missionary earned their living expenses and at the same time expanded their sympathizers in workplaces.

Comparing new comers' missionary with established denomination of Christianity, the former directed human resources towards missions. It was in sharp contrast with the missionary of Japanese churches that engaged in education, medication, and social works to construct a possible social image. Therefore, foreign missionaries are less known by Japanese and less influential in Japan.

Heresy and Cults

The third group is heresy or cults. Some of these groups founded their Japanese branch in early twentieth century and gradually expanded their membership. Jehovah's Witness have approximately 200,000 members who become active missionary to distribute "Awake!" on streets and conduct door-to-door canvassing. Mormons were acknowledged as "western duo cyclists" who engaged in English-teaching missionary but in vain. Unification Church also has officially 500,000 members (in fact approximately 50,000) and succeeded in proselytizing and fundraising in recent years. This religion provoked cult controversy due to illegal masked recruitment method and fraudulent sales of spiritual goods to citizens (Sakurai 2010). In addition to UC, Jesus Morning Star, whose founder Jeong Myeong-seok was in jail due to serious offense, also holds approximately 2,000 member among university students and the young.

Catholic undergoes internal reform movements that influenced some Japanese. However, there were heresy disputes just among Catholics. The priest of Little Pebble Church in Japan set up religious commune where priests and female adherents had sexual rites. They also uploaded these scandalous pictures for sale to earn living expenses (Table 4).

Table 3 Foreign missionaries in Japan

Name of foreign missionary	Founded year
The Family International	1972
Japan Keswick Convention	1962
Christopher Sun Evangelical Association	2005
Japan Pensacola Church	1990s
Saddleback Church	2006
Raymond Mooi (Japan Gospel Mission)	2008
Creation Research	1986
Bridging The Gap	2007
Saffron Ministries[a]	2006
New Hope International Fellowship Tokyo	1999
Purpose Driven Japan	2009
Asian Outreach Japan	1990s
Power For Living	2007
Japan Campus Crusade for Christ	1990s
The Taizé Community	1998
Franklin Graham Festival	2006
Christian International Asia	1975
Willow Creek Network Japan	2005
Youth With Mission	1980s
Alpha Japan	2000s

Source: Sakurai and Miki (2012: 154)
[a]No official English name

Table 4 Heresy or cults

Name of religion	Founded year
The Tokyo First Church of Christ, Scientist	1920, 1946
Church of Jesus Christ of Latter-Day Saints	1946
Jehovah's Witness	1946
Unification Church	1964
Jesus Morning Star	1985
Little Pebble Church	2000
Neo-Catechmenate	1990
Movimento Sacerdotale Mariano Japan	1980s
Fraternitas Sacerdotalis Sancti Pii Decimi	1993

Source: Sakurai and Miki (2012: 156)

Others: Foreign NRM, Spiritualism, and HPM

The fourth group is miscellaneous that can be divided into several groups such as Yoga, psycho therapy, Theosophy, spiritualism, cults, and various human potential movements. Even if these audience cults and client cults can gather maniacs, they cannot attract much citizen's interest widely because they promote cultural singularity and bear a strong sense of personal palatability. Moreover, natural scientists often criticized their dogma and activities as pseudoscience, although these organizations expanded their activities even to mainstreams culture, such as psychotherapy, education, and medical treatment (Table 5).

Table 5 Other religions

Name of group	Founded year
Daha World Japan	1997
Scientology, Tokyo	1980s
Vedanta Society of Japan	1959
Ahmadiyya Muslim Community of Japan	Unknown
Japan Baha'i Network	1932
Raelian Movement of Japan	Unknown
The Theosophical Society in Japan	1971
Krishnamurti Study Group	1990s
NPO Anthroposophical Society in Japan	2000
OSHO-JAPAN	1980s
Maharishi Research Institute	Unknown
Falun Dafa Japan	2004
Dhammkakaya International Meditation Center of Japan	2000s
Tendo Soutenda (YiGuanDao)	1958

Source: Sakurai and Miki (2012: 158)

Attitude to New Comers' Religion

The author demonstrates that new comers' religions have diversified Japanese religions since the 1980s and attracted a certain number of religious and spiritual seekers through a wide variety of recruitment strategies and supply of healing, caring, and salvation. The next part discusses the reaction to new comers' religions by the majority of Japanese, who are self-claimed irreligious people.

First, ethnic religions have expanded their branches in proportion to the increase of migrants. Even if their churches are located in the downtown, general public was not aware of their existence because masjids or ethnic churches for Brazilian, Peruvian, Filipino, Myanmar, and Korean have not propagated their religion to Japanese. The practitioners of Umbanda Espiritismo usually focus on Brazilian believers. Masjid leaders lead foreign students and workers with their families from Islamic countries and refrained from promoting to Japanese due to negative image of religious extremism. Members of Ahamadiyya Muslim Community Japan engaged in social work with Japanese volunteers who show sympathetic understanding to these people.

Ethnic religions were initially monitored and gradually welcomed when Japanese residents understood that foreigners just kept their faith and custom within their own community with no intention to expand. Even leaders of established religions held a relaxed attitude to promote interreligious dialogues and became helpmates of these religions. These trends are treated with favorable impressions by the media and intellectuals. Multiculturalism became the slogan of municipalities that promotes the integration of foreign migrants and their children. Moreover, universities set up courses to promote multiculturalism, even if they did not recognize that multiculturalism actually premised the idea of religious pluralism. Japanese do not consider that religions shall express their opinion in public sphere because of religio-politico separation. Given that the amount of ethnic religion and their influence was limited, ethnic religions would be considered harmless to "us."

Second, as for missionary religions, the general public, except for those who were proselytized, have no interest and/or distrust against them. However, established religions are suspicious of those emerging religions. Whether new comers' religion or Japanese new religions increased membership at a stunning rate, the characteristics of charismatic founder, discipleship, and extraordinary activities would be equated to cults and that their spiritual manipulation could enable their organizational growth. Under the stagnation of mission, mainline churches actively seek justification for their mission.

No matter what denominations of Christianity in Japan are, they historically received assistance from foreign mission board in terms of financial and missionary resources so that they could establish mission schools, hospitals, and charitable organizations. Even nowadays pastors as well as believers think that the role of mission should be entrusted to religious leaders. Alternatively Korean churches traditionally remained independent in terms of mission and financial management of churches from foreign countries, hence, mission-oriented churches urged ordinary members to propagate and donate considerable amount of time and money to church. This method is completely the same as the policy adopted by new religious movement in Japan

Moreover, missionary religions encourage their members to change their daily practice and relationship with others and society, which might be regarded as being dangerous. Japanese religious consciousness has rightly or wrongly legitimated the value of household (ancestor worship by Buddhist commemoration service), community (guardian spiritualism by Shinto festival), and nation (Tennoism).

Despite discomfort with and vigilance to missionary religions, general public has been instructed to be tolerant with those religions through cult controversy. The public reacted to the Aum incidents in the 1990s with avoidance. As a result, criticism of cults in the mass media by academics and laypersons grew markedly. However, excessive criticism of cult members who had not faced criminal charges provoked human-rights backlash in Japan. Human-rights advocates and intellectuals who were protective of Aum declared cults to be "religious minorities." The refusal by some municipalities to prohibit residency of Aum members were judged unconstitutional by courts. Although security police have kept Aleph (changed name from Aum) under surveillance, approximately 1,500 members are still active. Japanese people doubt that liberal intellectuals and courts are protecting civil rights of cult members and that they refrained from playing a preventative role towards cults (Sakurai 2009).

Conclusions

This study examines how the transnational religions brought by immigrants and missionaries diversified hegemonic religious order in Japan from the institutional perspective of religious and social history. Several important conclusions can be derived.

First, religious diversity has been the original characteristics of Japanese religiosity since the ancient times. The fundamental religious consciousness and customary practice include the worship of ancestors and guardian deities and shamanism. Foreign religions such as Chinese Buddhism, Confucianism, and Taoism were introduced by Tenno and aristocrats who aimed at governing nations through civilization and religious forces. From eighth to nineteenth century plural religious cultures were syncretized to form Japanese Buddhist denominations, Shugen-do, and popular religions.

Second, the control of religion by secular authority relies on historical and social institutions. Despite the fact that Japanese were passionate about the acceptance of foreign religious culture and were tolerant to religious diversity, the Tokugawa dynasty prohibited Christian missionary due to the fear of western colonization and thereby rigorously ordered every lords' serfs to be parishioners of Buddhist denominations. Religious control by authority continued to the end of World War II, until that time the government forced its people to bow in front of Shinto shrines designated as the place of worship for the dead during colonial aggression wars. After the war, the US and new government imposed religious freedom and the policy of religio-politico separation on Japan. Because of these policy changes, liberal Japanese have been reluctant to discuss religious issues in public sphere and administration conducted non-interactive control to religious matters. Therefore, although religious pluralism is protected by law and multiculturalism, however, general public and established religions seem to feel uneasy about cultic and missionary religions that emerged recently.

Third, new comers' religions were divided into two types, ethnic churches and missionary religions, both of which had to develop their mission strategies and organizational management under the conditions of pluralism and very loose control from administration and general public. Ethnic churches from various countries have not always established good relationships with residents, but at least they have not been rejected because they withheld mission to Japanese. In contrast, aggressive missionary religions were generally deemed to invade into the tranquil live of people whether their religious backgrounds were historical religions or new religions. Although there is no regulation on religions or authenticated or particular religious orders to monitor new comers' religions, Japanese tend to gear themselves well towards religions matters. That is, religions matters are better considered not as individual secular preference but as collective actions that are historically institutionalized.

The present study intends to explore the socio-historical development of Japanese religions. However, this chapter may offer some insights to the conceptual analysis of religious pluralism. My study contributes to a growing literature and suggests the importance of comparative studies of religions in understanding the effect of globalization and religious pluralism.

References

Beckford, A. James. 2003. *Social theory & religion*, 73–81. Cambridge: Cambridge University Press.

Bellah, Robert N. 1970. *Beyond belief: Essays on religion in a post-traditionalist world.* New York: Harper & Row. Japanese edition: Bellah. 1973. *Shakai Kaikaku to Shukyo Rinri* (trans: Hidekazu Kawai). Tokyo: Miraisha.

Berger, Peter, Brigitte Berger, and Hansfried Kellner. 1973. *Homeless mind: Modernization and consciousness.* New York: Random House. Japanese edition: Berger. 1977. *Kokyo Soshitsushatachi* (trans: Machiko Takayama). Tokyo: Sinyosha.

Bruce, Steve. 1999. *Choice and religion: A critique of rational choice theory.* Oxford: Oxford University Press.

Bryan, Wilson.1976. *Contemporary transformations of religion.* Oxford: Oxford University Press. Bryan. 1979. *Gendai Shukyo no Henyo* (trans: Fujio Ikado and Tsuyoshi Nakano). Tokyo: Jordan sha.

Casanova, Jose. 1994. *Public religions in the modern world.* Austin: University of Chicago Press. Casanova. 1997. *Kindai Sekaino Kokyoshukyo* (trans: Hirofumi Tsushiro). Tokyo: Tamagawa University Press.

Dobbelaere, Karel. 1981. *Secularization: A multi-dimensional concept.* London: Sage Publications. Dobbelaere. 1992. *Shukyo no Dyanamics* (trans: Jan Swyngedouw and Kenji Ishii). Tokyo: Jordan sha.

Iannaccone, Laurence R. 1992. Religious markets and the economics of religion. *Social Compass* 39(1): 121–131.

Ito, Masatoshi. 2008. *Jisha Seiryoku no Tyusei (Temple Buddhist Regime in Medieval Times Japan).* Tokyo: Chikuma shobo.

Lee Wonbom, and Sakurai Yoshihide. 2011. *Ekkyosuru Nikkan Shukyobunka: Kankokuno Nikkei Shukyo Nihonno Kanryu Kirisutokyo* [Transnational religious culture: Japanese new religions in Korea and Korean Christianity in Japan]. Hokkaido: Hokkaido Daigaku shuppankai

Luckmann, Tomas. 1967. *Invisible religion: The transformation of symbols in industrial society.* New York: Macmillan Japanese edition: Luckmann. 1976. *Mienai Shukyo* (trans: Noriaki Akaike and Jan Swyngedouw). Tokyo: Jordan sha.

Mcfarland, H. Neill. 1967. *The rush hour of the gods: A study of new religious movements in Japan.* New York: The Macmillan Company.

Sakurai, Yoshihide. 2009. Conflict between Aum critics and human-rights advocates in Japan. *Cultic Studies Review* 7(3): 254–278.

Sakurai, Yoshihide. 2010. Geopolitical mission strategy: The case of the unification church in Japan and Korea. *Japanese Journal of Religious Studies* 37(2): 317–334.

Sakurai, Yoshihide, and Hizuru Miki. 2012. *Religious lives of immigrants to Japan: The multidimensional development of religion brought by newcomers.* Kyoto: Minerva Shobo.

Shimazono, Susumu. 2004. *From salvation to spirituality: Popular religious movements in modern Japan.* Melbourne: Trans Pacific Press.

Shimazono, Susumu. 2005. State Shinto and the religious structure of modern Japan. *Journal of the American Academy of Religion* 73(4): 1077–1098.

Stark, Rodney, and William Sims Bainbridge. 1985. *The future of religion: Secularization, revival, and cult formation*. Berkeley: University of California Press.

Stark, Rodney, and William Sims Bainbridge. 1987. *A theory of religion*. New York: Peter Lang.

Yang, Fenggang. 2012. *Religion in China: Survival & revival under communist rule*. New York: Oxford University.

Religious Tendencies in Brazil: Disenchantment, Secularization, and Sociologists

Roberto Motta

Introduction

This chapter deals with two issues related to recent religious change in Brazil. First, the attempt by some Brazilian social scientists to change highly syncretic, Afro-Brazilian *Candomblé* into a full-fledged, self-sufficient religion, a church on its own right, severing its ties with Catholicism and functioning as a religion that would lead, or contribute, to the exit from all religion. Second, I will make some considerations about the Theology of Liberation. I contend that the rise of this movement in Brazil was associated with a kind of "sociologization", or secularization, of Catholicism. And this, to my mind, is the basic reason why it came to fail, opening the way to the fabulous growth of the Pentecostal or "Neo-Pentecostal" churches and sects in the country. For I also contend that there cannot be a religion without an enchanted core.[1] As simple as this: no enchantment, no religion.[2] And if one should claim, in Marxist terms, that religion, and therefore enchantment, is the "opium of the people", I would admit that indeed, *from such perspective*, it cannot be but the opium of the people. Let us take it as it is and as it cannot be otherwise. If one happens to agree with the Marxist or, at that, with the Nietzschean premises, efforts to unopiate religion are necessarily doomed to fail, except, at the very best, as an interim situation, based on a more or less generalized wish to cover the issue with a cognitive penumbra.

I also contend that, in Brazil, sociologists or, more broadly, social scientists, including anthropologists, or, even more broadly, social thinkers of many kinds

---

[1] As I see it, my implicit conception of religion is akin to those of Durkheim (1985), Eliade (1969), Lowie (1924), and Otto (1958).

[2] And this in spite of what Weber said, or is interpreted to have said, about disenchanted Calvinism in the *Protestant Ethic*.

R. Motta (✉)
Recife University, Rue Santo Elias, 109. Apt. 701, 52020-090 Recife, PE, Brazil
e-mail: rmcmotta@uol.com.br

G. Giordan and E. Pace (eds.), *Religious Pluralism*,   171
DOI 10.1007/978-3-319-06623-3_12, © Springer International Publishing Switzerland 2014

have taken upon themselves the task of overseeing and guiding the transition from (to put it in Comtean terms) the theological into the positive, scientific stage. In other words, the management of religion, for as long as it lasts, would be incumbent upon them.[3]

The Holy Alliance

There is an extensive literature, in several languages, about the so-called Afro-Brazilian religions, the *Candomblé* being first and foremost among them.[4] Under the influence of authors such as Arthur Ramos (1940), Roger Bastide (1960), and Pierre Verger (1957), these religions have been interpreted as the survival, in Brazil, of African society, culture, and memory. *Candomblé*, in fact, is a syncretic religion if ever there was one. It resulted from the fusion, or confusion, between the worship of the saints of popular Catholicism and that of some gods of African, mainly Yoruba derivation, according to a code of correspondences based on attributes seen as common to supernaturals belonging to both origins.

Candomblé can, indeed should, be viewed as a form of popular Catholicism, adopted, in some coastal and commercial cities of Brazil, by some people with mainly, but by no means only, West African roots, who also shared some forms of economic and social insertion. What is perhaps most disconcerting about the Afro-Brazilian religions is the fact that only 0.35 % [sic] of all Brazilians, according to the 2009 census, claim allegiance to one of them.[5] This is a sociological puzzle. Why such high number of papers, books, theses, [6] and so on, written by Brazilian and foreigners, have been devoted to a religion or to religions with such a scant number of adepts? This would seem to represent an instance, to use Grace Davie's words, of "believing without belonging", or perhaps of believing, belonging, but not admitting to it (Davie 1990).[7] Actually, far more than 0.35 % of Brazilian are terreiro-goers.[8] A first preliminary conclusion is that, despite all kinds of political

---

[3] About the role of sociologists in the process of secularization (or mundanization), indeed of Social Science as a transformation of religion, references can be multiplied indefinitely. I will limit myself to just two: Sombart (1955) and Löwith (2002).

[4] The name *Candomblé* used to apply but to one of the varieties of the Afro-Brazilian religions, the one practiced at Salvador da Bahia. Due to its outstanding prestige, the name spread to all the religions of like origin.

[5] Many saw this as progress due to the "movement of Black consciousness", since in the previous count (2003) only 0.23 % of the whole population claimed to belong to one of them.

[6] Including my own Ph. D. dissertation (Motta 1988).

[7] Exact figures are very difficult to obtain, if at all. I dealt with this problem in Motta (1988), which, in some essential points, including in its methodological approach, is not outdated. See also, for a more recent treatment of the question, Motta (2007).

[8] *Terreiros* are the shrines in which worship takes place, comprising animal sacrifices (a basic rite), dance, trance, divination, etc.

and intellectual efforts, the Afro-Brazilians religions have not yet acquired enough respectability to be acknowledged as theirs by their practitioners.

Intellectuals, among them some of the most distinguished sociologists and anthropologists of *Universidade de São Paulo, Universidade Federal do Rio de Janeiro*, and other outstanding centers of higher learning and research, have strongly supported their growth. This is not so much due to their religious propensities (although in the process they may experience a few mystical thrills and some other psychological and theatrical gratifications), but rather, paradoxically, to their dislike for any form of religion. Sociologists and social anthropologists are, after all, the progeny of Auguste Comte and the representatives of a form of priesthood we tend to consider higher than that of conventional religion. We are the priests of the "religion de l'humanité" and it is incumbent upon us to preside over the transition from the theological to the positive stage. It is true that, in doing so, we often create our own systems of metaphysics, indeed our own theology, our outright mythology, under the guise of social theory.

Perhaps in no other country social scientists have been as bold as in Brazil in assuming the management of this process.[9] Let us now quote from a leading sociologist who often held positions of the highest prestige, not only in his own university, but in some of the most important learned societies of South America. In a book that resulted from a conference, held in Porto Alegre in 1996, on *Globalization and Religion*,[10] he contributed an article with the telltale title "Religious Interests of the Sociologists of Religion" (Pierucci 1997). In a chatty, but forceful style, he starts by inveighing against "the blurred frontiers and the double game" of presumably Catholic and Protestant sociologists.[11] He claims that

> nowadays one hears more and more often from sociologists of religion (are they faithless or shameless?) that religion gives empowerment to people. It leads to an increase of self-esteem among the most disadvantaged strata because it leads them to shun undesirable forms of behavior, like addiction to alcohol, drugs, homosexuality and the like. They come near to saying that religion frees the poor from their own laziness. (Pierucci 1997: 255–256).

He grants all of the above, but with some qualifications:

> It is true. But they [the sociologists] have forgotten to say to students and readers that every religion is a historical form of domination, every ethical religion a form of repression of our best energies and that the sociology of religion is only possible because it finds in the modern critique of religion its post-traditional possibility as a science (ibid.: 257).

---

[9] I think this situation is far from being unique to Brazil. But Brazilians express themselves (the present writer not excepted) in a somewhat blunt, at times even crude fashion. Dealing with a similar matter, a European author would wear multilayered gloves of distance and politeness.

[10] The conference was sponsored by the "Mercosul", the Southern South America Association of Sociologists of Religion (one of a thriving species in our lands) and he speaks with the full authority of a leading senior scholar.

[11] With Bourdieu he exclaims: "There are even bishops who are sociologists!".

This author is not only a sophisticated interpreter of religion with, among others, a Nietzschean tinge. He is also an active and astute partisan of secularization and liberation. Thus, he adds that

secularization must be seen as implying the destruction of the roots of individuals and, as such, as the dessacralization of culture. If it does not lead to liberating the individual from his traditional ties and allegiances, it has no meaning, it is not worthwhile (ibid.: 258).

For his purposes, he sees as regrettable the transit from Catholicism to Protestantism:

A meager cultural gift, a gloomy fate for humans is the one represented by passage from Catholicism to Protestantism. Have you realized that this means that a growing part of our people, as it embraces Protestantism, abandons polytheism? [...] I regret as an enormous loss the decline of our traditional polytheistic Catholicism. If we do not take into account the Black religion – and from this standpoint we can hardly overstate the strategic importance of the Afro-Brazilians – the present religious panorama does not offer us anything better (ibid.: 260). [12]

He finishes his lecture expressing, somewhat unexpectedly, a wish for the growth of Islam in Brazil:

May the great Allah become stronger among us, and Islam more visible and active, with its ethical and religious contribution, with its splendid literature, but preferably without its dessecularizing fundamentalism (ibid.: 261).

But above all he longs to witness

the multiplication, among us, in value, influence, and sheer demographic numbers, of the Afro-Brazilian cults: *Candomblé*, *Xangô*, *Batuque*, and *Umbanda* (ibid.: 261).

The Afro-Brazilian religions, in spite of their conspicuous sacrificial character, seem to agree with a certain modernity due both to their rejection of the notions of sin and guilt and to their being, or to having been, when they first appeared in Brazil, religions of the oppressed. They were adopted by many social scientists in Brazil not so much on strictly religious terms, but under the assumption of the establishment of a kind of a protectorate by social scientists over these religions. Thanks to the writings of sociologists and anthropologists, *Candomblé* was invested with highly rationalized theological reinterpretations. Congresses and conferences, attended by both researchers and devotees, have functioned as councils in which faith is defined and proclaimed.[13] A holy and scholarly alliance was therefore

---

[12] Well to the right end of the political spectrum, French writer Charles Maurras (1868–1952), along lines in part, at least, compatible with Pierucci's, writes that "it is questionable whether the idea of God, of an only Deity, present to man's conscience, is always beneficial. It does raise the feeling that conscience can establish a direct relationship with that absolute, infinite and almighty Being. But, on the other hand, Catholicism's merit and honor lie precisely in the organization it was able to confer to the idea of the Deity. On the way leading to it Catholics finds legions of intermediaries, along a continuous chain. Heaven and earth are full of them. Thus, this religion gives back to our world, in spite of its monotheistic foundation, its natural character of multiplicity, harmony, and composition" (Maurras 1972: 116–117).

[13] I have dealt at length with this issue in Motta (1998) and Motta (2010).

established in Brazil between the devotees of the Afro-Brazilian cults and the sociologists and anthropologists who represent the values of modernity.

Mainline social scientists have not hesitated to take sides in the religious medley. A recent collection of essays, authored by some of the most distinguished sociologists of religion in Brazil, is presented in the following way:

> This book is a collective effort to analyze, from various points of view, the impact caused by the growth of the Pentecostal churches, with their speeches and practices of aggression and religious intolerance toward the Afro-Brazilians and their violations of civil rights by discrimination due to sexual preference (Gonçalves da Silva et al. 2007).

I myself, during some time, adhered to a somewhat evolutionist interpretation of *Candomblé*. To my mind, it was nearing the completion of a process of "ecclesification", whereby it was severing its links with Catholicism and this at the triple level of ritual, belief and organization (Motta 1998). It would thus turn into a self-sufficient religion, on an equal footing with, say, the Roman Catholic and the Presbyterian churches, and competing with them for the same "market" of religious goods and services. I am now convinced that researchers, including myself, had largely created, or imagined, the *Candomblé* as an autonomous religion.

To my mind, this process can already be recognized in the late 1930s and early 1940s of the twentieth century, with the Brazilians Arthur Ramos (1940) and Edison Carneiro (1981, or. 1936). The former was a psychiatrist by training, conversant in several European languages, who, in addition to having read the literature available on the native religions of West Africa, had the luminous idea of applying to the interpretation of these religions and to their Brazilian offshoots the theories of Freud and Jung. He thereby pioneered, in Brazil, the concept of the "African mind", which has since ruled over Brazilian or Brazilianist social science of religion.

Edison Carneiro, a militant Marxist, for some time a friend and later a foe of Ramos's, contributed largely to the effort of codifying or legitimizing the *Candomblé* by consecrating one of its rites as canonical and excommunicating all the others as spurious, deviant or revisionist. The rite he chose was associated with some of *terreiros* (shrines) of Salvador da Bahia[14] that claimed a *Nagô* (Yoruba) origin. As a religion of the oppressed, *Candomblé* and similar cults, elsewhere in Brazil, were called to play an important role in the social struggle that would revolutionize Brazil. Carneiro, like many of his peers, did not have any religious beliefs. Above all, he rejected the notion of "the one Deity held by the highest forms of religion" (Carneiro 1981: 98). What mattered to him was really "the revolutionary potential of the Brazilian Negro". In order to reach and to direct or control this energy along the desired lines, he thought that the first thing to be done should be the rupture with the syncretic links that tied the *Candomblé* to Catholicism.

---

[14] This city is often called "the Black Rome of Brazil".

Many are called, but few are chosen. *Filhos-de-santo*[15] have conspicuously failed to answer the call to partisan politics.[16] But there was another way intellectuals, both foreign and Brazilian, could put *Candomblé* to good use. And this has been its reinterpretation as a "liberated" kind of religion. Pioneers in this trend were Georges Lapassade and Marco Aurélio Luz (1972), who jointly wrote a seminal, if underquoted, little book titled *O Segredo da Macumba*.[17]

The issue of gay rights is often intertwined with intellectual sympathy for the *Candomblé*. For the Afro-Brazilians, so to speak, square the circle. The notions of sin, guilt, redemption and the like play but a scant role in their devotion such as it has existed or has been reinterpreted in Brazil. Or rather, these notions, which in some form or other, are inseparable from any kind of religious experience, do exist, but are reified in the guise of material, blood (animal) sacrifice. Devotees live in permanent awareness of what they owe to the supernaturals. And this includes not so much, in strict terms, an ethical regulation, but rather the imitation, in daily life, of the character and the behavior of the gods, with their peculiarities (at times of a sexual character) and even their whims. In addition to this, feast, dance, and trance, allow the gods to show that they exist. For devotees have implicitly adopted George Berkeley's (1685–1753) principle, according to which to be is but to be perceived.

Scholars studying religions often tend to evaluate them according to their conformity to the criteria they consider as representative of modernity and progress. The Afro-Brazilian religions, in spite of their conspicuous sacrificial character, agree, as already highlighted, with a certain modernity both in their practical rejection of the notions of sin and guilt and in their allegedly being religions of the oppressed. Thanks to the writings of sociologists and anthropologists, they were invested with highly rationalized theological reinterpretations. Congresses and conferences, attended by researchers and religious leaders, function as ecumenical councils during which faith is defined and proclaimed.

Such as they are understood nowadays, the Afro-Brazilian religions are largely the product of this latter-day variety of syncretism. But this did not change the strong concreteness of their form of devotion, very much oriented to the relief of everyday problems through ritual operations, believed to be effective if adequately

---

[15] "Filhos-de-santo" (children of the holy) is an expression commonly applied to the devotees of Candomblé and similar religions.

[16] Concerning politics, their motto could be "plus ça change, plus ça reste le même", the more it changes the more it remains as it is. But this is far from preventing "Candomblezistas" from engaging in clientelistic alliances with politicians of many or no persuasions.

[17] This point was certainly well understood, in spite of severe mythologization in many details, by the author of Jorge Amado's obituary in French newspaper *Le Monde*): "He distinguished himself from other Brazilian writers of his time by supporting the African religions hitherto brutally repressed by the Police. A Communist deputy in the Constituent Assembly of 1945, he caused them to be considered legal in the Constitution. During his whole life he supported their *terreiros* and received many distinctions from the priests of *Candomblé*. Under his influence, the Brazilian youth abandoned the Catholic churches and came in throngs to Bahia in order to be initiated [in Candomblé *terreiros*] and to discover the new values of joy, communion, and finally liberation, since these philosophies fight evil but ignore sin" (Soublin 2001).

performed. And thus we reach, or come back to, a core problem in the interpretation. Due precisely to their concreteness, to their care for the banal, practical, everyday problems they intend to solve through sacrifices and analogous rites, *Candomblé* and similar religions are, at the same time, receptive to many kinds of intellectual or theological explanations and resistant to all of them. This does not annul, but sets limits, as it seems evident, in the second decade of the twenty-first century, to the process of *ecclesification*, which requires a theological consistency going well beyond a ritual manipulation of events.

The same core problem can be stated in a different way: these religions provide short term relief for affliction, but they lack a comprehensive theodicy, which is, or intends to be, the ultimate form of relief for human suffering and the apparent nonsense of life. And thus their main advantage in the competitive religious "market" of Brazil, Latin America, and possibly other areas, is at the same time their main disadvantage. They do provide short term relief to affliction and this in a context of feast and enthusiasm. But they seem to be less effective than other religions in providing the faithful with a comprehensive system able to give sense to man's existence and mortality. Let us notice that it is precisely its short term character that renders it so attractive to intellectuals who tend to consider *Candomblé*, especially when properly managed by social scientists, as an adequate interim religion before the final exit from religion finally takes place.

The Illusion of Liberation

The rise of the Theology of Liberation[18] in Brazil should be understood within its historical, political, and religious context. To present but a simplified picture, on one hand Brazil seemed to be ripe for Revolution. Fidel Castro took power in Cuba exactly on the 1st January 1959. This, from the standpoint of theory of revolution (especially so Marxist theory), was a "divine surprise". In point of fact, Castro's victory aroused not only enthusiasm, but also embarrassment in circles of the Left and even of the extreme Left. It represented, as expressed in the very title of Regis Debray's essay, "a revolution in the revolution".[19] The Cuban Revolution seemed to demonstrate that, in spite of open or tacit arrangement between the Superpowers concerning the division of the world, Revolution followed its own laws, or no laws at all. Let us also take due notice of the rise of the radical left in Brazil, especially so in the Northeast region and even more so in the state of Pernambuco (capital Recife), with its Peasant Leagues, which, in the late 1950s and early 1960s, had not been influenced, in any discernable way, by the preconciliar Brazilian Catholic Church, which rather opposed them.

---

[18] Henceforth referred to as TL.

[19] Debray (1967). Let us remark that in the actual title there is a question mark: "revolution in revolution?".

On the other hand, let us take into account some all-important transformations in the Catholic field. These were largely international in scope. I refer, in a general way, to *aggiornamento*, the II Vatican Council and all that followed them, in Brazil and elsewhere. Among other things, the Council and its aftermath entailed (or perhaps rather were consequential to) a wide trend toward generalized cognitive capitulation to modernity, a marked loss of plausibility, a strong loss of enchantment of the Church, in Brazil and elsewhere. It was really the end of a world.[20]

Let us keep in mind that abrupt end came very much as a historical surprise. Brazilian Catholicism, even before the turn of the twentieth century, had started undergoing a process of modernization, with a new stress on the word and/or on organized thought, as opposed to baroque iconolatry and to the ritualism of processions, feasts, pilgrimages, and the like. This process has been called the "Romanization" of Brazilian Catholicism,[21] associated with a wider process of Europeanization of Brazilian society. By 1960, the Brazilian Church had reached a kind of social, cultural, indeed theological and intellectual zenith. All of this would drastically change under the pressure of the *aggiornamento* associated with II Vatican Council and of the TL.

The TL, according to the thesis I have tried to uphold in several papers (Motta 2009, 2011, etc.), consists in an attempt to secularize Catholicism and render it relevantly "public" by transferring it from an enchanted, often private and subjective domain, to the social and political arena. The Church would legitimize its continued existence by the services of a basically secular nature it could perform in order to change society, acting, as it were, as the very voice of the otherwise voiceless. Coherent with the spirit of the time – basically the period between, on one hand, the victory of the Cuban Revolution (1959) and the II Vatican Council (1962–1965) and, on the other, the Fall of the Berlin Wall (1990) – there was a strong Marxist strain in the TL.

Gustavo Gutierrez's *Teología de la Liberación* (1971)[22] represents one of the basic statements of the theories and aims of the TL.[23] It moves, in the freest of ways, from Hegel, with the development, or awareness, of consciousness through the dialectics of the master and the slave, to Marx, and, among many others, to Freud and Sartre. From the latter, Gutierrez quotes approvingly the dictum: "Marxism, as the culmination of the whole of our time's philosophical thought, cannot be surpassed" (Gutierrez 1986: 22).

---

[20] I am obviously quoting from the title of Danièle Hervieu-Léger's book, *Catholicisme: La Fin d'un Monde* (2003).

[21] Bastide (1951) refers explicitly to "Romanization". de Oliveira (1985) is a standard reference about this process and its sociological implications. Freyre (1986) deals extensively with the wider process of "Europeanization" of Brazil. See also Bruneau (1974), Della Cava (1970), DeKadt (1970), and Serbin (2006).

[22] Quoted here according to its Brazilian translation (1986).

[23] I consider Gutierrez as a prototypical theoretician of the TL. The ideas of Brazilian (also a Dominican friar) Francisco Cartaxo Rolim (1985, 1992) are also representative of the TL.

After having said that "with the Theology of Liberation we have reached a political interpretation of the Gospel" (ibid: 26), he further describes it as

> a new way to make theology. It is theology as a critical reflexion on historical praxis. Thus it is a liberating theology, the theology of the liberating transformation of the history of mankind. [...] It is a theology which does not limit itself to thinking the world, but which rather wishes to place itself as a moment of the process through which the world is transformed (Gutierrez 1986: 27).

"Salvation" does not entirely vanish, but it is reinterpreted as *liberation*. Or, put another way, supernatural, otherworldly salvation is replaced by innerworldly, historically immanent, *political* liberation, resulting from the end of oppression and brought about by class struggle.

We face here some indeed big problems. First, but perhaps not foremost, there is the problem of a religion that, as such, leads to exit or to the end of religion. And, no doubt foremost, this theology, which has changed itself into "a critical reflexion on historical praxis", wants, nevertheless, to enjoy all the privileges of the status it would have as a religion. It wants to have its cake and eat it. This is made less implausible thanks to the basic syncretic character of the TL. In it religious elements coexist with political elements derived from Marx, Hegel or other authors, syncretizing but not really synthesizing with them. The long term results of the TL are thus compromised on both the religious and political arenas. Yet, nothing has prevented TL from possessing, or having possessed, a certain effectiveness, as it has represented a kind of "interim ethics", meant – and this very likely done in full awareness by at least some of its proponents – to assure a smooth transition from religion into secularized politics. This was made possible precisely because of its *syncretic* character. Its religious and political components are simply juxtaposed. The cognitive penumbra of syncretism was an adequate strategy to ease the transition, during which the vested interests resulting from previous commitments could be decently safeguarded.

For the practical and theoretical evaluation of the TL we have a more decisive criterion than those represented by the analyses and the wishes of either theologians or social scientists. It is the criterion of the praxis.[24] Let us first to look at it from an ethnographic standpoint. There is a plentiful literature bearing on the thought and the activities of the TL in Brazil. This literature should be critically evaluated, with no concession to the mythologies from several sources that have collected around it. From all I have so far read, I know no other study as eloquent and poignant and, indeed, disenchanted, as that of Jadir Morais Pessoa (1999), *A Igreja da Denúncia e o Silêncio do Fiel.*[25]

---

[24] In other words, "the proof of the pudding is in the eating".

[25] Pessoa's *jeu de mots* can be translated as *the Church that accuses and the faithful who is silenced.*

The scenery is the diocese of Goiás,[26] in central Brasil, where, Pessoa adds,

> beginning with the diocesan assembly of 1975, the terms *Igreja do Evangelho* [Gospel Church], and *Caminhada* [27] were to define the new social and religious identity of all Catholic individuals who adhered prophetically to the process of change that was taking place in the diocese. These changes comprised above all the rupture with traditional religious habits centering around the 'consumption' of sacraments and the courageous denunciation of the situations of injustice, especially of the exploitation of the rural workers by the landowners (Pessoa 1999: 17).

This implied, to put it in Casanova's (1994) terms, a huge effort of "deprivatization" of religion, leading to ambiguous consequences:

> the uses were dogmatically changed. Whoever attributed to religion the task of explaining, or giving a meaning to, personal or family situations that have no sense at all (illness, death, failures, disasters) had now to restrict it exclusively to the decodification of social relations and of politics of oppression (Pessoa 1999: 118).

Thus, when

> several persons of the same family, who were practicing Catholics, were killed in a car crash at Nova Glória, the priest was called to celebrate their funeral mass. But he not only refused to go but, in addition, ridiculed the demand of the bereaved (Pessoa 1999: 134).[28]

Likewise, while conceding that "the violence of the landowners against the workers was extremely serious, being the source of the problems that really mattered and toward which all lights were directed" Pessoa also remarks that

> problems of a personal kind, like conjugal difficulties, alcoholism, clashes between neighbors, sentimental and sexual problems among the young, raising children, and do on, and so forth, did not get the same attention, since, from a political standpoint, they had little to do with people's development of consciousness (ibid.: 161).

In Goiás, the whole story of the *Caminhada*, with its erosion of religiosity, ends by a vengeful return of privatization, whether Catholic or other, which did not even spare the most militant:

Pessoa tersely reports that a priest, who was

> one of the leaders of the [liberationally militant] pastoral work [of the diocese] moved to São Paulo, where he took a Master's degree in Social Anthropology and later became a *pai-de-santo* [*Candomblé* priest][29] in Curitiba, where he died in 19. (ibid.: 177).

There is also the less portentous case of the sister

---

[26] The diocese and the city of Goiás should not be confused with the state of Goiás, where they are located, nor with the city of Goiânia, the capital of that state, nor with the Northeastern city of Goiana.

[27] This term implies walk, march, path and is suggestive of Peru's *Sendero Luminoso*, shining path, as well as of Mao's Long March.

[28] As a matter of fact, "cure of souls" has been very largely phased out in today's Brazilian Catholicism.

[29] This turn of events does not imply that the priest in question had any African Brazilian ethnic roots.

whose activity was very important in the beginning of the *Caminhada*. She quit religious life and married the former president of the syndicate, who was also one of the main lay agents of the Gospel Church. They are still the leaders of the congregation of the small valley where they now live. They cultivate a small garden and seldom visit other places (ibid.: 177).

It is indeed not clear what, in terms of costs and benefits, the rise and fall of the TL has represented to the Catholic Church. One of the indicators of those costs and benefits could be presumed to consist of the demographic evolution of Brazilian Catholicism. According to census[30] data, [31] relative to the total population of the country, the percentage of Catholics fell from 92 % in 1970, to 74 % in 2000, and to 68 % in 2009.

Meanwhile, in the same years and according to the same sources, the combined membership of the Pentecostal churches leaped from 3.2 % in 1980 (the first time the census treated them as a separate category) to 11 % in 2000, to 13 % in 2009. If we add to them the more conventional "historical" churches, Protestants amounted, in 2009, to very nearly 20 % of the whole country's population. Pentecostals and other Protestants have obviously been filling a religious void.[32]

The "historical" Protestant churches have largely, but not always, lagged behind. [33] Thus, unanglified Episcopalians in the area of Recife have experienced impressive growth. Their membership, however, should be carefully distinguished from that of Pentecostals. Episcopalians are oriented to the upper and upper-middle classes of professionals, businessmen, politicians and others. Their main church in Recife grew from 14 (fourteen) permanent members in 1975 to very nearly 10,000 (ten thousand) in 2010 (de Queiroz 2012). This underreported phenomenon is, to my mind, one the best examples of Brazilian religious entrepreneurship.

Casanova's *Public Religions in the Modern World* (1994), with its chapter on "Brazil: From Oligarchic Church to People's Church", is not mentioned in Pessoa's book, published 5 years later. It is likely that Pessoa was simply not cognizant of Casanova's book, although the former contains a consistent effort to refute the latter's descriptions.[34] To the present writer's mind, Casanova's chapter is marred

---

[30] Religious affiliation has been a standard item of nearly all Brazilian censuses down to the present.

[31] Brazil underwent very rapid demographic growth in the second half of the twentieth century. Thus, from very nearly 93,000,000 in 1970, the total population had increased to very nearly 170,000,000 in 2000.

[32] Concerning the Pentecostals in Brazil, an early and, to this writer's mind, still unsurpassed interpretation is that of Frase's (1975).

[33] In Brazilian parlance, the "historical churches" are ideal-typically represented by the Presbyterians, the Methodists and the Baptists, who have actively missionized in the country. Episcopalians (in spite of recent successful attempts), and Lutherans, have not so much attempted to expand beyond their original ethnic borders. In any event those churches have been very largely outdone by the Pentecostals, who also outdid, to the great chagrin of many commentators, the Afro-Brazilians and the Theology of Liberation-minded Catholics.

[34] I think this apparent coincidence is too strong to be purely coincidental. Pessoa, as a matter of fact, does not quote or mention any publications in English. But news and ideas travel fast. It may

by the frequent use of sheer mythology. Among other instances, it is highly doubtful that a "people's church" has really existed in Brazil, in spite of many appeals to the "people", like in the letter of the bishops of the Northeast, *I Heard the Cry of My People* (1973). Similarly, even though Casanova may have borrowed it from earlier (and no less mythological) sources, historical credibility is strained when he asserts that

> the popular Church and the ecclesial base communities (CEBs) that emerged in the 1970's [...] had their historical origins in Brazil's colonial reality of [...] popular religiosity autonomous from clerical control (1994: 115).

In point of fact, probably in no other time the Brazilian Catholic Church was more subject to the control of theologians and other intellectuals than in the last decades of the twentieth century. It may also be doubted whether the CEBs, such as described in the literature, have ever concretely existed, having no other consistent and coherent reality but in the wishful thinking and abstract constructs of the same theologians and intellectuals, Brazilian and foreign.

Yet that religious void is not the subject of this chapter. To state that it was caused by the (all too real) contradictions of the TL, even if understood in the broadest of ways, would go beyond the premises of this chapter. Many other factors may be responsible for it. But it can be stated that the TL did not fill the void. And it did not seem qualified to do so due to its lack of a consistent theodicy, oriented to more than the public coming of a new Heaven, indeed of a new Earth. In order to be successful it should also take into account the private, personal, subjective, ordinary needs of people. "Comfort ye, comfort ye, my people" (Isaiah 40: 1). I mean things like disease, aging, addictions, love, rivalries, employment, financial difficulties, and all the many dismal failures of everyday life.

This is what theodicy, salvation and religion are all about. Let us call it the opium of the people if we so wish. But it can as well be argued that there is an opium aspect in the promise of the coming of a Kingdom of Justice through the action, or with the decisive support, of progressive churchmen, who, after 2,000 years of Christianity, would have deciphered the mysteries of World History with the help from their Hegelian, Marxist, or plainly sociologist friends. Indeed, by attributing to themselves such grandiose role in the impending Millennium, those churchmen are the first and foremost consumers of the religious opium.

It can be safely concluded that in the past scholars promoted the study of *Candomblé* for their own reasons, neglecting a broader Brazilian pluralism. Likewise, the Theology of Liberation in Catholicism, failing to heed the appeal to "comfort my people" by not supporting the care of souls, created a vacuum. New religions, often imported from other lands but capable of very rapidly gaining national specificities, represented, first and foremost, by the Pentecostal and Neo-Pentecostal churches, came in to fill the vacuum, strengthening the religious pluralism typical of early twenty-first century Brazil.

---

have so happened that Pessoa was indeed trying to refute Casanova's ideas, without perhaps realizing that they derived from Casanova or from some other precise source.

References

Bastide, Roger. 1960. *Les Religions Africaines au Brésil: Contribution à une Sociologie des Interpénétrations de Civilisation*. Paris: PUF.

Bastide, Roger. 1951. Religion and the church in Brazil. In *Brazil: Portrait of half a continent*, orgs. T. Lynn Smith and Alexander Marchant, 334–355. New York: The Dryden Press.

Bruneau, Thomas C. 1974. *The political transformation of the Brazilian Catholic Church*. New York: Cambridge University Press.

Carneiro, Edison. 1981 (or. 1936). *Religiões Negras: Notas de Etnografia Religiosa*. Rio de Janeiro: Civilização Brasileira.

Casanova, José. 1994. *Public religions in the modern World*. Chicago: The University of Chicago Press.

Davie, Grace. 1990. Believing without belonging: Is this the future of religion in Britain? *Social Compass* 37(4): 455–469.

de Oliveira, Pedro A. Ribeiro. 1985. *Religião e Dominação de Classe: Gênese, Estrutura e Função do Catolicismo Romanizado no Brasil*. Petrópolis: Vozes.

de Queiroz, Cristiany Morais. 2012. *Rumos, Rumores e Reconstruções: Um Estudo Antropológico na Catedral Anglicana do Recife*. Doctor's thesis in Anthropology, Recife, Universidade Federal de Pernambuco.

Debray, Regis. 1967. *Revolution in revolution?* New York: The Monthly Review Press.

DeKadt, Emanuel. 1970. *Catholic radicals in Brazil*. London: Oxford University Press.

Della Cava, Ralph. 1970. *Miracle at Joaseiro*. New York: Columbia University Press.

Durkheim, Émile. 1985 (or. 1912). *Les Formes Élémentaires de la Vie Religieuse*. Paris: PUF.

Éliade, Mircea. 1969. *Le Mythe de l'Éternel Retour: Archétypes et Répétition*. Paris: Gallimard.

Frase, Ronald Glen. 1975. *A sociological analysis of the development of Brazilian protestantism: A study in social change*. Unpublished Doctor's dissertation, Princeton University Theological Seminary, Princeton.

Freyre, Gilberto. 1986. *Order and progress: Brazil from monarchy to Republic*. Berkeley: University of California Press.

Gonçalves da Silva, Vagner, et al. 2007. *Intolerância Religiosa: Impactos do Neopentecostalismo no Campo Religioso Afro-Brasileiro*. São Paulo: Edusp.

Gutierrez, Gustavo. 1971. *Teología de la Liberación: Perspectivas*. Lima: CEP.

1986. *Teologia da Libertação*. Petrópolis: Vozes.

Hervieu-Léger, Danièle. 2003. *Catholicisme, la Fin d'un Monde*. Paris: Bayard.

Lapassade, George, and Marco-Aurélio Luz. 1972. *O Segredo da Macumba*. Rio de Janeiro: Paz e Terra.

Lowie, Robert H. 1924. *Primitive religion*. New York: Liveright.

Löwith, Karl. 2002. *Histoire et Salut : Les Présupposés Théologiques de la Philosophie de l'Histoire*. Paris: Gallimard.

Maurras, Charles. 1972. *De la Politique Naturelle au Nationalisme Intégral*, textes chosis par F. Natier et C. Rousseau. Paris: Vrin.

Motta, Roberto. 1988. *Meat and feast: The Xangô Religion of Recife, Brazil*. Ph.D. dissertation, Department of Anthropology, Columbia University.

Motta, Roberto. 1998. The churchifying of Candomblé: Priests, anthropologists, and the canonization of African religious memory in Brazil. In *New trends and developments in African religions*, ed. Peter B. Clarke, 45–57. Westport: Greenwood Press.

Motta, Roberto. 2007. Environment and religion in a developing country: The role of Sacrifice in the Xangô of Recife (Brazil). In *Religion, Culture, and Sustainable Development*, ed. Roberto Blancarte Pimentel, 220–215. Paris: UNESCO-EOLSS.

Motta, Roberto. 2009. Enchantment, identity, community, and conversion: Catholics, Afro-Brazilians and Protestants in Brazil. In *Conversion in the age of pluralism*, ed. Giuseppe Giordan, 163–188. Leiden: Brill.

Motta, Roberto. 2010. Filhos-de-Santo e Filhos de Comte: Crítica, Dominação e Ressignificação da Religião Afro-Brasileira pela Ciência Social. In *Diálogos Cruzados: Religião, História e Construção Social*, org. Mauro Passos, 111–131. Belo Horizonte, Argumentum.

Motta, Roberto. 2011. Theology of liberation and some problems of religious changes in Brazil. *International Review of Sociology (London)* 21(1): 231–242.

Otto, Rudolf. 1958 (or. 1917). *The idea of the holy*. New York: Oxford University Press.

Pessoa, Jadir de. Morais. 1999. *A Igreja da Denúncia e o Silêncio do Fiel*. Campinas: Alínea.

Pierucci, Antônio Flávio. 1997. Os Interesses Religiosos dos Sociólogos da Religião. In *Globalização e Religião*, ed. Ari Pedro Oro and Carlos Alberto Steil, 249–262. Petrópolis: Vozes.

Ramos, Arthur. 1940. *O Negro Brasileiro: Ethnographia Religiosa*, 2nd ed. São Paulo: Companhia Editora Nacional.

Rolim, Francisco Cartaxo. 1985. *Pentecostais no Brasil: Uma Interpretação Sócio-Religiosa*. Petrópolis: Vozes.

Rolim, Francisco Cartaxo. 1992. Pentecôtismes et Visions du Monde. *Social Compass* 39(3): 401–422.

Serbin, Kenneth P. 2006. *Needs of the heart: A social and cultural history of Brazil's clergy and seminaries*. Notre Dame: University of Notre Dame Press.

Sombart, Nicolaus. 1955. *Einige entscheidende Theoretiker, in Einführung in die Soziologie*. Alfred Weber (Herausg.), 81–119. München: R. Piper & Co.

Soublin, Jean. 2001. Mort de Jorge Amado, libérateur par la plume du peuple brésilien. *Le Monde*, 8th August 2001.

Verger, Pierre. 1957. *Notes sur le Culte des Orisa et Vodun*. Dakar: Institut Français d'Afrique Noire.

Index

A

African Pentecostalism, 98, 104, 107
Afro-Brazilians, 4, 147, 172–176, 181
Ahmed, T.S., 23
Allievi, S., 96
Allott, A., 20
Ammerman, N.T., 10, 78
Aurélio Luz, M., 176

B

Bainbridge, W.S., 159
Barker, E., 52
Bastide, R., 172, 178
Baumann, C., 74, 76, 78
Beckford, J.A., 9, 10, 15–26, 38, 52, 56,
    57, 157
Behloul, S.M., 76
Belgium, 10, 63, 65–70, 120
Belief, 3–10, 18, 19, 21, 23, 31, 40, 49, 50, 52,
    55, 57, 58, 64–66, 68, 71, 93, 95, 109,
    111, 115, 121, 135, 139, 152, 160,
    161, 175
Bellah, R., 141, 152
Berger, M., 41
Berger, P., 4, 41, 50, 158
Berkeley, G, 176
Bertolani, B., 102
Black, D., 39–43
Bochinger, C., 74
Bombardieri, M., 96
Bouma, G.D., 75
Bovay, C., 75
Branch, 36, 146, 163, 164, 166
Bréchon, P., 23
Bruneau, T.C., 178
Buddhism, 58, 78, 80, 105, 152, 160–162, 168

C

Campbell, E., 139
Carneiro, E., 175
Caroline, S., 68
Carroll, L., 15
Casanova, J., 2, 129, 180
Catholicism, 4, 11, 66, 93–112, 122, 123, 134,
    171, 172, 174, 175, 178, 180–182
Cava, D., 178
Census, 10, 11, 73–88, 98, 99, 119, 172, 181
Chafetz, J., 135, 141
Chambliss, W., 39, 42–44
Chaves, M., 77, 140
China, 32, 35–37, 53, 55, 57, 105, 150, 151,
    159, 160
Civil religion, 58, 141–143, 150–156, 158
Civil society, 9, 11, 56, 58, 65, 157–169
Clark, W., 23
Cole, G.D.H., 18
Collectivistic religions, 117, 121–125,
    128, 129
Communism, 17, 38, 57, 58, 118, 149
Comparative Institutional Approach, 11,
    157–169
Comparison, 10, 22, 51, 63–71, 74, 76, 77,
    79–88, 95, 98, 100, 106, 115
Conception, 66, 67, 69–71, 171
Congregations, 11, 19, 73, 75, 77–82, 84, 85,
    88, 102, 103, 135, 141, 149, 181
Connolly, W.E., 16
Cooney, M., 41, 42
Croatia, 11, 115–128, 136
Cult controversy, 164, 167
Culture, 2, 5, 8, 9, 19, 20, 22, 31, 34, 36, 37, 65,
    68, 96, 109, 110, 118, 121–123, 133,
    137, 142, 143, 155, 160, 165, 168,
    172, 174

G. Giordan and E. Pace (eds.), *Religious Pluralism*,
DOI 10.1007/978-3-319-06623-3, © Springer International Publishing Switzerland 2014

D

Davidian, 36, 146, 147
Debray, R., 177
Defensive Civil Society, 11, 157–169
Definition of religion, 5, 10, 56–58, 79
DeKadt, E., 178
DeParle, J., 134
Dethier, H., 70
Dobbellaere, K., 158
Douglas, G., 19
Durham, W.C., Jr., 126
Durkheim, E., 141, 171
Dyer, A.E., 76

E

Ebaugh, H.R., 135, 138, 141
Eck, L.D. 75, 133, 134, 138, 140
ECtHR. *See* European Court of Human
    Rights (ECtHR)
Education, 2, 22, 23, 25, 31, 50, 64, 67, 68, 70,
    83–85, 118–120, 161, 164, 165
Eisenhower, D., 135, 148
Eliade, 171
Enchantment, 11, 171–182
Europe, 1, 3, 4, 7, 9, 10, 17, 23, 38, 43, 54,
    64, 69, 70, 73, 75, 76, 78, 80, 93–95,
    100, 115–117, 120–129, 133, 136,
    143, 160
European Court of Human Rights (ECtHR),
    38, 40, 43, 44, 120
Everyday, 16, 21, 24–26, 56, 74, 118, 120,
    129, 176, 177, 182

F

Ferrari, S., 75, 126
Ferry, J.M., 64, 65
Figgis, J.N., 18
Finke, R., 53, 55, 95
Fischer, C.S., 139
France, 4, 9, 10, 35, 36, 39, 63–66, 127, 133
Frase, R.G., 181
Free exercise, 11, 145–156
Freyre, G., 178
Furnivall, J.S., 17

G

Gauchet, M., 5
Giordan, G., 1–11, 100
Globalization, 23, 49, 111, 150–158
"God Bless America", 151, 152

Governance, 10, 33, 36, 37, 40, 94, 115–129
Grim, B., 55

H

Habermas, J., 71
Herberg, W., 141
Hervieu-Le'ger, D., 4, 5
Hinduism, 78, 80
Hirst, P.Q., 18, 21
"Holy Alliance", 172–177
Hout, M., 139
Hunter, J.D., 22
Husistein, R., 75
Husson, J.F., 68

I

Iannaccone, L., 159
Ibn Khaldûn, 137, 138, 142
Immigration, 9, 95–106, 126, 134–136,
    138, 141
Intolerance, 68, 124, 155, 175
Islam, 9, 19, 39, 58, 66, 71, 76, 78, 80, 85, 94,
    97–99, 110, 115, 116, 118–124, 128,
    129, 139, 142, 147, 149, 150, 153,
    155, 157, 166, 174
Italy, 1, 3, 11, 54, 93–109, 111, 112

J

Jakelić, S., 121, 128
Japan, 15, 105, 150, 157–169
Javeau, C., 66
Judicial autonomy, 35, 36

K

Kay, W.K., 76
Khaldûn, I., 137, 138
Knott, K., 76

L

Laïcité, 36
Laski, H.J., 18
Lassman, P., 22
Law, 4, 16, 19–21, 23, 24, 34–45, 53–56, 66,
    67, 75, 79, 115, 116, 118–120, 122, 125,
    126, 136, 137, 145, 148, 150, 154,
    168, 177
Leavelle, T., 17
Le Bras, G., 4

Lee, W., 152, 163
Legal pluralism, 19–22, 31–45
Lewis, C., 15
Lewis, J., 20
Lewis, W., 78
Lowie, R.H., 171
Löwith, K.
Luckmann, T., 158

M

Marty, M., 16
Marx, K., 94
Melton, J.G., 52
Methodology, 10, 11, 73–88, 162
Michel, P., 6, 97
Miki, H., 165, 166
Minority religions, 31–33, 35–38, 116,
    117, 129
Monnot, C., 73–88
Monopoly, 7, 11, 53–56, 93, 95, 109, 116
Motta, R., 171–182

N

New comer religions, 157, 158, 162–168
New religions, 98, 116, 127, 157, 159, 161,
    167, 168
New religious movements (NRMs), 31, 43,
    116, 127, 129, 147, 158, 159, 161,
    162, 165–167
Niebuhr, H.R., 141

O

Oligopoly, 10, 49–58
Orthodox Churches, 34, 43, 66, 97, 98, 100,
    110, 118, 119
Otto, R., 171

P

Pace, E., 7, 11, 93–112
Pastorelli, S., 75
Pentecostals, 3, 4, 11, 76, 94, 96–98, 102–105,
    107, 120, 124, 157, 159, 162, 163, 171,
    175, 181, 182
Pessoa, J.M., 179
Philosophy, 15, 17, 51, 67–69
Plurality, 50–54, 58, 74, 94, 133, 143
Pluralization, 24, 51–53

Politics, 2, 5, 7, 9, 10, 16–19, 21–24, 26, 31,
    33–36, 40, 42, 43, 50, 51, 53, 55–58, 64,
    65, 71, 94, 95, 98, 102, 111, 116, 118,
    121, 122, 129, 139–141, 145, 146, 149,
    151, 153, 154, 161, 167, 168, 172, 174,
    176–181
Pollack, D., 75
Polytheism, 159, 174
Poole, E., 23
Possamai, A., 41
Post-communism, 118
Poulat, E., 5
Protestantism, 66, 88, 139, 141, 152, 154,
    163, 174
Putnam, R.D., 139

R

Racial diversity, 115
Rademacher, S., 75
Ramos, A., 175
Recognition, 2, 6, 7, 16, 19, 20, 23, 24, 37, 41,
    43, 44, 67, 68, 70, 71, 82, 95, 117,
    119–122, 124, 125, 129, 157
Reformation, 81
Regulation, 5, 9, 11, 16, 19, 20, 23, 24, 41,
    53, 54, 58, 115–118, 126, 128, 129,
    159–161, 168, 176
Religio-politico separation, 167, 168
Religious freedom, 32, 36–38, 40, 42, 43,
    49–56, 58, 115, 117, 145, 146, 148,
    150, 152, 160, 161, 168
Religious mapping, 11
Religious monopoly, 53, 54, 116
Richardson, J.E., 23
Richardson, J.T., 9, 10, 31–45
Rolim, C., 178
Roof, W.C., 6
Runciman, D., 18, 20

S

Sakurai, Y., 157–169
Salzbrunn, M., 74
Sandberg, R., 20
Secularism, 10, 63–71, 161
Secularization, 1–3, 11, 50, 64, 71, 111, 158,
    159, 171–182
Serbin, K.P., 178
Shintoism, 158, 161
Sikh, 80, 94, 96–98, 100–103

Social control, 10, 31–45, 94
Social scientists, 50–52, 57, 158, 171,
    173–175, 177, 179
Social solidarity, 137
Sociology of Law, 39–42, 44, 45
Sombart, N., 172
Spickard, J.V., 11, 133–143
Spickard, P., 135
Spirituality, 5–7, 83, 85, 161
Stark, R., 53, 159
State, 3, 17, 31, 50, 64, 73, 94, 115, 133,
    145, 158, 177
Stolz, J., 73–88
Swatos, W.H., Jr., 11, 145–156
Switzerland, 9, 11, 36, 73–81, 83, 84, 86,
    88, 97

T
Taylor, C, 5
Theodicy, 177, 182
Theology of Liberation, 171, 177, 179,
    181, 182
Todd, J.T., 23
Torfs, R., 66
Trans-border religions, 11, 157–169
Transnationalism, 49
Trigg, R., 18
Tucker, A., 20

U
United States, 3, 4, 11, 36, 37, 40, 42, 51,
    75, 77, 134–136, 138–139, 143,
    145–155, 163
US Constitution, 146, 147

V
Verger, P., 172
Vertovec, S., 75

W
Warner, R.S., 135, 138, 141
Watson, J., 70
Willaime, J.P., 10, 23, 63–71, 75
Wittner, J.G., 135, 141
Worldview, 64, 65, 67, 69–71, 153, 155
Wuthnow, R., 6, 7, 51

Y
Yang, F., 10, 49–58, 159
Yoshihide, S., 11, 157–169

Z
Zrinščak, S., 11, 115–129
Zubrzycki, G., 17